African-American Medical Pioneers

AFRICAN-AMERICAN MEDICAL PIONEERS

Charles H. Epps, Jr., M.D.
Davis G. Johnson, Ph.D.
Audrey L. Vaughan, M.S.

Williams & Wilkins

BALTIMORE • PHILADELPHIA • HONG KONG
LONDON • MUNICH • SYDNEY • TOKYO

A WAVERLY COMPANY

Printed in the United States of America.

Library of Congress Cataloging-in-Publication Data

Epps, Charles H. (Charles Harry), date
    African-American medical pioneers / Charles H. Epps, Jr., Davis G.
Johnson, Audrey L. Vaughan.
        p.   cm.
    Includes bibliographical references and index.

    ISBN 0-941406-46-6

    1. Afro-American physicians--Biography.   I. Johnson, Davis
Gilman, date. II. Vaughan, Audrey L., date. III. Title.
R695.E67 1994
610'.92'273--dc20   94-5267
                                                          CIP

Dedication
To William Montague Cobb, M.D., Ph.D. (1904–1990)

This volume is gratefully dedicated to W. Montague Cobb, M.D., Ph.D., who was universally acknowledged during his long and distinguished career to be "the principal historian of the African American in medicine."

Dr. Cobb was a prize-winning 1925 graduate of Amherst College, an honors 1929 M.D. graduate of Howard University College of Medicine (HUCM), and an outstanding 1932 Ph.D. graduate (in anatomy and physical anthropology) of Western Reserve University. He was a leading faculty member at HUCM from 1932 to 1973 and chaired its Department of Anatomy from 1947 to 1969.

For 27 years, from 1950 to 1977, Dr. Cobb was editor of the *Journal of the National Medical Association (JNMA)*. His more than 600 publications include scores of editorials and over 100 biographical sketches of African-American leaders in medicine. Accordingly, his writings were among the major references for our research on black medical pioneers.

Dr. Cobb's outstanding leadership included his founding of the American Association of Physical Anthropologists and serving as its president from 1957 to 1959. Dr. Cobb was also president of the National Medical Association (NMA), 1963–1964, and the first African-American president of the National Association for the Advancement of Colored People (NAACP) from 1976 to 1982.

The three authors of this book were privileged to know Dr. Cobb personally. Dr. Epps knew him over several decades as his medical school teacher and faculty colleague, and he served as one of Dr. Cobb's assistant editors of the *JNMA*. Dr. Johnson knew him for approximately 20 years as a fellow Washington, D.C., area alumnus of Amherst College and as a colleague at HUCM. Ms. Vaughan knew him during the last few years of his life—in part through their joint efforts regarding the 1990 dedication of a Howard University medical school building in the name of its first African-American dean, Dr. Numa P. G. Adams.

For all of these reasons, the authors warmly and enthusiastically dedicate this book to Dr. Cobb's illustrious memory.

Contents

Dedication v

List of Tables ix

Foreword xi

Preface xiii

Acknowledgments xv

Part I: The History of African-American Medical Education
in the United States 1

  1. Assembling the Record: The Study and Its Sources 3

  2. Medical Education of Black Americans from 1868 to 1993 7

  3. Historic Achievements of African Americans
in U.S. Medicine 23

Part II: Representative African-American
Medical Pioneers 37

  4. Biographies of 33 Pioneers 39

  5. Voices and Patterns 131

Part III: The Pioneering "Firsts" of 556 African Americans
in Medicine 143

  6. First African-American Graduates of
U.S. Medical Schools 145

  7. Black Pioneer Graduates of Howard University
College of Medicine 167

  8. Black Pioneer Graduates of Meharry Medical College 177

  9. Black Pioneer Graduates of Other Colleges 183

Contents

10. Comparison of Pioneer Graduates of Howard, Meharry, and Other Schools 203

Part IV: Challenges for the Future 211

11. Summary and Recommendations 213

Appendix

A. Key Findings of the Study: Black Pioneers in Medical Education
Charles H. Epps, Jr., M.D. 219

B. Scope and Value of the Study: The Evolution and Significance of Black Medical Pioneers
Louis W. Sullivan, M.D. 221

C. Directory of United States Medical Schools 223

Bibliography 231

About the Authors 233

Index of Specialties 234

Index of Names 239

List of Tables

1. Predominantly Black U.S. Medical Schools,1868-1993 20

2. Chronological Summary of Selected Black Pioneers in Medical Education 24

3. Chronological Summary of Selected Black Pioneers in Organized Medicine 29

4. Chronological Summary of Selected Black Pioneers in Activities Closely Related to Medical Education and Organized Medicine 33

5. Summary Information about 33 Individuals with Biographical Sketches 132

6. Representative "Firsts" from the 33 Biographical Sketches 133

7. First Male and Female African-American Graduates of U.S. Medical Schools 146

8. Year of Graduation of First Male and Female African-American Graduates of U.S. Medical Schools 157

9. Number of Years from Medical School Organization to Graduation of First Male and Female African-American Students 159

10. Home States of First African-American Graduates of U.S. Medical Schools 161

11. Undergraduate Colleges of First African-American Graduates of U.S. Medical Schools 162

12. Black Pioneer Graduates of Howard University College of Medicine 169

13. Black Pioneer Graduates of Meharry Medical College 178

14. Black Pioneer Graduates of Medical or Graduate Schools Other Than Howard and Meharry 183

List of Tables

15. Medical or Graduate Schools Attended by Black Medical
    Pioneers From Institutions Other Than Howard and Meharry 201

16. Comparative Information About Graduates of Howard,
    Meharry, and Other Medical or Graduate Schools 203

17. Birthplace of African-American Pioneer Graduates of
    Howard, Meharry, And Other Medical or Graduate Schools 205

18. Undergraduate Colleges of African-American Pioneer Graduates
    of Howard, Meharry, and Other Medical or Graduate Schools 206

Foreword

As Howard University College of Medicine celebrates its 125th anniversary, the occasion affords an excellent opportunity to review the progress that has been made since its founding in 1868.

Progress has been made on many fronts. Initially, a single small medical department; today there is a college of medicine with 17 departments and two major centers. The first entering class numbered eight students; as of 1993 there are 434 undergraduate medical students and 74 graduate students (25 M.S. and 49 Ph.D. candidates) in HUCM's basic science departments. The first building was a frame house; today there are six buildings with over 350,000 square feet of classroom, laboratory, and office space. The faculty, which first numbered five, now numbers approximately 300 full-time and 500 part-time and volunteer members.

Throughout this 125-year period, HUCM faculty and graduates have included many men and women of unusual ability and professional achievement. Until three decades ago, institutional segregation and discrimination were the law of the land. Despite this formidable handicap, many of these individuals achieved professional distinction while making significant contributions in medical service, research, and education. The story of these individual and collective achievements must be recorded for posterity.

Admittedly, there have been previous biographical dictionaries and historical works that have included some of these individuals, but there has been no systematic accounting of the outstanding graduates of HUCM. It seemed, therefore, that a compilation under one title of the pioneering achievements of College of Medicine graduates would fill a historical and literary void—and at the same time, provide an inspirational vehicle for the current College of Medicine community. It also seemed that such a document could serve as a motivational agent for other African Americans to consider medicine as a career.

To keep the project to a manageable size, it was decided to limit it to pioneers in academic medicine and in organized medicine. Thus some outstanding medical practioners have been excluded intentionally. It is also possible that unintentional omissions of authentic African-American pioneers in medical education and organized medicine have occurred. If any such omissions or other errors are brought to our attention, we will try to include or correct them in a later printing.

Given the tendency for historical accounts from the majority medical community to omit or minimize contributions of African Americans, it is important to document these contributions now, especially because the nature of institutional memory is brief. For all of these reasons, the concept of this book was developed, and I had the good fortune to be joined by two colleagues, Davis G. Johnson, Ph.D., and Audrey L. Vaughan, M.S. Without their help, this undertaking would not have been possible. For example, Dr. Johnson did almost all of the library research, and he and Ms. Vaughan prepared all of the biographical sketches.

As our joint project developed, it soon became apparent that three additional components were natural supplements to the initial summary of HUCM pioneers in medical education and organized medicine and the study was expanded to include the following categories:

1. Pioneers who graduated from Meharry Medical College. For many years, Howard and Meharry graduated 80 to 85 percent of the African-American physicians in the United States.[1]
2. African-American pioneers who graduated from the other 124 existing U.S. medical schools or from schools now defunct.
3. The first African-American male and female graduates from each of the 126 U.S. medical schools.

In the latter instance we were generously assisted by the Association of American Medical Colleges (AAMC) and by the respective schools.

We have been fortunate to obtain the encouragement and support of Calvin C. Sampson, M.D., editor of the *Journal of the National Medical Association.* Significant contributions also were made by Sterling M. Lloyd, Jr., HUCM Assistant Dean for Student Affairs, and by Marion Mann, M.D., Dean Emeritus of HUCM. Both of these individuals made valuable suggestions about the content of the project and were kind enough to review early drafts of our publication. We are indebted to all the people and organizations who have provided assistance in this effort.

Charles H. Epps, Jr., M.D.
Dean, Howard University College of Medicine
April, 1994

---

[1]Today, the four historically black medical schools (Howard, Meharry, Morehouse, and Drew) graduate less than 20 percent of all African-American physicians.

Preface

"If we do not tell our own story, no one will."

William Montague Cobb, M.D., to whom this book is dedicated, was the 64th president of the National Medical Association (NMA), the major professional organization of African-American physicians, and the fourth editor of its journal. He is the renowned and acknowledged historian of African Americans in medicine, and author of the quotation reprinted above.[1]

It may well have been these words and the feelings they express that served as the catalyst to inspire Charles H. Epps, Jr., M.D., dean of Howard University College of Medicine, along with coauthors Davis G. Johnson, Ph.D., former division director of the Association of American Medical Colleges, and Audrey L. Vaughan, M.S., Public Information Officer, Editor, and Writer, at HUCM, to accept the challenge of researching and subsequently publishing this expanded version of their study of African-American Medical Pioneers. As editor of the *Journal of the National Medical Association* (*JNMA*), I was proud to have the initial version of this book appear as a series in the August, September, and October 1993 issues of the *JNMA* under the title "Black Medical Pioneers: African-American 'Firsts' in Academic and Organized Medicine."

In expanding the original *JNMA* articles to book length, the subjective portions of the 33 biographical sketches are now included along with a content analysis of both the objective and subjective sections of these sketches. In these entries, the pioneers who were interviewed tell of their obstacles, disappointments, and hardships, and frequently express their appreciation for the help they received from family and friends. The biographies also recount how, largely through hard work and perseverance, these pioneering men and women were able to enjoy the satisfaction of reaching their goals.

While portraits of the individuals appeared in the magazine articles, additional photographs of all of the 33 pioneers have been added to this book. These pictures, some of them informal snapshots from family albums, show personal moments in their growing professional lives, with friends on college campuses, and with patients and colleagues in the hospitals and in practice.

Adding to the value of this expanded version of the Journal series are appended materials that include historical articles about black medical education from 1868 to 1993 by Drs. Vanessa Gamble and Kenneth Manning, summary information about all of the predominantly black medical schools in the United States, and a list of the full names and locations of all 126 existing U.S. medical schools.

Other touchstone references included in appendixes are Dr. Epps' July 1993 letter to the editor of *Academic Medicine* describing the key findings of the study, as well as a guest editorial (*JNMA*, December 1993) on the scope and value of the study by Louis W. Sullivan, M.D., founding president of the Morehouse School of Medicine and former secretary of the U.S. Department of Health and Human Services.

Finally, this volume has a valuable index of names that includes the 556 medical pioneers identified in this study and 250-plus additional persons cited in the book; another index includes the specialties of the 289 pioneering individuals whose names are listed in the book's three tables about the pioneer graduates of Howard, Meharry, and other schools.

African-American Medical Pioneers will serve to stimulate those who are interested in medical history in general, and most particularly, in the historical role of blacks in American medicine. It is hoped that it may be only the first of many similar future volumes that will continue to meet Dr. Cobb's challenge of "telling our own story."

Calvin C. Sampson, M.D.
Editor, *Journal of the National Medical Association*

---

[1]"The Black American in Medicine." *Journal of the National Medical Association*, 1981; 73 [suppl]: p. 1187.

Acknowledgments

The authors express their sincere appreciation to the hundreds of individuals who contributed to the preparation of this book. Prominent among them is Calvin C. Sampson, M.D., editor of the *Journal of the National Medical Association (JNMA)*. Dr. Sampson not only encouraged us to publish our initial articles in the "Medical History" sections of that publication, but also was instrumental in inviting Louis W. Sullivan, M.D., founding president of Morehouse School of Medicine and former secretary of the U.S. Department of Health and Human Services, to write a guest editorial for those articles. Dr. Sullivan's editorial, which appeared in the December 1993 issue of *JNMA,* describes the scope and value of the study that formed the basis for this book and the *JNMA* articles that preceded its publication.

Other individuals worthy of special mention include Sterling M. Lloyd, Jr., Assistant Dean for Student Affairs, and Marion Mann, M.D., Dean Emeritus of Howard University College of Medicine (HUCM). Both of them made valuable suggestions about the content of our project and reviewed early drafts of some sections of our *JNMA* articles.

The 33 biographical sketches that appear in our book were made possible by the 31 living individuals who agreed to extensive interviewing and provided us with their photographs. In the case of Drs. Cobb and Drew, we are indebted to their children, Amelia Cobb Gray and Bebe Drew Price, who helped us obtain some of their photographs. Credit is also due to Messrs. Jeffrey J. Fearing, Alan D. Haile, and Gregory Robertson, of the HUCM Department of Biomedical Communications, for their help in recording some of Ms. Vaughan's interviews and in locating some of the photographs.

We are also grateful to Vanessa Gamble, M.D., and Kenneth Manning, Ph.D., the eminent black medical historians who allowed us to include in this book their excellent presentations at the HUCM 125th Anniversary Symposium held on November 9, 1993.

Others who merit acknowledgment by name include Vivian O. Sammons, M.S., author of *Blacks in Science and Medicine*, who met with the authors in the early stages of our planning, and Mr. Salvador B. Waller, former director of the Howard University Health Sciences Library, who facilitated our research at that facility. Our great indebtedness to W. Montague Cobb, M.D., is detailed in the dedication to this book.

Acknowledgments

The largest category of individuals who contributed to this work are the approximately 200 registrars and minority affairs officers of the 126 existing U.S. medical schools who provided us with information about their first African-American graduates. This information was gathered under the generous auspices of the Association of American Medical Colleges, through its Section for Student Services, which is headed by Mr. Richard R. Randlett.

With regard to publication, we are indebted to Ms. Mary L. Jerrell, managing editor of SLACK, Incorporated, and to her assistant, Ms. Randi D. Kershaw, for their skillful editing of the original *JNMA* articles; and to Ms. Kathryn A. Fisher, whose expert knowledge of book production transformed text into type with speed and precision, we extend our appreciation for her diligence and constant good humor.

Finally, the authors would like to thank their families for their strong moral support and valuable technical assistance so lovingly contributed to the completion of this project. Specific technical assistance was provided by Mrs. Mary C. Johnson and Ms. Tracie L. Vaughan.

PART I

THE HISTORY OF
AFRICAN-AMERICAN
MEDICAL EDUCATION
IN THE UNITED STATES

This section describes how our information was compiled for this study, and it provides the general historical background of medical education of African Americans in the United States. It includes a unique table concerning the 15 predominantly black medical schools that have existed in the U.S. from 1868 to 1993. It also highlights approximately 200 selected historical milestones in medical education, organized medicine, and closely related activities.

1

Assembling the Record: The Study and Its Sources

Readers will make optimum use of this book by gaining a better appreciation of its sources of information, its self-imposed limits, and its overall organization.

Sources of Information

To identify as many as possible of the African-American pioneers in medical education and organized medicine, several approaches were taken to gather the information needed for the study. These included a review of the literature, mailings to living pioneers, mailings to all U.S. medical schools, and interviews of selected pioneers.

The starting point for the literature review was to search the more than 1,500 biographical sketches in *Blacks in Science and Medicine* (Sammons, 1990) for those African Americans who were "firsts" in medical education and organized medicine. Other basic readings included *Howard University: The First Hundred Years* (Logan, 1969), *Educating Black Doctors: A History of Meharry Medical College* (Summerville, 1983), *A Century of Black Surgeons: The U.S.A. Experience* (Organ and Kosiba, 1987), *The History of the Afro-American in Medicine* (Morais, 1978), *Before the Mayflower* (Bennett, 1982), and "The Black American in Medicine" (Cobb, 1981).

Secondary references included *Afro-American Biographies* (Hawkins, 1982), *Contemporary Black Biography* (LaBlanc, 1992), *Dictionary of American Negro Biography* (Logan and Winston, 1983), *In Black and White* (Spradling, 1980), *Who's Who Among Black Americans* (Matney, 1985), *Who's Who in America* (Reed Publishing Co., 1993), and the *Directories of Medical Specialists*, particularly that of the Macmillan Directory Division, 1991. Finally, a review was conducted of more than 100 biographical articles, most of them by Dr. Cobb, that were published in the *Journal of the National Medical Association*.

Requests for biographical information were mailed in June 1991 to 44 living African-American medical pioneers identified in *Blacks in Science and Medicine*. Recipients were asked to provide the following:

1. The nature of their "firsts" in medical education and/or organized medicine.
2. The obstacles they encountered, and overcame, in achieving their "firsts."
3. The help received from blacks and others in becoming these "firsts."
4. Their advice to young blacks considering a career in medicine.
5. The names of other pioneers who might be included in this study.

Through the generous help of the Association of American Medical Colleges (AAMC), a request for information about each school's first African-American graduates was sent in February 1992 to the registrars and minority affairs officers of all 126 AAMC member U.S. medical schools. The AAMC's cooperation was secured in part because of the relationship of our activity to their *Project 3000 by 2000* (Petersdorf, 1992), which is attempting to have at least 3,000 underrepresented minority students per year admitted to U.S. medical schools by the year 2000. The initial mailing was followed up with phone calls and a verification mailing in June 1992.

The June 1992 mailing not only allowed the schools to verify the accuracy of what would be published, but it also invited them to make additional nominations about other African-American medical pioneers who had graduated from their institutions. To guide them in making these nominations, a document titled "Criteria for Inclusion as a Black Pioneer in Medical Education and/or Organized Medicine" accompanied this mailing and specified these basic criteria:

1. Usually, one must be the very first African-American man or woman to have achieved significant success in a given aspect of medical education or organized medicine.
2. In some cases, one may be the very first in an activity that is not directly in medical education or organized medicine but is very closely related to it.
3. In relatively few cases, one may not be the very first to have achieved a milestone but may have such outstanding accomplishments that he or she should be included for the historical record.

The criteria document also listed a number of specific examples of the types of accomplishment that would qualify individuals for inclusion as pioneers in medical education, in organized medicine, and in closely related activities. Examples from medical education ranged from being the first African-American graduate of a specific school or program to being the first dean of a predominantly white medical school. Examples from organized medicine include being either the first African-American official in a local, state, regional, national, or international medical organization, or the first founder, member, diplomate, fellow, examiner, officer, editor, or residency review board member of a medical specialty society. Examples of closely related activities included being the first African-American director of the American Red Cross Blood Bank, president of the American Cancer Society, and secretary of the U.S. Department of Health and Human Services.

Special mailings also were made during 1992 to the other three traditionally black medical schools, Meharry, Morehouse, and Drew. The purpose of these mailings was to ensure that as many as possible of their alumni who met the above criteria would be included. Interviews were conducted during 1991 and 1992 at the offices and homes of selected pioneers and at the 1991 Annual Meeting of the AAMC in Washington, D.C. The topics covered in the interviews were essentially the same as those indicated above for the June 1991 mailing to the 44 living pioneers.

Although these interviews were the major source for the 33 biographical sketches that appear in chapter 4, other sources included *curriculum vitae* and printed articles about several of these individuals. Other than making certain that females were adequately represented, no great effort was made to have the 33 sketches scientifically representative of the 556 pioneers who are cited in this study. The slight overrepresentation of individuals connected with Howard University College of Medicine (HUCM) is due mainly to the original plan of limiting the project to pioneers from HUCM and to the difficulty of arranging interviews elsewhere.

Limits of Study

As an example of the extent to which our study is limited to the areas of academic and organized medicine and closely related activities, attention is directed to the entry for Dr. Daniel Hale Williams in Table 14. Although we were able to include several significant "firsts" for Dr. Williams, such as his having been a founder of the National Medical Association and a charter member of the American College of Surgeons, the scope of our study precluded us from citing in that table one of the medical accomplishments for which he is best known—namely, having performed in 1893 the first successful surgery on the human heart.

Similarly, the entry for Dr. Patricia E. Bath in Table 12 includes seven of her African-American "firsts" in academic and organized medicine but omits what she believes to be one of her major medical achievements, namely, the invention of a new laser device for cataract surgery. Even though she received a U.S. patent for his device in 1988, and, according to her biographer, became "the nation's first African-American physician inventor," the parameters of our study precluded the mention of her invention in that table.

These examples are cited to emphasize that the overall medical achievements of the 556 individuals in our study are quantitatively greater than what our self-imposed limitation to academic and organized medicine have allowed us to report. Perhaps someone at a later date will research and write about African-American "firsts" in other important aspects of medicine in the United States, such as patient care or medical inventions.

Overview of Book

The results of the study were first published as a series of three articles in the August, September, and October, 1993, issues of the *Journal of the National Medical Association* and are published here as *African-American Medical Pioneers,* expanding the text and photographic records of the articles. The book has four major divisions, which include the historical background of African Americans in medicine, the 33 biographies, the historic "firsts," and a summary of the challenges faced by the pioneers.

The appendixes at the end of the book afford the interested reader pertinent background and reference information. Dean Epps' letter to the editor of *Academic Medicine* highlights not only some of the key findings of the study, but also the excellent cooperation received from both the AAMC and its member schools. Dr. Sullivan's editorial in *JNMA* expresses his personal appreciation for the scope and value of our project. In the information about the 126 existing U.S. medical schools, details are provided about the sometimes abbreviated school names in the body of the book.

The more than 30 references are limited to those publications which were most widely used in preparing this book. Finally, the index of names includes not only the 556 African-American medical pioneers in the book, but also the more than 250 other individuals cited by the authors or the 33 individuals with biographical sketches. The index of specialties lists the medical and other specialties of the 289 pioneers in the tables about the graduates of Howard, Meharry, and other medical and graduate schools.

2

Medical Education of Black Americans from 1868 to 1993

One of several major events celebrating the 125th anniversary of the founding of the Howard University College of Medicine (HUCM) was a symposium entitled "The Path We Tread." Held at HUCM on November 9, 1993, and moderated by syndicated columnist Carl T. Rowan, the symposium included historical presentations about the four existing predominantly black medical schools. Speaking for Howard was its dean, Charles H. Epps, Jr., M.D.; for Meharry Medical College was its dean, Henry W. Foster, Jr., M. D.; for Morehouse Medical College was its vice president for health and social policy, Ronny Lancaster; and for the Charles R. Drew University of Medicine and Science was its president, Reed Tuckson, M.D.

These four specific presentations were followed by general commentaries by African-American historians Kenneth R. Manning, Ph.D., and Vanessa N. Gamble, M.D., Ph.D., about the medical education of black Americans during the previous 125 years. Dr. Manning covered the 62-year period from 1868 to 1929; and Dr. Gamble commented on the 63-year period from 1930 to 1993. This chapter consists mainly of slightly revised versions of these two general historical commentaries.

To supplement these two narratives, the authors of this book also developed a summary (Table 1) regarding the 15 predominantly black medical schools that existed in the United States over these 125 years. To the best of our knowledge, this is the first time that such a summary about these 15 schools has ever been published.

Table 1 is organized chronologically according to the year that each school was founded. It indicates how long each school has been or was in existence, provides its full name and location, and, in some cases, additional explanatory comments. As indicated in the table's footnotes, its information comes from four major sources, including the presentation by Dr. Manning.

A History of Black Medical Education, 1868–1929
Kenneth R. Manning, Ph.D.

Dr. Manning is Thomas Meloy Professor of Rhetoric and of the History of Science at the Massachusetts Institute of Technology, Cambridge, Massachusetts.

As we celebrate the 125th year of the founding of the Howard University College of Medicine, let us briefly explore its rich early history. It is a proud history—unique in its integrity of purpose; in its ongoing struggle for justice in professional opportunity; and in its hard-earned success in formulating and implementing progressive educational goals. The medical school was conceived to provide opportunities—extremely rare if not unheard of at the time—for African-American men and women to acquire the education, training, and experience necessary to go out among their people and practice the healing arts. Healing arts essentially meant pharmacy and medicine in the first decade and a half at Howard; courses in dentistry were added in 1881, and the first dental degrees were awarded in 1884.

In a speech to the assembled class, delivered on 5 November 1868 at the opening of the first course of pharmaceutical and medical lectures, the school's first professor of physiology and microscopy—Lafayette C. Loomis—captured the enthusiasm of the moment with the following homily:

"What a field of honorable toil is here! How limitless its opportunities for good! How worthy the life that uses them well! Such toil, such opportunities, and such honor open to the patient, conscientious, and faithful student of medicine. May the after years of your lives, my young friends, justify the hopes of the present hour, and along your sometimes weary student's life may you never forget that success comes only of patient toil, and that patient toil never fails of success."

In avid anticipation, and with Loomis's words no doubt ringing in their ears, the first group of students convened for their first class at 5 p.m. on Monday, 9 November 1868—exactly 125 years ago to the day of this speech. Their first classroom occupied the second floor of an old frame house on Seventh Street just above Florida Avenue (then known as Boundary Road), where the business of teaching and learning proceeded until the opening, in 1869, of the medical building on the corner of 5th and W streets.

Diversity was the school's watchword. No efforts were spared to ensure that those who had been traditionally excluded from opportunities for professional training in American educational institutions—African Americans and women, in particular—would be not only admitted but encouraged and welcomed as part of a community of professionals striving towards a common goal: that of expanding and improving health services for a nation entering a post-Emancipation and post-Civil War era.

The faculty and student body exhibited qualities of diversity at the outset. The first faculty, five members in all, included four whites and one black, Dr. Alexander T. Augusta, who taught anatomy. Another black, Dr. Charles B. Purvis, arrived the following year to teach *materia medica,* therapeutics, botany, and medical jurisprudence. The first degree, the Pharm.D. (doctor of pharmacy), was awarded to an African American, James T. Wormley, on 3 March 1870. The first students admitted to the three-year medical program included eight men, seven blacks and one white, while the first five M.D. graduates in 1871 comprised three whites and two blacks. The first woman graduate, Dora Spackman, a white, earned the M.D. in 1872.

The interracial composition of the early faculty and student body was remarkable, as were the school's conscious efforts towards gender integration. Women were admitted on an equal footing with men, and shared the same classrooms and forums for clinical instruction. This was true even in anatomy—a radical departure considering the standards of social propriety prevalent at the time. Few medical schools admitted women, let alone strived to render them fair and equal treatment. Yet Howard held the beacon in both regards. In 1872, the faculty received complaints from two women students about ill treatment by some men students and about lack of access to facilities in the course on practical anatomy. The faculty acted swiftly and adopted the following strongly worded resolution in March 1873:

"Whereas an unjust discrimination is being made against certain members of our profession on account of sex. Therefore be it Resolved: That we discountenance and denounce said discrimination as being unmanly and unworthy of the profession: That we accord to all persons the same rights and immunities that we demand for ourselves: That said discrimination rests upon the basis of selfish interest or ignorant prejudice: That we highly appreciate and honor intellect and capacity without regard to nationality or sex. . . ."

Such a highly principled stand, oddly enough, coincided with the beginning of a difficult economic period in Howard's history. Yet, while economic realities probably tested the school's idealistic resolve, they never undermined or broke it. The Great Depression of 1873 brought on a financial crisis that threatened to cripple the institution and its prospects for development, just as its unique mission was beginning to bear first fruits. Faculty salaries were drastically cut. The few teachers who stayed on did so for no other reason than to keep the dream alive; some worked gratis. Faculty and students eked out an existence the best way they could during the day, convening afterwards—in the evening hours—to take up the business of teaching and learning.

It was a decade when, fortunately, two other black schools—the medical department of Lincoln University (1870) and Meharry Medical College (1876)—were established to contribute to the task of producing the new generation of black health professionals needed to go out and work in African-American communities springing up around the country. While the Lincoln program was shortlived, closing in 1872 without turning out a single graduate, Meharry joined Howard as a premier institution for the training of black health professionals. They, in turn, were joined during the next two decades by a series of proprietary or church-affiliated schools that were never as prominent (or as permanent) but that nevertheless fed numerous graduates into the expanding core of African-American physicians, dentists, pharmacists, and nurses who were starting to take their place in the professional life of communities throughout America.

These schools, and their dates of founding, were: Leonard Medical School of Shaw University (1882), Louisville National Medical College (1888), Flint Medical College of New Orleans University (1889), Hannibal Medical College (1889), Knoxville College Medical Department (1895), Chattanooga National Medical College (1899), State University Medical Department of Louisville (1899), Knoxville Medical College (1900), University of West Tennessee (1900), and the Medico-Chirurgical and Theological College of Christ's Institution, Baltimore (1900).

In spite of economic hardship during its early years, Howard continued to attract a first-rate faculty and to maintain its commitment to high standards and achievement-oriented goals. A major concern was professionalization, how to ensure that opportunities were generated not just for teaching, learning, and training but for participation in the outside community as well. The first quarter century was one of struggle to penetrate the impenetrable white medical establishment. In 1869, for example, the all-white Medical Association of the District of Columbia denied applications for membership to Drs. Augusta and Purvis. The

Howard medical faculty, united in opposition to racial discrimination, fought the ruling but to no avail—and, in response, organized in 1870 an interracial group, known as the National Medical Society, whose purpose was to bring together "regular physicians in the District of Columbia in favor of extending equal rights and privileges to regular practitioners of medicine and surgery."

The National Medical Society was a precursor of the Medico-Chirurgical Society of the District of Columbia, established in 1884 to provide a forum and a spirit of professional camaraderie for African Americans, who were excluded from the all-white Medical Association of the District of Columbia until the mid-twentieth century. Such challenges extended to white Howard faculty as well, some of whom were ostracized by the white medical community for their involvement with a racially integrated institution.

Other struggles included efforts on Howard's part to seat its representatives at meetings of the Association of American Medical Colleges. This time the gender issue was raised. Jefferson Medical College of Philadelphia objected in 1877 to Howard's participation, citing Howard's practice of teaching men and women together in the same class—a practice widely perceived as detrimental to sexual morals and, on some level no doubt, as a threat to male privilege.

The obstacles faced by Howard faculty and students were prevalent elsewhere in the United States. In the late 1880s and early 1890s, African-American health professionals—many of them freshly minted graduates of Howard, Meharry, and the other so-called "race" schools—organized professional societies in Arkansas, Georgia, North Carolina, Texas, and elsewhere. These grass-roots efforts led to the formation of the National Medical Association, founded in Atlanta in 1895 during the Cotton States and International Exposition at which Booker T. Washington delivered his famous "cast down your buckets" address. The National Medical Association, well into the twentieth century, provided the only nationwide professional forum for African Americans who were excluded from admission to the American Medical Association by that organization's by-law denying membership to anyone not a member of a constituent state society—which was in almost all instances a racially exclusive body.

Even at Howard, however, multiracialism ultimately proved too radical a concept and experiment. American society was no more ready for it than it had been for Reconstruction during the 1870s. Several events—including the establishment of the all-black M Street High School in Washington, D.C.; and the 1896 "separate but equal" Supreme Court decision in the case of *Plessy v. Ferguson*—helped transform Howard from a racially mixed institution into a predominantly black one. By the turn of the twentieth century, the medical school's white enrollment had declined to almost nothing and the medical school was catering almost exclusively to colored races—not just African Americans but students from the Caribbean, Africa, and Latin America as well.

The crises and dramatic historical events of the time in medical education, however, were not all unique to Howard. After years of criticism and efforts at reform, the first decade of the twentieth century saw final acceptance of the notion that medical education throughout North America was in need of an overhaul. To that point, there had been minor adjustments but no consistent entrance and exit examinations, no general agreement about standards or curriculum. This all changed with the publication, in 1910, of Abraham Flexner's report, *Medical Education in the United States and Canada,* conducted under the auspices of the Carnegie Institution for the Advancement of Teaching. The report was the single most influential document in the history of medical education in this century, perhaps in any century. Flexner's sweeping criticisms resulted in the extinction of some schools, and in the revamping of curricula at others.

The black schools, like the white, came in for their fair share of criticism. Flexner considered five black schools—Flint at New Orleans, Leonard at Raleigh, and the Knoxville, Memphis, and Louisville schools—as "ineffectual . . . sending out undisciplined men." Some of these schools closed immediately, and all had shut their doors by 1923. According to Flexner, the future of Howard was—as he put it—"assured." In fact, Howard fared better in many respects than the two white D.C. schools awarding the M.D. degree: George Washington University and Georgetown University. Whereas Howard required a high-school diploma for admission, George Washington and Georgetown did not.

Moreover, Flexner considered Freedmen's Hospital "an asset the like of which is in this country extremely rare." In seeking a close affiliation with Freedmen's Hospital, and by integrating the academic curriculum with ward work for students and interns, Howard had early recognized the importance of clinical training in a way that many schools had not by the time Flexner's report was published. By contrast, Meharry was (in Flexner's words) "in urgent need . . . (of) improved clinical facilities—a hospital building and a well-equipped dispensary," but was otherwise a "creditable" institution worthy of development.

In effect, the Flexner report left only two black medical schools

(Howard and Meharry) intact to train future generations of African-American health professionals. This was a challenge that both schools met ably, if not without struggle, supplemented over a half century later by the work of the Charles R. Drew University of Medicine and Science and the Morehouse School of Medicine.

In leaving African Americans just two viable schools, Flexner did not intend to underestimate the importance of their role. In fact, he considered that role essential to overall improvements in health care of black and white communities alike. As he observed:

"The medical care of the negro race will never be wholly left to negro physicians. Nevertheless, if the negro can be brought to feel a sharp responsibility for the physical integrity of his people, the outlook for their mental and moral improvement will be distinctly brightened. The practice of the negro doctor will be limited to his own race, which in its turn will be cared for better by good negro physicians than by poor white ones. But the physical well-being of the negro is not only of moment to the negro himself. Ten million of them live in close contact with sixty million whites. Not only does the negro himself suffer from hookworm and tuberculosis; he communicates them to his white neighbors, precisely as the ignorant and unfortunate white contaminates him. Self-protection no less than humanity offers weighty counsel in this matter; self-interest seconds philanthropy. The negro must be educated not only for his sake, but for ours. He is, as far as human eye can see, a permanent factor in the nation. He has his rights and due value as an individual; but he has besides, the tremendous importance that belongs to a potential source of infection and contagion."

Flexner's candid paternalism, combined with his somewhat circumscribed vision for the role of African-American professionals, might sound a little strange to us today, but it was typical of the thinking among progressive whites at the time and it produced essential financial and moral support for the development of black educational institutions. The years following the publication of the Flexner Report saw revitalized efforts to build a program of which the Howard community—and, by extension, the African-American community at large—could be proud.

These efforts at Howard included establishment of an endowment; the erection of a new building (opened in 1927) with matching funds provided by the General Education Board of the Rockefeller Foundation; the upgrading of the curriculum in content, length, and overall rigor; and the development of a research program—involving recruitment and motivation of faculty members to pursue postgraduate work and, if possible, to acquire Ph.D.'s in addition to M.D.'s—to complement the teaching program. Many of these efforts were initiated, completed, or furthered by Howard University's first African-American president, Mordecai Johnson (appointed 1926) and its first African-American dean of the medical school, Numa P. G. Adams (appointed 1929).

As my colleague Professor Gamble prepares now to provide us with an overview of the period since 1930, I am certain that, as a fellow historian, she will join with me in expressing a note of deep appreciation for the work of those historians who have gone before in chronicling the Howard experience with care and insight. I think here of Daniel Smith Lamb, Walter Dyson, Rayford Logan, and—in particular, the late W. Montague Cobb—whose efforts have inspired all those who follow their lead in interpreting the role and experience of African Americans in the health professions; a role and experience in which Howard has figured so prominently for 125 years.

Thank you, and may the next 125 years be as fruitful and productive as the first!

A History of Black Medical Education, 1930–1993
Vanessa N. Gamble, M.D., Ph.D.

Dr. Gamble is Associate Professor, History of Medicine, at the University of Wisconsin School of Medicine, Madison, Wisconsin.

Twenty years ago (in 1973) I applied for admission to medical school. I sent applications to several schools, including Howard University College of Medicine. My application to Howard proved successful and I was accepted here. Yet when I went to medical school I did not come here or to Meharry Medical College, the other historically black medical school then in existence. My action was not an isolated one. Throughout the 1970s and 1980s most black students who matriculated went to predominantly white institutions. This, however, is a relatively recent phenomenon.

As a result of the civil rights movement and affirmative action programs, the range of options available to black medical students today are much wider than those available to our professional foremothers and forefathers. I went to the University of Pennsylvania School of Medicine. But the doors to the school had not always been open wide to African Americans, especially women. Between 1910 and 1925, my alma mater graduated 37 white women and eight black men. It graduated its first black man in 1882, its first white woman in 1918, and its first black woman in 1964, 46 years after the first white woman had graduated.

Between 1910 and 1947, Howard and Meharry graduated approximately 3,400 students, 100 of whom were women (Morais, 1967). By 1950, the two schools together were graduating about 100 black physicians annually, and all the predominantly white schools were only graduating an additional 10 or 20 per year (Savitt, 1992).

These figures illustrate a significant fact—that throughout most of the twentieth century black medical institutions have been critical to the professional survival of African-American physicians. Because racial discrimination denied them access to many of the institutions essential for their professional development, they moved to establish and support parallel institutions: hospitals, medical journals, medical schools, and professional organizations. Until very recently, few African Americans had options beyond the separate black medical world.

The four black medical schools that exist today—Howard, Meharry, Morehouse, and Drew—and the others that operated during the late nineteenth and early twentieth centuries all shared a common philosophy—a belief that African Americans possess the capabilities and skills needed to become physicians. I bring this point up because if one examines the history of American medicine, one sees that a contradictory view has often permeated and influenced the profession.

Dr. Manning has already discussed the impact of the Flexner Report on black medical education. However, I think that it is important to reiterate one of the conclusions of that report. Specifically, Abraham Flexner prescribed a restricted role for black physicians, contending that their practices would be limited to black people and that they should be taught to master the principles of hygiene rather than the techniques of surgery (Flexner, 1910).

Such views about the capabilities of African-American physicians were not limited to Abraham Flexner. During December 1927, a committee appointed by the city manager of Cleveland visited several medical schools. Its objective was to make recommendations about the feasibility of admitting black nursing students and interns to the programs at Cleveland City Hospital. The next month it filed its final report. An examination of this report graphically documents the pervasiveness of racism in medical education in the late 1920s and the justifications used to exclude African-American health professionals from majority institutions.[1]

The report vividly depicted the enormous pressures and obstacles that black men and women faced as they sought to enter medicine and nursing. It underscored the assessment of an assistant dean at Harvard Medical School who informed members of the committee that the black medical students at his institution had "very tough sledding." He told them that the black students were housed in separate accommodations and that the white medical students usually did not socialize with them. Furthermore, he noted that the presence of black students on clinical rotations "creates much ill feeling." The medical school administrator added that African-American medical students "invariably" graduated in the lower third of the class and that this indicated "the lower mentality" of the black race.[2]

The committee found that similar conditions existed for medical students at the University of Pennsylvania School of Medicine. Since the 1882 matriculation of Nathan Francis Mossell, the school had admitted two or three black male students each year. The school's dean, Dr. William Pepper III, informed the committee that the "mortality is heavy" among these students and that usually only one graduated annually. He also concurred with his colleague from Harvard that the presence of black students led to difficulties. For example, he noted that in the autopsy room they had difficulties "unless care [was] taken that the other three men working at the same time [had] no special prejudices." Black medical students were usually prohibited from working with white patients "except in exceptional instances" where the patients had been "hand-picked or otherwise prepared." Furthermore, the students were not allowed in the dormitories, but had to find accommodations off campus. It should be emphasized that at both Harvard and Pennsylvania the officials viewed the source of the problem as the presence of African-American medical students, not the existence of racial discrimination.[3]

On the other hand, the black medical schools did not view the education of African-American students as a "problem." Instead, it was the essence of their mission. Their task has not been an easy one. Throughout the twentieth century the schools have had to grapple with meager endowments, struggle to provide care to low income patients, combat racist attitudes about the intellectual capabilities of African Americans and, more recently, have had to wrestle with the effects of the desegregation of the predominantly white schools.

In the years after World War II, many black physicians focused their energies on the burgeoning civil rights movement. One especially vigorous activist was a Howard University faculty member, Dr. W. Montague Cobb. The civil rights activists argued that a poorly-financed, segregated black medical ghetto of which Howard and Meharry were major components could not adequately meet the health and professional needs of black people (Cobb, 1947). Instead, they called for the desegregation of medical schools.

At the end of World War II, one third of the approved medical schools—26 out of 78—barred African-American students. All 26 schools were located in southern or border states. In 1948, as a result of a series of lawsuits filed by the NAACP, the University of Arkansas Medical School opened its doors to a black student. The student was Edith Mae Irby. This was not the last time that she was a pioneer. In 1986, Dr. Edith Irby Jones became the first woman president of the National Medical Association.

As a result of civil rights legislation and affirmative action programs, the number of black students matriculating in predominantly white medical schools has progressively grown since Dr. Jones entered the University of Arkansas. In 1948 only 25 percent of the African-American students entering medical school enrolled in predominantly white institutions; by 1968 the figure was 47 percent; by 1983 it was 61 percent; and by 1990 it had grown to 84 percent (Shea and Fullilove, 1985; and Tomasson, 1992). In contrast to earlier generations of black physicians, black medical students today are not as dependent on black medical institutions for their professional survival and advancement.

The gains of the civil rights movement pose new challenges for black medical institutions. For example, the desegregation of medical facilities has been the primary factor accelerating the demise of the historically black hospitals and contributing to the vulnerability of the few that remain. As Haynes Rice, the former executive director of Howard University Hospital put it, "Integration provided for the elimination of black institutions. The community could not support black institutions *and* integration."[4] Civil rights legislation increased the access of black people to previously white medical facilities. Consequently, black medical schools face an ironic dilemma. They now compete for applicants and faculty members with institutions that had once excluded African Americans.

The declining percentage of black students receiving their medical educations at the historically black schools suggests to some that the gains of the civil rights movement have rendered these institutions obsolete. However, in recent years, African Americans have begun to reassess the value of black-controlled institutions and organizations. Escalating racial tensions, frustration over the unfulfilled dreams of the civil rights movement, increased attacks on affirmative action programs, and anger over the continued estrangement of African Americans from the country's political and economic systems have prompted the reevaluation.

Let us look at some of these issues a bit more closely within the context of black medical education. As I stated earlier, the percentage of African-American students attending the historically black medical schools has steadily declined over the past forty-five years. In 1990, Howard, Meharry, and Morehouse admitted 15.9 percent of the first-year black medical students (Tomasson, 1992). This percentage was matched only by the total black enrollment of six predominantly white schools. Thus it is clear that the historically black medical schools continue to play a vital and critical role in medical education. At a time when concerns have been raised about the number of black physicians, we must continue to support the black medical colleges. As I am sure that all of you know, the health status of black Americans lags behind that of white Americans. The continued existence of black medical schools can help bridge this gap. The schools have developed programs dedicated to the diseases and conditions that affect African Americans and have functioned as advocates of black health care needs.

We are here today to celebrate the 125th anniversary of the Howard

University College of Medicine and we are proud of its rich history. We are also proud of the histories of its sister schools. However, we should also be here to reaffirm the principle on which this school was founded—namely that African Americans are not members of an intellectually inferior race. We have produced and are continuing to produce academically and professionally competent physicians. A reaffirmation of this founding principle is especially needed today because of escalating racial tensions and increasing attacks on the humanity of African Americans. We must let the world know, especially our children, that we have successfully tread many paths and will continue to do so.

---

[1] The committee's tour included visits in Chicago, Ill., to Cook County Hospital, Municipal Sanatorium for Tuberculosis, and Provident Hospital; in Kansas City, Mo., to Kansas City General Hospital No. 2, Wheatley Hospital, and St. Luke's Hospital; in St. Louis, Mo., to City Hospital No.1 and City Hospital No. 2; in Washington, D.C., to Freedman's Hospital, Howard University Medical School, City Tuberculosis Sanatorium, and City General Hospital; in Philadelphia, Pa., to Philadelphia General Hospital, Mercy Hopital, and the University of Pennsylvania School of Medicine; in New York, N.Y., to Harlem Hospital, Lincoln Hospital, and Bellevue Hospital; and in Boston, Mass., to Harvard University Medical School and one anonymous hospital. Report, "Committee Investigating the Admittance of Colored Interns and Nurses to the Staff of Cleveland City Hospital," 12 December 1927, Western Reserve Historical Society Library.

[2] Ibid., p. 25 and Exhibit #2, p. 5.

[3] Ibid., p. 19. The University of Pennsylvania School of Medicine, however, did not admit a black woman until 1960. On the other hand, the doors of the school had been opened to white women since 1914 (Corner, 1965, p. 249, and personal correspondence, Office of Minority Affairs, University of Pennsylvania School of Medicine).

[4] Interview, Haynes Rice, Howard University Hospital, Washington, D.C., 8 October 1982.

In the following table, a coded entry is given for the "Source" column. These sources of information are:

A = Association of American Medical Colleges (specifically from the 1991–92 AAMC *Directory of American Medical Education*).
C = W. Montague Cobb (specifically from pages 1218–19 of "The Black American in Medicine." *Journal of the National Medical Association.* 1981:73 (suppl):1185–1244.
F = Abraham Flexner ("Medical Education in the United States and Canada." New York: Carnegie Foundation for the Advancement of Teaching, Bulletin No. 4, 1910).
M = Kenneth R. Manning (Talk given on November 9, 1993, at the HUCM Symposium, "The Path We Tread.")

Table 1—Predominantly Black U.S. Medical Schools, 1868–1993

DATES	NAME AND LOCATION OF MEDICAL SCHOOL	SOURCE	COMMENTS
1868–	Howard University College of Medicine, Washington, D.C.	ACFM	—
1870–72	Medical Department of Lincoln University, Lincoln University, Pa.	M	No graduates.
1876–	Meharry Medical College Nashville, Tenn.	ACFM	Original name was Medical Department of Central Tennessee; changed to Meharry Medical College of Walden University in 1900; became separate corporate entity in 1915.
1882–1918	Leonard Medical College of Shaw University, Raleigh, N.C.	CFM	First U.S. medical school to have a 4-year graded curriculum.
1888–1912	Louisville National Medical College Louisville, Ky.	CFM	—
1889–1911	Flint Medical College of New Orleans University, New Orleans, La.	CFM	—
1889–1896	Hannibal Medical College Memphis, Tenn.	M	—
1895–1910	Knoxville College Medical Department, Knoxville, Tenn.	CM	—
1899–1908	Chattanooga National Medical College, Chattanooga, Tenn.	CM	—

Table 1, *continued*

Dates	Name and Location of Medical School	Source	Comments
1899–1903	State University Medical Department of Louisville, Louisville, Ky.	M	Merged with Louisville National Medical College in 1903.
1900–1910	Knoxville Medical College Knoxville, Tenn.	F	Independent institution.
1900–1923	Medical Department of the University of West Tennessee, Memphis, Tenn.	CF	Originally located in Jackson, Tenn., 1900-1907
1900–?	Medico-Chirurgical and Theological College of Christ's Institution, Baltimore, Md.	M	—
1966–	Charles R. Drew University of Medicine and Science Los Angeles, Calif.	AM	Signed expanded affiliation agreement with UCLA in 1978 to develop undergraduate medical education for third and fourth years of clinical instruction leading to joint M.D. degree.
1978–	Morehouse School of Medicine Atlanta, Ga.	AM	Originally a component of Morehouse College; became independent in 1981.

3

Historic Achievements of African Americans in U.S. Medicine

Whereas chapter 2 focused on the institutional history of the 15 predominantly black medical schools that have existed in the United States from 1868 to 1993, this chapter emphasizes the individual milestones achieved by more than 100 different African-American medical pioneers from the 1780s on. The milestones are listed chronologically in order to demonstrate the relationship of these pioneering breakthroughs to the social and political history of the times. In a sense, this chapter is a preview of the detailed information about the more than 500 African-American pioneers that appears in chapters 6 through 10.

Table 2 highlights milestones in all aspects of academic medicine, Table 3 in organized medicine, and Table 4 in activities closely related to academic and organized medicine. These three tables demonstrate that African Americans made slow but steady progress in all of these areas. In each of these tables, the first entry explicitly includes the reminder that the individual in question was the "first African American" to make the given pioneering achievement. To save space, the term "first African American" is omitted from the remaining entries in these tables.

Of the 202 items selected to illustrate the chronological history of this pioneering, 38 percent are in the area of medical education, 37 percent in organized medicine, and the remaining 25 percent in related activities (Table 16). The items selected for the Howard and Meharry graduates tend to emphasize organized medicine, while those for the "other "schools are more in the area of medical education. For specific historical milestones, refer to tables 2, 3, and 4. These tables include the schools from which the pioneers graduated, coded as "H" for Howard, "M" for Meharry, and "O" for other.

Although limitations of space precluded the chronological listing of all the pioneering "firsts" listed in chapters 6 through 10 of this book, an attempt has been made to select enough of the highlights to demonstrate the relationship of these pioneering breakthroughs to the social and political history of the times.

For example, Table 2 reminds us that there was at least one African-American physician (James Derham) in the United States shortly after the American revolution and that several African Americans graduated from U.S. medical schools prior to the Civil War. During the Civil War, an African American (Alexander Augusta) became head of Freedmen's Hospital and the first African-American woman (Rebecca Lee Crumpler) received her M.D. from a U.S. school. Following that war, African Americans became members of the faculty at Howard and Meharry medical schools and started interning at predominantly white hospitals.

In the following table, a coded entry is given for the medical school from which individual graduated: H = Howard, M = Meharry, O = Other.

Table 2—Chronological Summary of Selected Black Pioneers in Medical Education

1780s	James Derham (Durham) is first African-American physician in the U.S. (learned from other physicians).
1837	James Smith (O) is first American to receive the M.D. degree (University of Glasgow).
1847	David Peck (O) is first documented graduate of a U.S. medical school (Rush).
1849	John DeGrasse (O) and Thomas White (O) become second and third U.S. M.D.s (Bowdoin).
1863–64	Alexander Augusta (O) heads Freedmen's Hospital in Washington, D.C .
1864	Rebecca Lee Crumpler (O) becomes first woman M.D. in the U.S. (N.E. Female Medical College)
1867	Rebecca Cole (O) becomes second woman M.D. in the U.S. (Female Medical College of Pennsylvania).
1868	Alexander Augusta (O) becomes member of a medical school faculty (HUCM).
1869	Charles Purvis (O) becomes second member of Howard University College of Medicine (HUCM) faculty.
1883	John McKinley (M) becomes faculty member at Meharry Medical College.
1891	Austin Curtis Sr. (O) becomes intern at predominantly white hospital (Provident in Chicago).
1898	Austin Curtis, Sr. (O) becomes chief of surgery at HUCM

Table 2, *continued*

1899	Solomon Fuller (O) becomes faculty member at Boston University Medical School.
1908	Ferdinand Stewart (O) becomes chief of surgery at Meharry.
1917	Julian Lewis (O) becomes first M.D., Ph.D. (M.D., Rush and Ph.D., University of Chicago).
1918	George Hall (O) establishes postgraduate course at Chicago's Provident Hospital.
1918	Ubert Vincent (O) becomes intern at a major U.S. hospital (Bellevue).
1919	Louis Wright (O) becomes member of the medical staff at Harlem Hospital.
1920	William Quinland (M) receives first Rosenwald Fellowship for advanced medical study.
1929–40	Numa P. G. Adams (O) is dean of HUCM.
1930	Roscoe McKinney (O) earns Ph.D. in anatomy (University of Chicago).
1930–57	Julian Ross (H) chairs department of obstetrics/gynecology at HUCM.
1931	Joseph Johnson (O) earns M.D., Ph.D. (University of Chicago).
1931	Arnold Maloney (O) earns M.D. and Ph.D. degrees (M.D., Indiana; Ph.D., Wisconsin) and becomes professor of pharmacology at HUCM.
1931	Frederick Stubbs (O) interns at a white teaching hospital (Cleveland City).
1932	Robert Jason (H) earns Ph.D. in pathology (University of Chicago).
1932	Vernon Wilkerson (O) earns Ph.D. in biochemistry (University of Minnesota).
1933	Ruth Moore (O) earns Ph.D. in bacteriology (Ohio State).
1934	Paul Cornely (O) earns Dr.P.H. (University of Michigan).
1934	Moses Young (H) earns Ph.D. in anatomy (University of Michigan).
1934–70	Moses Young (H) teaches anatomy at HUCM.
1935	Flemmie Kittrell (O) (female) earns Ph.D. in nutrition (Cornell).
1937	Hildrus Poindexter (O) earns M.D. plus Ph.D. in bacteriology and M.P.H. (M.D., Harvard; Ph.D. and MPH, Columbia)
1941	Michael Bent (M) becomes dean at Meharry Medical College.
1941	Ruth Lloyd (O) earns Ph.D. in anatomy (Western Reserve).
1941–46	John Lawlah (O) is concurrently dean at HUCM and director of Freedmen's Hospital.
1948	Marie Daly (O) earns Ph.D. in chemistry (Columbia).

Table 2, *continued*

1949	Clarence Greene (H) becomes chief of HUCM's Division of Neurosurgery.
1949–53	William Hinton (O) is a professor at Harvard Medical School
1952	Albert Wheeler (O) becomes full-time professor at the University of Michigan Medical School.
1952–56	Calvin Sampson (M) is resident (in pathology) at Episcopal Hospital in Philadelphia.
1952–66	Harold West (O) is president of Meharry Medical College.
1953–58	W. Lester Henry (H) is Markle Foundation Scholar in Medical Science.[1]
1955	Doris Shockley (O) becomes first woman to earn a Ph.D. in pharmacology in the U.S.
1960	Lloyd Elam (O) becomes chief of psychiatry at Meharry Medical College.
1960–62	Middleton Lambright (M) is assistant dean at the Medical University of South Carolina.
1965–66	Russell Miller (H) interns in internal medicine at the University of Michigan Medical School.
1966–68	Carroll Leevy (O) is chair of internal medicine at a predominantly white medical school (Seton Hall).
1968–75	Jeanne Spurlock (H) is first woman woman chair of psychiatry at Meharry Medical College.
1969	Carlton Alexis (H) becomes vice president for health affairs at Howard University.
1969	Anna Cherrie Epps (H) founds Medical Education Reinforcement and Enrichment Program for Minorities in the Health Professions (MedREP) at Tulane Medical Center.
1969	W. Montague Cobb (H) becomes distinguished professor of anatomy at HUCM.
1969	James Comer (H) becomes associate dean at Yale Medical School.
1969	Helen Dickens (O) becomes associate dean at the University of Pennsylvania Medical School.
1969	Melvin Jenkins (O) becomes tenured faculty member at the University of Nebraska Medical School.
1969	Alvin Pouissant (O) becomes associate dean (of students) at Harvard Medical School.

---

[1]Markle scholars were competitively selected individuals who received substantial funding from the John and Mary Markle Foundation to advance their careers in medical research and academic medicine.

Table 2, *continued*

1969–77   Mitchell Spellman (H) is president/dean of Drew Postgraduate Medical School (and assistant dean at UCLA Medical School).

1970   Eleanor Franklin (O) becomes first female administrative officer (associate dean for academic affairs) in Dean's Office at HUCM.

1971–72   Claude Organ (O) is chair of surgery at a predominantly white medical school (Creighton).

1972   Asa Yancey, Sr., (O) becomes associate dean at Emory Medical School.

1972–88   Jack White (H) founds and directs HUCM Cancer Center.

1973   Samuel Kountz (O) becomes chair of surgery at SUNY-Downstate Medical Center.

1976   Joycelyn Elders (O) becomes full professor at the University of Arkansas Medical School.

1976   Charles Whitten (M) becomes associate dean at Wayne State Medical School.

1977–78   Levi Watkins (O) is chief resident in surgery at Johns Hopkins.

1977–82   Russell Miller (H) is Burroughs-Wellcome Scholar in clinical pharmacology.

1977–80   Pauline Titus-Dillon (H) is first woman to direct a training program in internal medicine (D.C. General Hospital).

1978   Maurice Clifford (M) becomes vice president for medical affairs at the Medical College of Pennsylvania.

1978   Mitchell Spellman (H) becomes executive vice president (and dean for medical services) at Harvard University Medical Center.

1978   Augustus White (O) becomes professor of orthopaedic surgery at Harvard Medical School.

1980   Pauline Titus-Dillon (H) becomes highest female M.D. administrator in HUCM dean's office.

1980–86   Maurice Clifford (M) is president of the Medical College of Pennsylvania.

1981   Louis Sullivan (O) becomes president of Morehouse School of Medicine.

1987   William Matory (H) initiates HUCM Magnificent Professor Recognition Program.

1988–90   LaSalle Leffall (H) is president of the Society of Surgical Department Chairmen.

1991   Levi Watkins (O) becomes assistant dean at Johns Hopkins University School of Medicine.

1991   Donald Wilson (O) becomes dean of a predominantly white medical school (University of Maryland).

1993   Haile Debas (O) becomes dean of a predominantly white medical school (University California, San Francisco).

As illustrated in Table 2, African Americans began in the early 1900s to earn advanced degrees at predominantly white institutions. In 1929, HUCM appointed Numa Adams as its first African-American dean; Meharry Medical College appointed Michael Bent in 1941. By the mid-1950s, African Americans began to be appointed to the faculty of predominantly white medical schools and to become Markle scholars. These developments were accelerated by the Civil Rights movement of the 1950s and 1960s and by the assassination of Dr. Martin Luther King, Jr., in 1968.

By the late 1960s, a number of African Americans had been appointed as associate deans at Ivy League medical schools, and between 1969 and 1981 African Americans were named as presidents of two new predominantly black medical schools (King/Drew and Morehouse). Finally, in 1980, Maurice Clifford became president of the predominantly white Medical College of Pennsylvania; and in 1991, Donald Wilson became Dean of the predominantly white University of Maryland School of Medicine. He was followed in 1993 by Dr. Haile Debas who became dean of the predominantly white University of California, San Francisco, School of Medicine.

Table 3 reveals a somewhat similar chronology for the participation of African Americans in organized medicine. Prior to the Civil War, at least one African American (John de Grasse) became a member of a medical society in a northern state. Shortly after the Civil War, several eminent African-American physicians were presented to the District of Columbia Medical Society for membership but were refused. Partly as a result of such refusals, the National Medical Association was founded in 1895.

In the following table, a coded entry is given for the medical school from which individual graduated: H = Howard, M = Meharry, O = Other.

Table 3—Chronological Summary of Selected Black Pioneers in Organized Medicine

1854	John De Grasse (O) becomes first African-American member of a medical association (Massachusetts Medical Society).
1869	Alexander Augusta (O), Charles Purvis (O), and Alpheus Tucker (O) are presented to the District of Columbia Medical Society for membership but are refused.
1888	Nathan Mossell (O) becomes a member of the Philadelphia County Medical Society.
1895	Miles Lynk (M) suggests organization of the National Medical Association (NMA).
1895	Daniel Williams (O) founds and is vice president of the NMA.
1895	Henry Butler (M) becomes chair of the executive board of the NMA.
1895–98	Robert Boyd (M) is president of the NMA.
1897–1904	Charles Purvis (O) is a member of the District of Columbia Board of Medical Examiners.
1913	Daniel Williams (O) becomes charter member and fellow of the American College of Surgeons.
1918	Ulysses Dailey (O), John Hunter (O), and John Kenney, Sr., (O) found Andrew Clinical Society.
1919	Dorothy Brown (M) becomes first woman fellow of the American College of Surgeons.
1921	John Turner (O) is founder and president of the Pennsylvania State Medical, Dental, and Pharmacy Association.
1927	William Barnes (O) is certified as specialist (otolaryngology).
1931	William Barnes (O) founds Society for the Promotion of Negro Specialists in Medicine.
1931	Peter Murray (H) is certified by the American Board of Obstetrics and Gynecology.
1933	Chester Chinn (O) is certified by the American Board of Ophthalmology.
1935	William Allen (H) becomes a diplomate of the American Board of Radiologists.
1935	G. Hamilton Francis (M) founds the NMA House of Delegates.
1935	Justin Hope (O) is certified by the American Board of Psychiatry and Neurology.
1935	Theodore Lawless (O) is certified by the American Board of Dermatology and Syphilology.
1935	Julian Ross (H) is certified in both obstetrics and gynecology
1936	R. Frank Jones (H) becomes a diplomate of the American Board of Urology.

Table 3, *continued*

1936	Alonzo Smith (O) is certified by American Board of Pediatrics.
1937	Jesse Peters (O) is certified by the American Board of Radiology.
1937	William Quinland (M) becomes a member of the American Association of Pathologists and Bacteriologists and is certified by the American Board of Pathology.
1938	Roscoe Giles (O) becomes a diplomate of the American Board of Surgery.
1940	Henry Callis (O) becomes a diplomate of the American Board of Internal Medicine.
1942–46	Ulysses Dailey (O), Carl Roberts (O), and Frederick Stubbs (O) are among first four members of the American College of Surgeons.
1943	Frederick Stubbs (O) becomes a member of the American Board of Surgery
1949	James Gladden (M) is certified by the American Board of Orthopedic Surgeons.
1949	J. Richard Laurey (O) is certified by the American Board of Thoracic Surgery.
1949	William Morman (H) is one of first two admitted to the St. Louis Medical Society and the first to be admitted to the Missouri State Medical Society.
1950	Peter Murray (H) becomes a member of AMA House of Delegates.
1951	James Gladden (M) becomes a fellow in the American Academy of Orthopaedic Surgeons.
1951	Julian Ross (H) is a founding fellow of the American College of Obstetrics and Gynecology.
1953	Clarence Greene (H) becomes a diplomate of the American Board of Neurosurgery.
1954–55	Peter Murray (H) is president of the New York County Medical Society
1955	Edward Crump (M), Axel Hansen (M), and Matthew Walker (M) become members of the Nashville (Tenn.) Academy of Medicine.
1959	Howard Venable (O) becomes an examiner for the American Board of Ophthalmology.
1961	Paul Cornely (O) becomes president of the Physician's Forum.
1962	Bobby Harris (O) is certified in colorectal surgery.
1965	R. Frank Jones (H) becomes a member of the American Urological Association.
1968	Vincent Porter (H) is certified in plastic surgery.
1969	Paul Cornely (O) becomes president of the American Public Health Association.
1969	Helen Dickens (O) is first woman admitted to the American College of Surgeons.

Table 3, *continued*

1969	Walter Leavell (M) becomes president of the Minority Affairs Section of the AAMC Group on Student Affairs.
1971–78	W. Lester Henry, Jr. (H) is a governor of the American Board of Internal Medicine and a member of its Residency Review Committe
1972	Arthur Coleman (H) becomes president of the Golden State Medical Association.
1972–80	Jeanne Spurlock (H) is a member of the Committee on Certification in Child Psychiatry (and chairperson in 1979).
1973	John Anderson (H) founds the Southwest Medical Association, Inc.
1973	James Comer (H) cofounds Black Psychiatrists of America.
1974–75	Samuel Kountz (O) is president of the Society of University Surgeons.
1974–78	W. Lester Henry, Jr., (H) is a representative to the American Board of Medical Specialties.
1974–80	W. Lester Henry, Jr., (H) is a regent of the American College of Physicians.
1975	Walter Leavell (M) cofounds the National Association of Minority Medical Educators (NAMME).
1975	Samual Rosser (H) is certified in pediatric surgery.
1977–83	Charles Epps, Jr., (H) is a member of the American Board of Orthopaedic Surgery.
1978	LaSalle Leffall, Jr. (H) becomes president of the Society of Surgical Oncology
1979	Charles Epps, Jr., (H) becomes president of the D.C. Medical Society.
1982–88	Charles Epps, Jr., (H) is a governor of the American College of Surgeons.
1983–89	Melvin Jenkins (O) is a governor of the American Board of Pediatrics.
1984–86	Claude Organ (O) is chairperson of the American Board of Surgery.
1985	Clarence Avery (O) becomes president of the California Medical Association.
1985	Charles Epps, Jr., (H) becomes president of the American Orthopaedic Association.
1985	Deborah Turner (O) is first woman certified in gynecological oncology.
1985	Asa Yancey, Sr., (O) becomes a member of the Southern Surgical Association.
1986	Edith Irby Jones (O) becomes first woman president of the NMA.
1986	Rosalyn Sterling (O) is first woman certified by American Board of Thoracic Surgeons.
1986	John Townsend (O) and Donald Wilson (O) found the Association for Academic Minority Physicians.

Table 3, *continued*

1987	W. Lester Henry, Jr., (H) becomes a master in the American College of Physicians.
1988–90	LaSalle Leffall, Jr. (H) is president of the Society of Surgical Chairmen.
1989	Vivian Pinn (O) becomes second woman president of the NMA.
1990	Roselyn Epps (H) becomes president of the American Medical Women's Association.
1992	Roselyn Epps (H) becomes first woman president of the D.C. Medical Society.

As shown in Table 3, African Americans began by the early 1900s to become certified as medical specialists and in 1931 a society was founded for the promotion of black specialists in medicine. In the mid-1900s, an increasing number of African Americans were admitted to local and county medical societies; and in 1950, Peter Murray became the first African-American member of the AMA House of Delegates. Concurrently with the Civil Rights movement, African Americans began moving into leadership positions in organized medicine. From the 1970s on, a number of both men and women became presidents of their respective local, state, and national professional organizations.

Table 4 shows a similar progression regarding the participation of African Americans in activities closely related to medical education or organized medicine. For example, at least one African American (Alexander Augusta) received a medical commission during the Civil War. Soon after the Civil War, African Americans founded several hospitals of their own and began serving on the staffs of at least a few predominantly white hospitals.

In the following table, a coded entry is given for the medical school from which individual graduated: H = Howard, M = Meharry, O = Other.

Table 4—Chronological Summary of Selected Black Pioneers in Activities Closely Related to Medical Education and Organized Medicine

1863	Alexander Augusta (O) is first African American to receive a medical commission in the U.S. Army.
1891	George Hall (O), Allen Wesley (O), and Daniel Williams (O) cofound Chicago's Provident Hospital.
1895	Nathan Mossell (O) founds the Frederick Douglas Memorial Hospital (Philadelphia).
1896	Austin Curtis, Sr. (O) becomes a member of the surgical staff at Chicago's Cook County Hospital.
1898?	Artisha Gilbert (H) becomes first woman physician in Kentucky.
1899	Solomon Fuller (O) becomes first psychiatrist in the United States.
1904	Thomas Jones (O) founds obstetrical school for blacks in Gonzales,Texas.
1908	John Kenney, Sr. (O) suggests establishment of *Journal of the National Medical Association* (*JNMA*).
1908–18	Charles Roman (M) edits *JNMA*.
1914	Ernest Just (O) receives first Spingarn medal.
1917	Charles Garvin (H) receives commission as Army officer in World War I.
1920	Charles Garvin (H) appointed as urologist at Western Reserve University's Lakeland Hospital.
1924–36	Joseph Ward (O) heads Veterans hospital at Tuskegee.
1929	Louis Wright (O) becomes police surgeon for New York City.
1930	Ernest Just (O) becomes vice president of American Society of Zoologists.
1931–41	John Turner (O) is police surgeon for the city of Philadelphia.
1932	Whittier Atkinson (H) founds an interracial hospital in Pennsylvania.
1940	Charles Drew (O) organizes a blood bank to supply plasma to the British.
1940	Roscoe Giles (O), Clarence Payne (O), and Carl Roberts (O) get "COL" (colored) removed from AMA directory.
1941	Charles Drew (O) directs first American Red Cross Blood Bank.
1941	Vance Marchbanks (H) becomes surgeon for the 332nd Fighter Group and for Tuskegee Army Air Force Base.
1944	Eugene Dibble (H) is commissioned as colonel in the U.S. Army Medical Corps.

Table 4, *continued*

1947–65	Hildrus Poindexter (O) is surgical and medical director of the U.S. Public Health Service.
1951–52	Howard Payne (H) is vice president of the National Tuberculosis Association.
1954	John Johnson, Jr. (O) and R. Frank Jones (H) become staff members of Georgetown University Hospital.
1955	William Cardozo (O) helps found the Alpha Omega Alpha Honorary Society at HUCM.
1957	W. Montague Cobb (H) founds and becomes president of the American Association of Physical Anthropologists.
1960	Whittier Atkinson (H) is named General Practioner of the Year by the Pennsylvania State Medical Society.
1964	Lena Edwards (H) receives the Presidential Medal of Freedom (for her work with migrants, etc.).
1968	Jesse Barber (H) founds the Howard University Medical Stroke Project.
1968	Clotilde Bowen (O) becomes first woman lieutenant colonel in the U.S. Army.
1969	Dennis Dove (O) becomes AAMC Administrative Assistant for Minority Affairs.
1970–74	James Cowan (M) is state commissioner for health in New Jersey.
1971	Calvin Sampson (M) founds HUCM Department of Allied Health Professions.
1971	Jeanne Spurlock (H) is first woman to receive the Strecker Psychiatric Award.
1973	Arthur Coleman (H) cofounds the American Health Care Plan.
1974	James Cowan (M) becomes the assistant secretary of defense (for health and environment).
1974–77	John Holloman (O) is president of the NYC Health and Hospital Corporation.
1975	Marion Mann (H) becomes one of first M.D. generals in the U.S. Army.
1979	LaSalle Leffall (H) becomes president of the American Cancer Society.
1984	Clive Callender (M) becomes a member of the National Task Force on Organ Procurement and Transplantation.
1986–88	Herbert Nickens (O) directs HHS Office of Minority Health.
1987	Mae Jemison (O) becomes first female astronaut.
1988	Harold Freeman (H) becomes second president of the American Cancer Society.
1988	Herbert Nickens (O) becomes vice president of the AAMC Division of Minority Health, Disease Prevention, and Health Promotion.

Table 4, *continued*

1989–93	Louis Sullivan (O) is M.D. secretary of the U.S. Department of Health and Human Services.
1990	Bernard Harris (O) becomes first male astronaut
1991	Vivian Pinn (O) becomes director of the NIH Office of Research on Women's Health.
1992	Edward Cooper (M) becomes president of the American Heart Association.
1993	Joycelyn Elders (O) becomes the surgeon general of the United States.

In the early 1900s, the *Journal of the National Medical Association* was established, and during World War I, some African Americans were commissioned as Army physicians. In the 1920s, an African American (Joseph Ward) was appointed as head of a Veterans hospital and another African American (Whittier Atkinson) founded an interracial hospital in Philadelphia. In the 1940s Charles Drew directed the first Red Cross Blood Bank, and Vance Marchbanks became a surgeon at the Tuskegee Army Air Force Base.

During the decades of the Civil Rights movement, African Americans began to be elected as officers of medically-related organizations and to become staff members of predominantly white teaching hospitals. They also were appointed to important positions in the local, state, and federal governments. By the late 1980s, Louis Sullivan, an African-American physician, was serving as the secretary of health and human services. In 1993, Joycelyn Elders, an African-American woman, was appointed as surgeon general of the United States.

PART II

REPRESENTATIVE
AFRICAN-AMERICAN
MEDICAL PIONEERS

This section features detailed biographical sketches of 33 representative African-American medical pioneers. Formal portraits for each of the 33 pioneers and numerous informal snapshots showing them with colleagues, friends, patients, and students are also included.

Chapter 5 includes a content analysis of the achievements of the 33 individuals and of their interview responses regarding attitudes and advice.

4

Biographies of 33 Pioneers

Building on the general historical background summarized in chapter 2 and the specific historical milestones presented in the previous chapter, this chapter consists of detailed biographical sketches of 33 of the more prominent African-American pioneers in academic and organized medicine.

All of the biographies are based on personal interviews except for those of Drs. Cobb and Drew, who are deceased, and that for Dr. Organ, whose sketch is based on his book about black surgeons (Organ and Kosiba, 1987).

With the exception of Drs. Cobb and Drew, each sketch begins with a chronological history of the individual's life and ends with his or her personal observations concerning obstacles encountered, help received, and advice to others. The opening sentence of each sketch includes a "black first" which was selected somewhat arbitrarily as an example of that person's pioneering achievement.

The 33 individual sketches that follow are presented alphabetically and are accompanied by both formal and informal photographs. For an overall summary of the key contents of these biographies, see chapter 5.

Clive Orville Callender, M.D., F.A.C.S.

Chronological History

Clive O. Callender, the first (and as of 1993 the only) African-American member of a national Task Force on Organ Procurement and Transplantation, was born in New York City on November 16, 1936. His mother died giving birth to him and a twin brother. Consequently, he lived for a period in foster homes, then a short stay with his stepmother, and finally with an aunt. Living with Aunt Ella was the turning point in his life. She was an ardent churchgoer and it was with her at age seven that he became a Christian and decided he wanted to become a medical missionary.

Dr. Callender's public schooling in New York was interrupted at age 16 when he developed tuberculosis. While hospitalized, he took a battery of tests that indicated he was capable of succeeding at whatever he wanted to do. Once he reentered school, teachers and counselors told him he didn't have what it took to pursue a college education, let alone a medical career. What might have been a deterrent to many only fueled his determination, for his underlying belief was that "obstacles are but stepping stones to success if you have faith in God."

In 1955, Dr. Callender entered Hunter College, then a 97 percent white institution. Although he was told there was no way he could get into a medical school, he was the first in his class to be accepted. Even after the offer, classmates tried to discourage him, saying he would never make it because his father did not earn enough money. Moreover, at the end of a very successful freshman year at Meharry Medical College, he returned to Hunter to visit former teachers, anxious to tell them about his experiences there. One faculty member called him a liar, stated he had never been accepted to medical school, and refused to talk to him. That stimulated

Clive O. Callender, M.D., shown in 1988 lecturing to medical students and community members about the need for organ/tissue donations in the African-American community.

him to work even harder, and in 1963 Dr. Callender received a medical degree from Meharry, graduating as its top ranking student.

After completing his surgical training, first at the University of Cincinnati (1963–64), then at Harlem Hospital in New York (1964–65), and at Howard University's Freedmen's Hospital (1968–69), Dr. Callender pursued his goal to become a medical missionary and traveled to Africa. He spent a year there before realizing he might make an even more meaningful medical contribution in America. Investigating the opportunities, Dr. Callender discovered that there were few, if any, black physicians in organ transplantation and decided to enter that area. His entry was via an NIH postdoctoral fellowship to train from 1971 to 1973 in transplant immunology at the University of Minnesota.

A young Clive O. Callender graduates from Meharry Medical College in 1963 as the ranking student in his class.

In 1973, Dr. Callender returned to Howard and established a kidney transplant program. Although during this period the government was designating transplant centers, Howard University was not one of them. Consequently, until 1975, under Dr. Callender's direction, the hospital was performing transplants without remuneration. However, because of its excellent patient care results, as well as political warfare on its behalf, the secretary of the U.S. Department of Health and Human Services (HHS) designated Howard University Hospital as a transplant center with funding retroactive to 1973. In 1987 Dr. Callender completed a Special Clinical Liver Transplant Visiting Fellowship at the University of Pittsburgh. He was the first black physician to participate in liver and kidney transplantation.

Dr. Callender can claim several other "firsts," including being the first and only black member of the National Organ Transplant Task Force, the only black member on the End-State Renal Disease Study that was completed in 1991, the only black physician to have a transplant center named in his honor, the first black transplant center director in a minority institution and one which has the only minority-run histocompatibility laboratory in the world, codirector of the only minority-run dialysis and transplant center in the country,and the first black member of the HHS secretary's Advisory Committee to the End State Renal Disease Data Program.

Personal Observations

When asked about African Americans who had helped him along the way, Dr. Callender cited his cousins, Drs. Herbert and Vernal Cave (who were role models), his aunt, Mrs. Ella Waters (who was responsible for his religious development), his twin brother, Carl (who was always supportive), and the pastor and members of Ebenezer Gospel Tabernacle in New York City. He also named Drs. Burke Syphax (an early chairman of the Department of Surgery at Howard), LaSalle D. Leffall (its present chairman), Samuel Kountz (the first black transplant surgeon), Curtis Yeager (his transplant coordinator), and Lewis Kurtz as among the black professionals who had inspired his career and were responsible for much of his success. He also noted that his wife, Fern, is the strength behind everything he has done.

Relative to nonblacks who had influenced his career, Dr. Callender appreciated Dr. Katherine V. Kreidle and other physiology and chemistry faculty members at Hunter College, and four other individuals: Dr. John Nejarian, who accepted him into the transplant fellowship at the University of Minnesota and sponsored him for membership in professional organizations and societies; Dr. Richard Simmons, chairman, Department of Surgery, University of Minnesota, who was his surgical transplant mentor; Dr. Thomas Starzl, who trained him in liver transplantation; and Dr. Felix Rappaport, who helped organize the International Symposiums on Transplantation in Blacks.

Dr. Callender recognizes that every person has natural gifts that make him or her special. He stated, "God has created each of us in a beautiful yet unique way." His advice to young people is, "Relish this uniqueness, take God's gifts and use them to the utmost each day to become the best you can be. If I, an ordinary man with faith in God and hard work, can succeed, so can you!"

William Montague Cobb, M.D., Ph.D.

Chronological History

William Montague Cobb, principal historian of the African American in medicine, was born in Washington, D.C., on October 12, 1904, the son of William Elmer and Alexzine Montague Cobb. Reared in Washington, "Will Cobb, the printer's son," as he often referred to himself, attended Paul Lawrence Dunbar High School, where he excelled in academics and was a varsity letterman in cross country and track. Upon graduating from Dunbar in 1921, Dr. Cobb headed for New England, where he matriculated at Amherst College.

At Amherst, he was his class's ranking student in biology and was awarded the Blodgett Scholarship for study at the Marine Biological Laboratory at Woods Hole, Massachusetts. He also won championships for Amherst in cross country and boxing before graduating in 1925. In 1929, Dr. Cobb earned his medical degree from Howard University, where he taught embryology during his senior year.

In June of that year, he married Hilda B. Smith of Washington, D.C., and they eventually had two daughters, Carolyn Wilkinson and Amelia Gray. From Howard he went to Western Reserve University where he received his doctoral degree in anatomy and physical anthropology in 1932.

In 1932, Dr. Cobb returned to Howard as assistant professor of anatomy. By 1942 he had been promoted to full professor and he served as chairman of the department of anatomy from 1947 to 1969. In 1969 he was the first to be elevated to the rank of distinguished professor at Howard University and in 1973 he achieved emeritus status. After retiring, Dr. Cobb was a visiting professor at several universities. He was visiting professor of anatomy at Stanford University and at the University of Maryland, distinguished university professor at the University

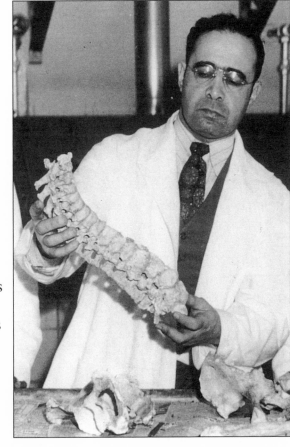

W. Montague Cobb, M.D., Ph.D., shown during the 1940s examining specimens in the HUCM gross anatomy laboratory.

of Arkansas, and visiting professor of orthopaedic surgery at Harvard University, Beth Israel Hospital.

Dr. Cobb loved the written word. He frequently could be found in his "inner sanctum" writing or reading. He published over 600 articles, editorials, biographical sketches, and other works. As editor of the *Journal of the National Medical Association (JNMA)* for 27 years (from 1920 to 1947), he developed that publication into a highly respected journal. He is also recognized as the principal historian of the African American in medicine.

During the course of his career, Dr. Cobb received numerous honors. These included founding and serving as president of the American Association of Physical Anthropologists, being a fellow of the American Anthropological Association, a board member and national president of the National Association for the Advancement of Colored People (NAACP), and president of the National Medical Association. He received the Distinguished Service Award of the Medico-Chirurgical Society of the

(L to R) Howard University President Franklyn G. Jenifer, Ph.D., Russell L. Miller, Jr., M.D., W. Montague Cobb, M.D., Ph.D., and Charles H. Epps, Jr., M.D., at October 1991 dedication of the medical school's Numa P. G. Adams Building.

District of Columbia, the Henry Gray Award of the American Association of Anatomists, the Scroll of Merit from the National Medical Association, and ten honorary degrees from noted universities. He also served as a member or chairman of the board of numerous organizations, foundations, and special study groups, including the American Heart Association, the American Eugenics Society, and the 1965 White House Conference on Health.

Throughout his lifetime, Dr. Cobb engaged in an unremitting struggle for human and civil rights. He championed many causes, including improved medical care rendered to African Americans, integrating hospitals, and lobbying for the passage of the Medicare-Medicaid legislation. His successful efforts to integrate the District of Columbia Medical Society made it possible for others to become pioneers in organized medicine because membership in a local medical society was a prerequisite for membership in many state and national medical organizations.

Dr. Cobb died on November 20, 1990, at George Washington University Hospital after a long illness. He had recently celebrated his 86th birthday. His memorial service was held on November 26, 1990, at Howard University's Andrew Rankin Memorial Chapel. The overflow crowd that paid him their last respects also heard tributes from a number of distinguished speakers, including Dr. James Whittico, representing the Past President's Council of the National Medical Association, and Dr. Benjamin Hooks, executive director of the NAACP. Other tributes to Dr. Cobb's memory included a memorial dinner sponsored by the Black Students' Union at Amherst College. The dinner was followed by a gathering at Amherst's Charles Drew House, which had been named after Dr. Cobb's fellow alumnus.

(Most of Dr. Cobb's biography is from his memorial service program.)

James Pierpont Comer, M.D.

Chronological History

James P. Comer, cofounder of the Black Psychiatrists of America, was born in East Chicago, Indiana, on September 25, 1934. He was raised there by his parents and attended both its elementary and secondary public schools. In 1956, he received the bachelor of arts degree from Indiana University. When the Howard University College of Medicine began its academic year in 1956, James was a member of the freshman class. He mastered the program in medical education with relative ease and in 1960 received a medical degree. Dr. Comer was admitted to the University of Michigan School of Public Health and awarded a masters degree in public health in 1964.

While receiving training in psychiatry, Dr. Comer was a staff member at the Yale University School of Medicine (1964–67), the Yale Child Study Center (1966–67), and the Hillcrest Children's Center, Washington, D.C. (1967–68). He was also a staff physician at the National Institute of

Mental Health (1967–68). Since 1969 he has been associate dean for students at the Yale University School of Medicine.

Dr. Comer has written several books discussing various topics that include race relations, the African-American family unit, educational and social welfare programs, and African-American child care. Among his book titles are *Beyond Black and White, Black Child Care: How to Bring up a Healthy Black Child, School Power: Implications of an Intervention Project,* and *Maggie's Dream: The Life and Times of a Black Family.* In addition, he is published in many scholarly and professional journals

James P. Comer, M.D., with third-grade students at the Katherine Brennan School, one of the more than 300 institutions in the School Development Program that he initiated. Courtesy of John Abbott, *Newsweek.*

covering topics that have a major interest for educators, counselors, administrators, and parents.

In 1968, Dr. Comer was a cofounder of the Black Psychiatrists of America. He also developed a school improvement program that is designed to promote student development and learning and to prevent behavioral and psychological problems. This approach is receiving both national and international attention. He is recognized for his pioneering efforts to combine the professional fields of psychiatry and education.

Personal Observations

With hard work and discipline, Dr. Comer indicated that he was able to overcome the hurdles of racism cluttering the path leading to his goals. A strong determination to succeed in spite of obstacles, either overt or covert, is responsible for Dr. Comer's worldwide recognition as one of its leading African-American psychiatrists.

Dr. Comer gives credit to those African-American school staff members, business and professional leaders, civil rights and political leaders, and medical members, especially from *Black Enterprise* and *Ebony* magazines, who, through their support, played a major role in his success. He stated that his family, including his parents and children, was also instrumental in his accomplishments.

The support from many foundations, Yale University faculty and mentors, school officials, and local and federal government officials helped Dr. Comer become a successful psychiatrist. Acknowledging all of this support, Dr. Comer unselfishly shares his knowledge, advice and experience with students at Yale and anywhere else they will listen. He offers encouragement whenever it is needed. For African-American youth considering a career in medicine, Dr. Comer advises, "Work hard and be disciplined."

Concluding his lengthy entry in the 1992–93 edition of *Who's Who in America,* Dr. Comer shares the following general observations concerning race relations and career planning: "As a black child, I sometimes had doubts about my future opportunities for success in our predominantly white country. My parents counseled me never to let the issue of race stand in my way; that the time of greater opportunity for blacks would come. They advised me to work hard, prepare myself, to strive to be the best or among the best in every undertaking, and at the same time be respectful of all people, regardless of their abilities, race, beliefs, or station in life. I have lived by this advice and it has served me well. I have learned not to strive for the top position but to let my work take me where it will in line with my interests."

Paul Bertau Cornely, M.D., Dr. P.H.

Chronological History
Paul B. Cornely, the first African-American president of the American Public Health Association, was born on March 9, 1906, as a French citizen on the island of Guadeloupe in the West Indies. His parents' quest for a better environment led them to Santurce, Puerto Rico, when Paul was three years old. After he had completed his grammar school education there, they moved to the United States where they lived in Harlem for a year and Paul won prizes in English and history. The family next moved to Detroit, where better paying jobs were available in the automotive industry.

Although Paul was interested in becoming an engineer, his father persuaded him that was not a promising field for a black man and encouraged him to enter a profession—such as medicine—where he could serve his own people. With the medical degree as his goal, Paul entered City College in Detroit and subsequently transferred to the University of Michigan from which he received a bachelor of arts degree in 1928. When admitted to this medical school, he was one of only four black freshmen

Paul B. Cornely, M.D., Dr.P.H., 1971 president of the American Public Health Association, passes the gavel to incoming president Lorin E. Kerr, M.D., M.P.H. Courtesy of Reni Photos.

out of a class of 250. In spite of having to do a large amount of part-time work while in medical school, he became the first black student elected to Michigan's Alpha Omega Alpha honor society and received his M.D. degree with honors in 1931.

While interning at Lincoln Hospital in Durham, North Carolina, Paul was approached by Dr. Numa P. G. Adams, dean of Howard University College of Medicine (HUCM), who was recruiting bright young black physicians for eventual careers in academic medicine. At the time, Paul was more interested in becoming a thoracic surgeon (because of a respected white role model, Dr. John Alexander), but Dean Adams was recruiting for the basic sciences and fellowships were available. Of the two-year $2,500 Rockefeller Foundation fellowships, the one in public health appealed to Paul most because it dealt more directly with people.

After completing his internship, Dr. Cornely returned to Michigan and became in 1934 the first black to earn the doctor of public health degree. He then moved to HUCM as an assistant professor of public health and rose steadily to become head of its department of bacteriology, preventive medicine, and public health in 1943 and chairman of its department of community health practice in 1950. He became professor emeritus in 1973 but was still giving occasional lectures at the time of this interview. In 1991 he received an honorary degree from Howard University.

In addition to Dr. Cornely's distinguished career in academic medicine, he was also very active in organized medicine. He founded and was the first president (from 1962 to 1964) of the District of Columbia Public Health Association and was the first black president (1970) of the American Public Health Association. He was also the first black president (1961) of the Physician's Forum, an activist organization founded in New York by Franz Boaz "to reduce prejudice in the health professions." Furthermore, in 1939 Dr. Cornely founded the National Student Health Association, which was aimed at raising the level of health care for students at the more than 100 black colleges in the United States at that time.

Personal Observations

When asked about obstacles encountered, Dr. Cornely said that they were mostly financial. He overcame them by lots of part-time work and by a $625 Julius Rosenwald Fellowship in his senior year of medical school. Even though his medical school tuition was less than $200 per year, he also needed to meet the costs of room, board, and books. Therefore, while in medical school, he waited tables at a university fraternity (a mile and a half from campus) and worked summers at an automobile foundry in Detroit.

One summer, he and his best friend and classmate, K. Albert Harden (who later became dean of HUCM), also earned $1,400 by promoting a "Monday Night Dance" at the Greystone Gardens, a popular ballroom in Detroit. Paul suggested to his father that he stay out of medical school for a year to build up his savings through this venture. His father was afraid that Paul might never return to school and convinced him not to interrupt his studies. In addition, he and Al earned their basement apartment rent in their senior year by doing chores for their landlord. At the time, black students were not admitted to the University of Michigan dormitories and restaurants did not serve the black community. This did not disturb Paul too much because he could afford neither one.

Dr. Cornely encountered several racial obstacles during his medical school days. A faculty member told him that he and the other black medical students would not be allowed to take the obstetrics and gynecology clerkship during the senior year. Al Harden obtained the help of Mr. Fred Butzel, a white lawyer from Detroit, who threatened the medical school dean with a possible lawsuit if the blacks weren't allowed on that clerkship. The bottom line was that "the students only lost two days from the clerkship, but the faculty member lost his job for the following year."

The second such obstacle was that, although an honor graduate, Dr. Cornely could not apply for an internship at his medical center because at that time it did not accept black house staff. Accordingly, he interned at a black institution. As the first black graduate of a predominantly white medical school to intern at predominantly black Lincoln Hospital in Durham, North Carolina, Dr. Cornely said that he was "given a hard time" at first by a few of his black supervisors. After they became better acquainted, however, this problem vanished and he had a good learning experience—partly because many of the professors from Duke medical school came over for lectures and ward rounds.

Regarding advice to other African Americans aspiring to leadership in academic medicine or organized medicine, Dr. Cornely emphasized that one should be ready and willing to "pay one's dues." For example, prior to becoming president of the APHA, he had been the first black chair of its medical care section and a member of the editorial committee of its *Journal.* It also helps to be "persistent and patient," as illustrated by his being elected APHA president on his second attempt. He further believes that black professionals should continue to join predominantly white organizations in large numbers and should become social activists in them, as well as in their local communities and in national affairs.

Dr. Cornely acknowledged the help he had received from a number of other people, both black and white. He cited, in particular, his parents who sacrificed and encouraged his educational aspirations and desire to help others, and his wife-to-be, Mae Stewart, for her belief in him. He also mentioned his appreciation for Dr. Rupert Markee, an early black graduate of his medical school, who advised him how to best approach his medical studies; Dr. Nathan Sinai, the white head of his graduate program who stimulated his interest in health and medical care accessibility for the underserved; and Dr. Lorin Kerr, a lifelong white friend whom he affectionately called "cousin," and who nominated him to become president of the APHA. Finally, the importance Dr. Cornely places on an integrated society was demonstrated when he and his wife sent their son (now an emergency room physician) to predominantly white summer camps so he could overcome the handicap of living daily in the segregated community which characterized Washington, D.C., in the 1930s, '40s, and early '50s.

Helen Octavia Dickens, M.D., F.A.C.S.

Chronological History

Helen O. Dickens, the first African-American woman in the American College of Surgeons, was born on February 21, 1909, in Dayton, Ohio. Her father, a former slave child and waterboy in the Civil War, was taken by a Union colonel and raised by his family in Ohio. Rather than keeping his original name, Helen's father changed it to Dickens after he had met the famous novelist. Her father attended Wilberforce and Oberlin for awhile and "read law." Because of racial prejudice, however, his occupation was that of a janitor in a Dayton, Ohio, bank. Helen's mother, Daisy Jane Dickens, was employed by the Reynolds paper manufacturing family and earned about $24 a week. Both of her parents placed great emphasis on education and had her travel to an integrated school in Dayton.

Helen's father, who died when she was eight, wanted her to become a nurse but her goal was always to become a physician. To that end, she lived with an aunt in Chicago while attending Crane Junior College (now Malcolm X College). When she applied to medical school, she was rejected by Howard for not having enough required chemistry and she "never heard from" Meharry. Her first choice was Illinois, however, because tuition was only $165 per semester and she could continue living with her aunt. Except for difficulty with one course involving lots of chemistry and physics, she did well in medical school and received her medical degree in 1934 as one of the University of Illinois's first black women physician graduates. (Dr. Elizabeth Hill preceded her.)

As a woman and an African American, Dr. Dickens had some difficulty finding suitable postgraduate training but was accepted at Chicago's Provident Hospital for a general internship and a residency in obstetrics. She then became one of the first African-American women to practice medicine in Philadelphia where she worked in obstetrics with Dr. Virginia Alexander, an African-American Quaker. Dr. Dickens then returned to Provident in 1942–43 for a residency in obstetrics and gynecology. There she met her future husband, Dr. Purvis S. Henderson, who was training to become a neurosurgeon. Following their marriage in 1943, she continued her training at Harlem Hospital while he received

Helen O. Dickens, M.D.
Photo by Bachrach.

further training in Pennsylvania. Dr. Dickens' family includes a daughter, a physician in Pennsylvania, and a son, in communications in Virginia.

Returning to Philadelphia, Dr. Dickens became a staff member and eventually chief of obstetrics and gynecology at Mercy-Douglass Hospital and a clinical professor at the Medical College of Pennsylvania. In 1946, she was certified by the American Board of Obstetrics and Gynecology and in 1950 became the first African-American woman to be admitted to the American College of Surgeons. She was also a staff member and eventually chief of obstetrics at Women's Hospital. When Women's was taken over in the mid-1960s by the University of Pennsylvania, Dr. Dickens was one of only five "holdovers" who were appointed to faculty positions there. Starting as an instructor in obstetrics and gynecology in 1965–66, she rose steadily through the ranks to become a full professor in 1976. In 1969, she was appointed the first African-American associate dean (for minorities) at the University of Pennsylvania School of Medicine. Her administrative responsibilities have included admissions and minority affairs.

Dr. Dickens, active in organized medicine, was president from 1970 to 1973 of the Pan American Medical Women's Alliance. She has received numerous awards and honors from the medical profession.

Personal Observations

When asked about obstacles she had encountered and overcome, Dr. Dickens said that they were mainly financial and were overcome by attending no-tuition (Crane) and low-tuition (Illinois) schools and by living with her aunt while attending college and medical school. She said that racism was not too much of a problem for her while in medical school, but a few faculty made offensive remarks such as "thick as a Negro's lips" and "his Negro mammy told him absurd information about mosquitoes." In one instance, the African-American students stopped attending a class where racist remarks were made but passed the course anyway because the incident occurred late in the semester. (Dr. Dickens noted that today, rather than just African Americans boycotting such a class, both African-American and white students would have walked out when the remark was made.)

When applying for a residency at a white hospital in Philadelphia, Dr. Dickens remembers being asked, "Why do colored people want to come where they are not wanted?" She also ran into gender discrimination when she applied for a staff position in obstetrics and gynecology at another Philadelphia hospital; her original male chairman left when she eventually became board certified and she replaced him as chief of the department.

In reply to questions about African Americans who had helped her along the way, Dr. Dickens mentioned not only her parents and her aunt, but also Dr. Elizabeth Hill who practiced in Evanston, Illinois, and helped her register for medical school. Dr. Virginia Alexander, with whom Dr. Dickens worked in Philadelphia, had relatives (Sadie and Raymond Alexander) in the legal profession who were also very supportive.

Concerning help received from nonblacks, Dr. Dickens cited Dean Alfred Gellhorn, who appointed her as associate dean at the University of Pennsylvania, and Dr. Luigi Mastroianni, chair of obstetrics and gynecology there and who promoted her through the ranks. She also mentioned Dr. Emily Mudd, who helped her obtain a grant for a teenage pregnancy program that was one of Dr. Dickens' major interests from 1965 to 1970.

Regarding advice to prospective African Americans in medical education and organized medicine, Dr. Dickens stressed that "you shouldn't let finances hold you back." She noted, "A $100,000 house can be taken away from you, but no one can take away your education." Her other emphases: "Education is primary"; "If you work hard, you can open doors"; and "Prepare yourself, stick to it, and follow your dream!" Finally, relative to racial harmony, she cautioned, "Don't prejudge people by the color of their skin because sometimes those of a different color can become your best friends and supporters."

Charles Richard Drew, M.D., C.M., Med.D.Sc., F.A.C.S.

Chronological History

Charles R. Drew, director of the first American Red Cross Blood Bank, was born in Washington, D.C., on June 3, 1904. He attended public schools there and received a bachelor of arts degree from Amherst College in 1926. Starring as a four-letter man at Dunbar High School, he continued his athletic feats at Amherst where his prowess in track and football won him the annual Mossman Trophy as the athlete who brought the highest honor to his school.

After working for two years at Morgan State College in Baltimore (now Morgan State University), as director of athletics and instructor in biology and chemistry, he resigned from these positions to enter the Faculty of Medicine, McGill University, Montreal, Canada. He received the medical and master of surgery degrees in 1933. Academically, he distinguished himself by being elected to Alpha Omega Alpha and by earning the Williams Prize awarded to the winner of a competitive examination taken annually by the top five students in the senior class.

Spending two years in postgraduate study at Montreal General Hospital as an intern and assistant resident in medicine, he returned to Washington, D.C., in 1935 and served one year as instructor in pathology at HUCM. In 1935, he was an assistant in surgery and the following year an instructor in surgery at the medical school and assistant surgeon at Freedmen's Hospital.

Because of the great promise he had shown, Dr. Drew received a General Education Board Fellowship in Surgery at Columbia University in New York, where he also served as resident in surgery at Presbyterian Hospital from 1938 to 1940. It was there that he met Dr. John Scudder, who was engaged in research related to fluid balance, blood chemistry, and blood transfusions. Dr. Drew prepared a 200-page doctoral thesis, entitled "Banked Blood: A Study in Blood Preservation," which his mentor, Dr. Scudder, called "a masterpiece—one of the most distinguished essays ever written, both in form and content."

In June 1940, Dr. Drew received the doctor of medical science degree from Columbia University and then returned to Howard as assistant professor of surgery. However, he was granted a leave of absence in September 1940 to serve as medical supervisor, Blood Plasma Division, Blood Transfusion Association, New York, in charge of collection of blood plasma for the British Army during World War II—often called the "Blood for Britain Project." The board of the association found Dr. Drew to be the "best qualified of anyone we know to act in this important development." In February 1941, he was appointed director of the first American Red Cross Blood Bank (at Presbyterian Hospital) and assistant director of blood procurement for the National Research Council, in charge of blood for use by the U.S. Army and Navy

In March 1941 Dr. Drew was certified as a diplomate by the American Board of Surgery. It is said that during Dr. Drew's oral examination at Johns Hopkins, his examiner was so impressed that he called in his fellow examiners to listen to Dr. Drew explain problems related to fluid balance and blood transfusions.

In October 1941, he became professor and head of the department of surgery at Howard and chief surgeon at Freedmen's Hospital. In these

Charles R. Drew, M.D., instructs postgraduate surgical residents at HUCM's Freedmen's Hospital in Washington, D.C.

roles, he was primarily interested in teaching medical students, training surgical residents, providing patients high quality care, and obtaining hospital privileges for African-American surgeons. As a teacher, he was dynamic, stimulating, and inspirational. One of his favorite statements was, "Excellence of performance will transcend the barriers of racial discrimination and segregation." Although Dr. Drew's tenure as chief of surgery was slightly under nine years, there were approximately 25 surgeons who became certified in their specialties having received all or part of their postgraduate training under his leadership.

Dr. Drew also served on the boards of the following organizations: District of Columbia Division of the American Cancer Society; Washington, D.C., Branch of the National Poliomyelitis Foundation; and The National Society for Crippled Children. In addition, he served as chairman, Surgical Section, National Medical Association; member of the Dean's Committee, Veterans Hospital, Tuskegee, Alabama; and surgical consultant to the Surgeon General, U.S. Army, assigned to duty in the European Command.

In July 1944, he received the Spingarn Medal—the highest award given by the NAACP—for work done in research and organization of the British and American Blood and Plasma Projects. Chief among places named for him is the Charles R. Drew University of Medicine and Science in Los Angeles. In 1981, on his birthday, June 8, a postage stamp in the Great Americans Series was issued in his honor. He is also honored at Howard in the annual Drew-Syphax Lecture and Prize named for Dr. Drew and Dr. Burke Syphax. (Dr. Syphax worked closely with Dr. Drew, succeeded him as chief of general surgery in 1950, and served as professor and chairman of the department from 1957 to 1970.)

Dr. Drew was killed in an automobile accident just outside Burlington, North Carolina, on April 1, 1950, on his way to speak at the John Andrew Annual Clinic in Tuskegee, Alabama. In a highly unusual action, the board of regents of the American College of Surgeons granted him posthumous fellowship in 1951. Shortly after Dr. Drew's tragic and untimely death, Dr. Mathew Walker, professor and head of the department of surgery at Meharry Medical College, was asked to comment on Dr. Drew. Along with other laudatory remarks, Dr. Walker stated, "He had the purest heart of any man I've ever known."

Dr. Drew's life was characterized by an unselfish devotion to high standards, by a sense of fair play, and by outstanding performance in all endeavors. During his tenure as head of the HUCM Department of

Surgery from 1941 to 1950, he guided the department to new heights and left a legacy and tradition that live today.

(Dr. Drew's biography is from the program for the March 1992 installation ceremony of Dr. LaSalle D. Leffall, Jr., the first occupant of the Charles R. Drew Chair in Surgery at HUCM.)

Charles Harry Epps., Jr., M.D., F.A.C.S.

Chronological History

Charles H. Epps, Jr., the first African-American president of the American Orthopaedic Association, was born in Baltimore, Maryland, on July 24, 1930. He was the oldest son in a family of six children. His father was a graduate of Coppin Teachers College and a public school teacher. Both of his parents died at an early age and the family encountered significant health and financial problems.

Because of his family situation, Dr. Epps worked from childhood at all types of jobs, including whitewashing basements and tarring roofs. Despite this necessary and time-consuming work, he did extremely well academically, graduating from Baltimore's segregated Frederick Douglass High School in 1947 as valedictorian, class president, and editor-in-chief of the school paper. He also won first prize in a science fair for high school students held at Howard University, which encouraged him to pursue scientific study at that institution.

His original career goal was to become a pharmacist, but he decided too late to meet Howard's application deadline. Accordingly, he pursued its liberal arts program and discovered that, in spite of substantial part-time work, he could more than hold his own in such premedical courses as biology, chemistry, and physics. He met his future wife during his third year, was president of the student body his senior year, and graduated magna cum laude in 1951.

While at Howard's medical school, he also did honors work despite driving a taxi at night. In addition to using these earnings to meet his own expenses, he sent money home whenever possible to help support the rest of his family. Partly due to the then lack of opportunity elsewhere for the graduate training of African-American physicians, Dr. Epps did his internship at Freedmen's Hospital in 1955–56 and his residencies in surgery at Freedmen's, D.C. General, and Mt. Alto Veterans Hospitals.

(While at D.C. General, he was the first African American to serve there as chief resident in orthopaedic surgery). He served as a captain in the Army Medical Corps Reserves from 1956 to 1965 and was on active duty with the 354th General Hospital for one year.

Dr. Epps returned to medical education at HUCM in 1961 as an instructor in orthopaedic surgery, became an assistant professor and chief of the division in 1964, associate professor in 1968, and professor in 1972. He has also held appointments in orthopaedic surgery at Johns Hopkins

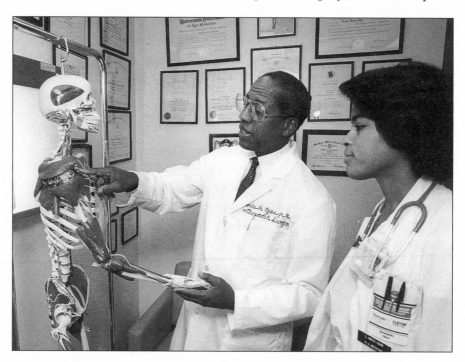

Charles H. Epps, Jr., M.D., shown during the 1980s explaining an orthopaedic condition to a junior medical student. Courtesy of HUCM Department of Biomedical Communications.

and at Northwestern University Medical Schools. Dr. Epps helped edit the *JNMA* and authored numerous scientific articles; he also edited three editions of *Complications in Orthopaedic Surgery*, the first and only text on this subject in the orthopaedic literature. Throughout most of this time, he maintained an active practice, specializing in work with handicapped and crippled children. Since 1988, Dr. Epps has been dean of the Howard University College of Medicine.

In organized medicine, Dr. Epps has been an outstanding pioneer. He was the first African-American to become: president of the District of Columbia Medical Society (1979), governor of the American College of Surgeons, (1982–88), and president of the American Orthopaedic Association (1985). Other African-American "firsts" include: president of the Washington Orthopaedic Society (1967–68), oral examiner for the

Board of Orthopaedic Surgery (1970–1990), and member of that board (1977–83). In 1981, he was president of the Association of Children's Prosthetic and Orthotic Clinics. He has also been a member of the Council on Ethical and Judicial Affairs of the American Medical Association (1982–87 and 1989–1992), and a member of the American Medical Association (AMA) House of Delegates, representing the American Academy of Orthopaedic Surgeons (1982–87).

Personal Observations

When asked about obstacles he had encountered along the way, Dr. Epps indicated that, in addition to the financial problems mentioned above, he had also experienced his share of racism. For example, as a student at segregated public schools, he often had to travel long distances from his home by bicycle or street car. When he arrived at Union Station in Washington, D.C. in 1947, he had difficulty finding a taxi driver who would take him to Howard University. Later, while doing his residency at a hospital staffed by white physicians, he and his wife were excluded from a Christmas party because of their race.

Because of his loving and supportive parents and wife, however, and thanks to a number of dedicated teachers and role models, Dr. Epps didn't let these experiences hold him back or diminish his basic confidence and self-esteem. Rather, he worked even harder and denied himself many immediate comforts and gratifications. At an early age, he recognized, "Life is not fair and in a white man's world, a black person has to work twice as hard to succeed."

In reply to questions about specific individuals who had helped him along the way, Dr. Epps cited not only his family members but also a number of public school teachers and college faculty. Included were Mr. Howard Hucles, a high school biology teacher and mentor who encouraged him to major in chemistry in college, and Dr. Lloyd Ferguson, who stimulated him intellectually by the way he taught organic chemistry. While in medical school, he was positively influenced by such outstanding surgery faculty as Dr. Burke Syphax and by such eminent basic science faculty as Dr. W. Montague Cobb, who encouraged him to develop his writing talents. Dr. Epps's wife, Roselyn P. Epps, M.D., who was a college and medical school classmate, is appreciated as not only his constant and staunchest supporter, but also his closest friend.

Dr. Epps also cited a number of white physicians who helped him obtain training in orthopaedic surgery and sponsored him for membership in various professional societies. These individuals included Dr. John

Adams, head of Orthopaedic Surgery at George Washington University Medical School, Dr. Henry Feffer, Dr. George T. Aitken, and Dr. Harvey Ammerman, past president of the Washington, D.C., Medical Society, all of whom encouraged him to become active in local and national professional associations.

Roselyn Payne Epps, M.D., M.P.H., M.A., F.A.A.P.

Chronological History

Roselyn P. Epps, the first African-American president of the American Medical Women's Association, was born on December 11, 1930, in Little Rock, Arkansas. She grew up in Savannah, Georgia, where her father was president of Savannah State College and her mother was an elementary school principal, high school teacher, guidance counselor, and college professor. The great emphasis her parents put on education led them to send Roselyn and her older brother to boarding school in Sedalia, North Carolina, from which Roselyn graduated as salutatorian in 1947.

From age 10, Roselyn knew she wanted to become a pediatrician and she never wavered from that goal. She attended Howard University, majored in zoology and chemistry, and graduated cum laude in 1951. While there she met her future husband, Charles H. Epps, Jr., and they were married on June 25, 1955, shortly after both completed medical school.

At Howard's College of Medicine, Dr. Epps won graduation prizes from the Departments of Pediatrics, Neuropsychiatry, and Obstetrics and Gynecology. She also received a certificate from the American Medical Women's Association as a ranking student from its Junior Branch, which she had helped establish and served as its first president.

After receiving her medical degree with honors in 1955, Dr. Epps served a rotating internship and pediatric residency at Howard's Freedmen's Hospital, where she was chief resident in 1958–59. During this postgraduate training, she was encouraged by Dr. Roland Scott, chief of the Department of Pediatrics, to do laboratory research, write papers, prepare exhibits, and to deliver them at national pediatrics meetings. At these meetings she came to more fully appreciate the esteem in which Dr. Scott was held and the strong impact that an African-American physician of his stature could make when he spoke up, for example, on behalf of better health care for disadvantaged black children.

Upon completion of her residency, she was in private practice with Dr. Scott for a short time and worked in Howard's Sickle Cell Research Laboratory during 1960–61. Although she had planned to remain at Howard, there were then strict nepotism regulations that prevented family members from working there concurrently. And since her husband had a longstanding interest in medical education and there was greater need in orthopaedic surgery than in pediatrics, the two of them decided that he should be the one to accept a long-term Howard appointment. Although nepotism rules were relaxed enough for both of them to work for the medical school in the 1980s, she left for federal employment at NIH when he became dean of HUCM in 1988.

Along with raising four children (born from 1957 to 1963), Dr. Epps held a number of important positions in the Washington, D.C., Department of Public Health, including that of acting commissioner (1980). She continued her formal education to include an M.P.H. degree in maternal

Roselyn P. Epps, M.D., speaks at an antismoking session of the American Medical Women's Association held in 1991.

and child health from Johns Hopkins University in 1973 and a masters in interdisciplinary studies (Health Services for Blacks in Higher Education) from American University in 1981.

Dr. Epps has also been very active in various professional and civic organizations, achieving the status of the first woman and the first African-American president of the Washington, D.C., Chapter of the American Academy of Pediatrics (1988–91), the first African-American president of the American Medical Women's Association (1990–91), and the first African-American woman president of the Washington, D.C., Medical Society (1992). She has also been national president of Girls Inc., formerly Girls Clubs of America.

Personal Observations

In reply to questions about personal obstacles she encountered, Dr. Epps replied that, largely due to her parents, she was brought up to believe that "there was no permanent obstacle, just opportunity!" She said that temporary obstacles might change one's course for a while but that such challenges may increase one's motivation, "Particularly if one has a broad vision and wide goals, any experience can be put to good use in the future."

Regarding individuals who had helped her along the way, Dr. Epps not only elaborated on the support and guidance she received from her parents and from Dr. Scott, but also appreciated Dr. Dorothy Boulding Ferebee, head of the health service while Dr. Epps was in college. Dr. Ferebee was a role model of a mother and national sorority president, as well as a physician. Other African Americans she singled out for special appreciation included her husband, Dr. Charles H. Epps, Jr.; Dr. W. Montague Cobb, a warm personal mentor and friend to their family; and Dr. Paul Cornely, a role model in the field of public health.

The main white person who significantly aided her career was Dr. Samuel Shwartz, chief of maternal and child health for the D.C. Department of Public Health. He not only gave her maximum opportunity to grow and develop under his guidance, but, on learning she might leave to work for the federal government, he retired early and strongly recommended her as his replacement. A number of other unnamed white colleagues were appreciated for nominating her for office and for supporting her leadership.

Dr. Epps' advice to young people is "to set lofty goals and to persist in reaching them in spite of the attempts of others, including one's peers, to discourage you." She believes that there is still room for many more black medical pioneers. While there may already be black "firsts" on a few certification boards and medical journal boards, for example, the barriers have not yet been broken for many others. She also stresses the obligation that highly educated black men and women have for public and volunteer service to benefit others of their race, and notes that an African-American physician, for instance, may make a greater contribution on a nonmedical board such as Girls Inc. than on a medical board.

Angella Dorothea Ferguson, M.D.

Chronological History

Angella D. Ferguson, the first African-American woman to be named associate vice president for health affairs at Howard University, was born in Washington, D.C., on February 15, 1925. She attended the area public schools, graduating from Cardozo High School in 1942. Since Cardozo prepared students primarily for careers in business, Dr. Ferguson at first thought she would become an accountant. During her senior year, however, she decided she wanted to go to college and took courses that prepared her to attend Howard University. In her sophomore year at Howard, she decided to become a physician. She recalled her father's remarks after informing him of this decision. He stated, "If you think you can work your way through, then by all means, go ahead." Dr. Ferguson received a bachelor of science degree from Howard University in 1945 and graduated from its College of Medicine in 1949.

Including time at Howard as a professor of pediatrics, Dr. Ferguson has spent more than 20 years of her professional life as a pediatrician. She headed Howard's division of pediatric research and is widely recognized for achievements related to her work in this area. She was among the first African-American women recognized by national professional organizations for research on sickle cell disease. In 1964, the New York-based Association for Sickle Cell Anemia, Inc., awarded her a bronze plaque for outstanding work in this field. In addition, her work and research received meritorious recognition from the American Medical Association and the National Medical Association. She is author or coauthor of over 35 publications on studies involving sickle cell anemia and the growth and development of African-American children. In 1970, Dr. Ferguson was included in *Who's Who of American Women*.

After many years in the field of sickle cell disease and pediatric research, Dr. Ferguson moved into administration. In 1969, when Dr. James E. Cheek, then president of Howard University, appointed Dr. Carlton P. Alexis vice president for health affairs, among his major tasks was to assemble a team to plan for the new Howard University Hospital. To oversee this project, Dr. Alexis appointed Dr. Ferguson as the director of programs and facilities in his office. With this appointment, she became Howard University's highest ranking woman in health affairs.

Her primary responsibilities regarding the hospital project were to advise the vice president regarding construction progress, recommend changes, review programs, academic research, and patient services, and understand their relationship in order to anticipate problems and assign and manage space. Dr. Ferguson stated that the experiences and assignments were both challenging and stimulating. She also noted, "I don't even think about the fact that I am the highest ranking woman in health affairs. I'm just a person assisting another person who has to do a

Angella D. Ferguson, M.D., shown in the 1970s checking construction of the new Howard University Hospital with (L to R) former HUCM Dean Robert S. Jason, M.D., and Mr. James F. Hilfiker, director of Health Center Engineering.

job." She is credited with being the force behind the construction of the Howard University Hospital, a $43 million facility frequently referred to as "the hospital that Dr. Ferguson built."

Eventually acquiring the title of associate vice president for health affairs, Dr. Ferguson has also been in charge of construction for several other buildings at Howard University. These include the Seeley G. Mudd Building of the College of Medicine, the fourth and fifth floors of the Russell A. Dixon Building of the College of Dentistry, the Animal Research Center in Beltsville, the Howard University Hospital Child Care Center, and the Howard University Cancer Center.

Personal Observations

Unlike most African-American medical pioneers we interviewed, Dr. Ferguson does not recall encountering any particular obstacles while pursuing a medical education or since moving into administration. She remembers that her parents always supported her educational goals. She does not recall being discouraged or questioned about her desire to be a physician. "I did not meet anyone along the way who said medicine is not a field for women," she stated. Since Dr. Ferguson's freshman medical class was the first to include a substantial number of females (17), she did not feel in a significant minority role because of her gender. Financing an education in medicine, with scholarships and other financial aid, was not a problem either. Nor did she encounter obstacles after the transition from pediatric research to administration. Confident in her ability to do an excellent job, she emitted this self-assuredness to all who worked with her. She felt that other health affairs administrators, university officials, and construction consultants trusted her judgment. Dr. Alexis stated, "I think history will record that she did an outstanding job."

Dr. Ferguson acknowledges the support she received from Drs. Roland B. Scott (former professor of pediatrics and director of the Center for Sickle Cell Disease), Blanche Bourne, and Melvin Jenkins for assisting her research in sickle cell anemia in children. From her father, who was an architect, she learned how to make good spatial judgments and to renovate buildings that best served users' needs. He encouraged her pursuit of a medical career, and she credits him as being largely responsible for the success she earned as an administrator in health affairs.

For those who aspire to be a pioneer, especially in the medical field, Dr. Ferguson suggests, "Expose yourself to the profession to ensure your interest in it. Medicine is arduous and can sometimes be traumatic, so become involved and get a feel for it to determine if it is really for you." Dr. Ferguson also feels that it is necessary for the young aspirant to feel and demonstrate compassion for humanity and for the profession before he or she can truly possess the ability required to be successful.

Eleanor Lutia Ison Franklin, Ph.D.

Chronological History

Eleanor L. Franklin, the first African-American woman to become a major administrative officer at the Howard University College of Medicine, was born in Dublin, Georgia, on December 24, 1929. She was encouraged in her early intellectual development by her mother, Rose, and by her father, Luther, who was a mathematician. She excelled in school and at age 15 entered Atlanta's prestigious historically black school for women, Spelman College. While there, about half of the faculty and administration were white and she received special encouragement from her white major professor, Dr. Helen Tupper Albro, a graduate of Brown University. Eleanor also took chemistry and physics courses at Morehouse College as part of their consortium arrangement and discovered she could compete very well with their all-male student body. She graduated in 1948.

Eleanor's father had encouraged her to become a physician but when he died in 1948, their family finances prevented her from pursuing that goal. Dr. Albro and others encouraged her to attend graduate school in one of the life sciences and informed her of opportunities for financial aid. Eleanor graduated magna cum laude from Spelman at age 18. Her Spanish teacher, Camilla Howard, helped Eleanor appreciate her own academic ability and strongly encouraged her to leave Spelman for graduate work.

Although the University of Georgia would have been the logical place to attend for graduate studies, it was not accepting any African Americans at that point in time. It did, however, help meet the expenses of African Americans who studied out of state. Accordingly, she applied at several schools and was accepted first by the University of Wisconsin, from which she received an master of science degree in zoology in 1951. While there, she discovered she could more than hold her own academically with students of all racial and ethnic backgrounds and with students of all ages—many of her classmates were older veterans of World War II.

Because her younger sister was still in college and her family needed financial help, Eleanor returned to Spelman and taught there for two years. During summer vacations, however, she continued her studies at Wisconsin. A key event happened in her life when four of her white male professors invited her to one of their homes and strongly encouraged her to continue to work toward a Ph.D. degree. They also assured her that her financial needs would be met by scholarships, fellowships, teaching assistantships, etc. Several black women graduate students (one of them a fellow-graduate of Spelman) also encouraged her, both by words and example, to continue her studies.

After completing her doctorate in endocrinology, Eleanor was invited to teach physiology and pharmacology at the Veterinary School of Tuskegee Institute. Although she was apprehensive about switching from human to animal physiology, she found there were many similarities and became over a period of six years one of their popular and respected faculty members. However, while her duties were mostly teaching, her major interest was research.

Because of her research interests, Eleanor was considering the possibility of postdoctoral study at the Sloan-Kettering Institute. However, she was encouraged to join the faculty at the Howard University College of Medicine. She was hired as an endocrinologist by Dr. Edward Hawthorne, chairman of the Department of Physiology, but eventually became more of a cardiovascular physiologist. She also married during her four-year tenure in that department and gradually took over many of Dr. Hawthorne's administrative duties.

When her colleague, Dr. Anna Cherrie Epps, married and moved to New Orleans, Dr. Franklin was asked to take over Anna's responsibilities for the medical school's Academic Reinforcement Program. Others closely involved in that program included Dr. Marion Mann of pathology, Dr. Ruth Lloyd of anatomy, and Dr. William West of pharmacology.

Eleanor L. Franklin, Ph.D., the first female dean for Academic Affairs at the Howard University College of Medicine, 1970–1980, maintained frequent contact with faculty and students.

Following the death of Dean K. Albert Harden, the search committee recommended Dr. Mann as his replacement. Because of his good working relationship with Dr. Franklin and his respect for her administrative abilities, Dean Mann promptly asked her if she would become the associate dean for academic affairs. When Eleanor replied that she was not sure she had the qualifications or experience for that position, Dean Mann replied that "they could learn their new jobs together." With that encouragement, Dr. Franklin became the first African-American woman to hold a major administrative office at the Howard University College of Medicine. In that capacity, she provided outstanding leadership in the areas of curriculum development, academic support services, and educational administration. Specific achievements included the development of a combined B.S.-M.D. program and the establishment of an Office of Medical Education.

Personal Observations

When asked whether being a pioneer woman in the dean's office was a problem, she replied that her gender was less of a barrier than her being a Ph.D. rather than an M.D. But she said that by applying common sense and "mother wit," she was gradually able to gain the confidence and respect of the predominantly male, M.D. faculty. The esteem in which she is held is also shown by her being elected president of the Spelman Alumnae Association and by her becoming dean of Continuing Education for all of Howard University.

In reply to questions about advice for other aspiring "black pioneers," Dr. Franklin emphasized the importance of parental support, of receiving the best possible education, of choosing a rigorous schedule for oneself, and of "earning one's way" through the academic and social system. She stressed the goal of earning the respect of one's peers, irrespective of the color of their skin and noted that "knowledge is nonracial." She also noted the importance for medical educators to acquire the ability and sensitivity to instruct without demeaning one's students. Finally, she expressed appreciation for the help and encouragement she had received along the way from men and women who were both black and white and said that she has tried to do the same for others—regardless of race.

Walter Lester Henry, Jr., M.D., M.A.C.P.

Chronological History

W. Lester Henry, Jr., the first African-American governor of the American Board of Internal Medicine, was born on November 19, 1915, in Philadelphia, Pennsylvania. His father had an eighth grade education and worked as a postal clerk. His mother had completed the eleventh grade and is remembered as being an avid reader—both to herself and to her children. Lester attended a black elementary school located in his neighborhood and a junior high school in a mixed neighborhood. He was one of only three blacks to be admitted to his class for the academic course of Philadelphia's prestigious predominantly white Central High School.

He and several of his high school classmates then attended Temple University where Lester did well academically and particularly enjoyed his small classes in chemistry. Although he was aware that most of the Philadelphia medical schools had admitted a few black students in the past, he applied only to Howard University. He excelled in his studies at HUCM, won a number of prizes, and graduated first in his class in 1941.

World War II broke out during Dr. Henry's 1941–42 internship at Howard's Freedmen's Hospital; and two weeks into his residency he was called to active duty in the army as a first lieutenant. His military service included commanding a company of the 317th medical battalion in combat in Italy from 1942–46 and being promoted to the rank of major.

W. Lester Henry, Jr., M.D., chairman of the HUCM Department of Internal Medicine from 1962 to 1973, addressing the audience at the "Magnificent Professors" ceremony of May 1991.

Because all of the HUCM residencies were filled when he was discharged from the army, Dr. Henry started a private practice in Philadelphia and had plenty of patients referred by a former HUCM teacher who was leaving for an extended vacation. Although he considered remaining in full-time practice after only a year's internship, which was common at the time, he realized that to be able to care for his patients in the best hospitals, he would need to obtain further training and become board certified. Accordingly, he arranged an interview with the dean of the University of Pennsylvania's Graduate School of Medicine and was admitted for study during 1948–49.

By then places had become available at HUCM and Dr. Henry served a residency in internal medicine there from 1949–51. This was followed by a fellowship in endocrinology from 1951–53 at Chicago's Michael Reese Hospital. Dr. Henry then returned to HUCM and rose steadily from assistant professor of medicine (1953–58) to associate professor (1958–63) to professor (1963–). While assistant professor, he was also the first black John and Mary Markle Scholar in medical science on the basis of competing with candidates from medical schools nationwide. He was also head of the department of medicine from 1962–73 and vice dean of the medical school from 1954–60.

Dr. Henry has been very active in organized medicine and is a black pioneer in several distinguished categories. These include governor of the American Board of Internal Medicine (ABIM), member of the Residency Review Committee in Internal Medicine, regent of the American College of Physicians (ACP), representative from ABIM to the American Board of Medical Specialties, and master of the American College of Physicians (MACP).

Personal Observations

Asked about obstacles he had encountered along the way, Dr. Henry said he was aware of very few. When he first entered junior high school in a new neighborhood, there were apparently some fights between the black and Italian students but they did not persist. While in high school, he was aware that some of the teachers, all of them white, let him know that they would have preferred all of their students to be white. After completing Temple (where all of the faculty were white), he learned that a young biology teacher had wanted to fail him, but his performance was too good to allow this to happen. Following seven years of instruction by all-white faculty at high school and college, Dr. Henry recalls that it seemed very good to have so many impressive black faculty at HUCM.

Relative to his fellowship at the predominantly Jewish Michael Reese Hospital and his activities in organized medicine, Dr. Henry reports very favorable memories. While at Michael Reese, he says that his mentor, Dr. Rachmiel Levine, "treated me like a son," and Dr. Henry's wife says that her husband "sometimes thinks that he is Jewish." At the many meetings he attended relative to his offices in organized medicine, Dr. Henry recalls that both he and his wife were received very cordially by his white colleagues and their wives. He does remember one instance when a colleague said, "There is no such thing as a good woman internist in the

U.S.," which made him wonder what that person had said about black internists when Dr. Henry was originally proposed for membership.

In reply to questions about black people who had helped him along the way, Dr. Henry cited not only his parents, but also an uncle who left him his ministerial library when Lester was about 10 years old; a neighbor, Mrs. Mattie Henson, who paid his fees at Temple to supplement his scholarship there; and Drs. R.K. Brown, W. Montague Cobb, Charles Drew, Edward Hawthorne, J.B. Johnson, Arnold Maloney, and E. Clayton Terry at HUCM. Whites whom he cited included not only Dr. Levine, but also Dr. Edward Howes, chief of surgery at HUCM before Dr. Drew, and Drs. Jack Myers (president of ABIM) and Robert Petersdorf (president of ACP) who appointed him to posts in those organizations.

Finally, Dr. Henry's advice to young blacks considering a career in medicine is to "study diligently, be curious, seek understanding rather than relying on rote memory, seek out role models among your teachers at all levels of education, join the Smithsonian Associates early or a similar organization [offering educational opportunities], and try to understand the benefits of academic medicine vs full-time practice." By implication, he also advocated becoming actively involved in organized medicine and earning one's way to recognition by doing a good job in one's initial assignments.

Gertrude Cora Teixeira Hunter, M.D.

Chronological History

Gertrude T. Hunter, first Director of Health Services for the Head Start Program, was born on March 23, 1926, in Boston but grew up in nearby Wollaston, Massachusetts. She was the oldest of four children of Antonio Dias Teixeira and Carrie Jackson Teixeira. Her father owned a successful wholesale food business and her mother was a homemaker. As the only African-American family in their town, they maintained their cultural roots by attending a black church in Boston and black summer camps.

Although Gertrude was an excellent student, school authorities tried to have her study domestic arts rather than academic course in high school. She remembers being asked, "What's a colored girl going to do with a college education?" Gertrude and her parents insisted that she take the academic curriculum and Gertrude graduated with an excellent record from North Quincy High School. She then enrolled at Boston University but transferred after two years to Howard University as a chemistry major.

Gertrude's becoming a physician was quite unexpected. She took the Medical College Admission Test and did so well on it that she applied and was admitted to HUCM after completing only three years of college. Dr. Hunter received her medical degree in 1950, interned at the Homer G. Phillips Hospital in St. Louis and served pediatric residencies both there and at Howard's Freedmen's Hospital. Ten of her classmates, including her eventual husband, Dr. Charles Hunter, who became a radiologist, accompanied her to St. Louis.

After completing her graduate medical education, Dr. Hunter not only raised six children, but also served as a teacher and researcher in HUCM's department of pediatrics. As a parent of children in the Washington, D.C., public schools, Dr. Hunter's volunteer work helped her become acquainted with Mrs. Dorothy Goldberg, wife of then Secretary of Labor Arthur Goldberg. Partly upon Mrs. Goldberg's recommendation, Dr. Hunter became from 1965-71 the first National Director of Health Services for the highly-acclaimed Head Start Program of the Office of Economic Opportunity.

The many "firsts" achieved by Dr. Hunter include: Region One health administrator of the U.S. Public Health Service (1972–76), founder and cochair of the Northeast Canadian-American Health Conference (1971–76), and chairman of HUCM's Department of Community Health and Family Practice (1976–80). From 1977–90, she was the first woman physician on the Board of Trustees of the Massachusetts College of Pharmacy and Allied Health Sciences. In 1988, Dr. Hunter retired from her professorship at HUCM and founded a private nonprofit organization, the Human Services Educational and Research (HUSER) Institute in Washington, D.C.

Personal Observations

When asked about obstacles she had encountered and overcome, Dr. Hunter noted that both of her parents died prematurely during her college years but that a younger sister took over the family business, and Gertrude was able to live with relatives while attending Howard. She also received fairly generous financial aid through the University. During her first semester at medical school, she found that she was much younger than most of her classmates, many of whom were World War II veterans studying under the GI Bill of Rights. She discovered a fear of blood and needles, but her strong background in science and her inherent interest in learning enabled her to eventually do so well in her medical education that she was invited to pursue graduate training in not only pediatrics, but also in medicine, obstetrics and gynecology, and surgery.

Undoubtedly due at least in part to racial discrimination, Dr. Hunter was turned down for graduate training by Boston's Children's Hospital and therefore completed all of it at predominantly black hospitals. When taking Part III of the National Board examinations in St. Louis, she was treated badly by a male monitor and assumed it was due to racism. In comparing notes with others, however, she learned it was due to sexism because the monitor had treated the black males well but had been universally insulting to all the females.

Gertrude C. T. Hunter, M.D., first director of health services for Head Start, shown in 1968 conferring with (center) Head Start Director Julius Richmond, M.D., and (L to R) Head Start consultants Samuel Watts, M.D., and Charles F. Whitten, M.D. Courtesy of EPS Studios, Inc.

Relative to help received from other African-Americans, Dr. Hunter cited not only her close-knit and supportive family (where her mother taught her as a child to appreciate the beautiful color of her black skin), but also the leaders of the church youth group she attended in Boston and of the summer camp (Atwater) she attended in East Brookfield, Massachusetts. All of these people encouraged her (and other blacks) to believe she could become anything she wanted to be and to "aim for the highest star." She also appreciated her teachers at Howard, who not only reinforced these values, but also helped her realize the opportunities and obligations of helping blacks in general achieve their maximum potential.

Whites who were particularly helpful to Dr. Hunter included her public school teachers of mathematics, chemistry, and sewing, and a Boston University professor who helped her appreciate the importance and fascination of history. As previously indicated, she was recommended for the Head Start job by Mrs. Goldberg. She was hired for that position by Dr. Julius Richmond and was appointed to her public health position by Dr. Vernon Wilson, head of the U.S. Health Services and Mental Health Administration.

Regarding advice to young blacks, Dr. Hunter encourages them to "recognize the power of knowledge" and to remember that one of the underpinnings of slavery was not allowing slaves to learn to read and write. She encourages young people to "view barriers as challenges to be overcome" and notes that "added burdens can actually increase rather than decrease one's productivity." She explains that, in the same way that nerve-muscle experiments in physiology demonstrate this "added burden" theory, it is reasonable to believe that "the added burden of racism can increase one's productivity, as long as one's environment is reasonably favorable." Finally, she urges young black men and women to not only recognize and develop their considerable talents, but also to use them for the betterment of society.

Melvin Earl Jenkins, Jr., M.D.

Chronological History
Melvin E. Jenkins, Jr., the first African-American governor of the American Board of Pediatrics, was born in Kansas City, Missouri, on June 24, 1922 but moved with his parents when six months old to Kansas where he was reared and educated. In Kansas, his father later became a postal clerk and supervisor while his mother remained a very supportive homemaker. Dr. Jenkins attended public schools in Kansas City, Kansas and graduated with honors from Sumner High School. He received his bachelor of arts degree from the University of Kansas in 1944 and his medical degree from the University of Kansas School of Medicine in 1946. He was only the fourth black to graduate from the medical school, since all blacks enrolled prior to 1935 were required to transfer to Howard or Meharry to complete their clinical years.

Following a 1946–47 rotating internship at Freedmen's Hospital in Washington, D.C., Dr. Jenkins remained for a pediatric residency until 1950 when he became a clinical instructor in pediatrics. He was promoted to assistant professor in 1957 and to associate professor in 1959. From 1955–57, he served in Japan with the 6110th U.S. Air Force Hospital as chief of pediatrics. From 1963–65 he trained as a research fellow in pediatric endocrinology at Johns Hopkins Hospital, following which Jenkins became the first black pediatric endocrinologist in the United States.

In 1969, Dr. Jenkins left Howard to become the first African-American tenured faculty member at the University of Nebraska's Medical School. He was appointed professor of pediatrics while he developed the academic, research, and clinical components of Nebraska's first endocrine programs and in two years assumed the added responsibility of being vice-chairman of the Pediatric Department. The Pediatric Endocrine Program at Nebraska has grown to additional prominence since its inception under Dr. Jenkins' leadership.

Melvin Jenkins returned to Howard in 1973 to chair the Department of Pediatrics and Child Health until his retirement in 1986. In that role, he strengthened and gained national recognition for this department. He became a member of the National Research Advisory Council at NIH in 1974 and has been appointed to numerous national committees, study sections, and task forces at the NIH, U.S. Public Health Service, Department of Agriculture, and at other government agencies and academic institutions.

From 1983–89 he was the first and only African-American member of the governing body of the American Board of Pediatrics, having been nominated to that position by the American Society of Pediatric Department Chairmen. Dr. Jenkins has also contributed significantly to health care and medical education in Nigeria, Guyana, Trinidad, and Jamaica as a consultant, lecturer, examiner, and researcher.

Personal Observations

When asked about obstacles along the way, Dr. Jenkins responded that while he recognized the realities of racism in the U.S. and challenged them when they stood in his way, he used them as a stimulus to do his best and refused to use racism as an excuse for less than excellent performance.

In response to questions about African Americans who had been especially helpful in his development, Dr. Jenkins noted that his father had encouraged him to become a physician rather than an architect, his first career choice. A maternal uncle, Dr. A.R. Maddox, who was a family physican in Sedalia, Missouri, had been an early role model. Dr. Jenkins also appreciated a neighbor, Mr. William Fluellen, who encouraged young

Melvin and some other 11- to 13-year-old boys to form a neighborhood debating team. This helped prepare Melvin to eventually win a state oratorical contest for black high school seniors and to earn a scholarship for his higher education. The high school teachers of Sumner, who were all black during that segregated era, were especially talented and stimulating to his development.

Among the whites who were influential in his development, Dr. Jenkins cited Dr. Cecil Wittson, vice chancellor for health affairs at Nebraska, who offered him the position there and who followed through faithfully on all of his promises regarding rank, salary, tenure, space, and support staff. Drs. Robert M. Blizzard and Claude Migeon, with whom he studied endrocrinology at Johns Hopkins, were also very helpful and supportive throughout his career.

Regarding advice to young people aspiring to careers in medicine, he

Melvin E. Jenkins, Jr., M.D., reassures a young patient during his pediatric rounds at HUCM in 1982.

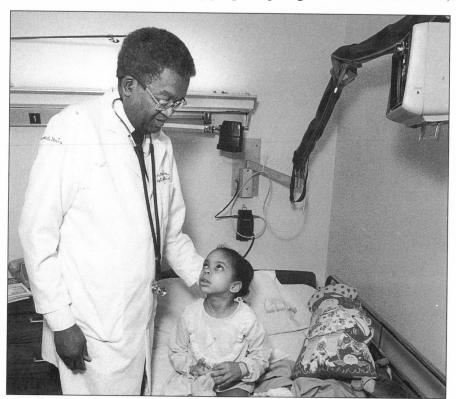

reminds them to appreciate the fact that options and opportunities are even greater now than they were when he was young. He encourages them to read widely and to listen seriously to adults who are interested in their welfare. Similarly, he encourages adults to serve as mentors and role models for young people, particularly for black males in the inner city.

Finally, Dr. Jenkins advises young people against using racism as an excuse. Rather, he encourages them to learn what other blacks have accomplished in spite of the odds against them and to aspire for similar or even greater accomplishments for themselves.

Renee Rosilind Jenkins, M.D.

Chronological History

Renee R. Jenkins, the first African-American president of the Society of Adolescent Medicine, was born in Philadelphia, Pennsylvania, on January 16, 1947. She attended suburban Philadelphia's Upper Darby High School until her senior year. In 1964 her family moved to Detroit, Michigan, where she completed her secondary education at Samuel C. Mumford High School, graduating cum laude. Renee then entered Wayne State University where she earned the bachelor of arts degree for work completed in 1967 and received the medical degree in 1971. Deciding to specialize in pediatrics, Dr. Jenkins was accepted in and completed the residency program at Albert Einstein College of Medicine, Jacobi Hospital, Bronx, New York. The Montefiore Medical Center of that college awarded her a fellowship in adolescent medicine in July of 1974. She completed this training in June of 1975.

Before choosing a medical career, Dr. Jenkins stated that her mother tried to encourage her to become a teacher. "My mother was concerned that by being a doctor, I would not get married and have children," she said. Dr. Jenkins is married to Charles Woodard and they have a daughter, Kristinza.

In December 1979, Dr. Jenkins cofounded the Center for Youth Services, the first comprehensive, multi-service, single site program for disadvantaged and troubled youth in the District of Columbia. Additionally, from 1989 to 1990, Dr. Jenkins served as president of the Society for Adolescent Medicine. She is the first African American to hold this leadership position. In July of 1990, the American Academy of Pediatrics appointed Dr. Jenkins chairman of the Committee on Community Health Services. She is the first African-American to chair a national committee for this academy. As of 1993, Dr. Jenkins directs the adolescent medicine program at Howard University Hospital. She is the first female to direct this program.

Personal Observations

When asked what obstacles, if any, were encountered in her pursuit of a medical career, Dr. Jenkins responded that she first incurred them as a student in junior high school She said, "Motivation was a problem for me, initially." She explained that excelling in school was relatively easy; it was not necessary to put forth any extra effort. The uncertainty created by her father's serious illness, together with the assistance of teachers who constantly reminded her that she was talented, caused her to realize that it

Renee R. Jenkins, M.D., confers with staff members in 1992 at the Center for Youth Services, which she cofounded in Washington, D.C., in 1979.

was necessary at this point in her education to become a serious student. "I had to be focused and motivated to move as far as I could, given my intelligence and the opportunity that I had," she explained.

Later, she encountered obstacles in medical school. Dr. Jenkins stated that at Wayne State University, a predominantly white institution, being female, especially an African-American female, she encountered subtle messages of prejudice particularly as they related to expectations. These messages, however, did not deter her. She consistently applied her personal philosophy of life, one that is optimistic and proactive. "I can get there. Some things that people perceive as obstacles are only mazes. As long as I am healthy, I have the potential to do almost anything," she said. Dr. Jenkins credits her aunt, Dr. Barbara Jenkins, a pathologist at Wayne State University, for encouragement and academic and moral support. She remembered that her aunt was always a role model and never let her forget that African-American women could be doctors. She also named Dr. Melvin Jenkins, who was her mentor.

Others, not African American, who helped Dr. Jenkins professionally along the way were: Drs. Lewis Fraad, chief of pediatrics at Jacobi Hospital, who encouraged her to give serious consideration to future goals in the profession once she completed her residency; Paul Wooley, chief of pediatrics, Wayne State University, who provided serious counsel regarding a career in pediatrics; and Elizabeth McAnarney, a professor at the University of Rochester, who has over the years been a mentor in adolescent medicine and who currently helps her weigh career decisions.

For those aspiring to be pioneers, Dr. Jenkins advises, "Have a positive attitude about what you want to do. Develop an unselfish approach. Performing certain activities for the benefit of others can be the kind of motivation that tends to send you in new directions and to people who are supportive as you explore new roads." Dr. Jenkins also feels that it is important to have other people share your dream and to work with those who can stir your creative energy.

Walter Fairchild Leavell, M.D.

Chronological History

Walter F. Leavell, the first African-American president of the Minority Affairs Section of the Association of American Medical Colleges (AAMC) Group on Student Affairs, was born to Ernest B. and Grace Leavell in Chicago, Illinois, on May 19, 1934. When six months old, he went to live with his aunt and uncle in Cincinnati, Ohio. He attended the public schools in that city and graduated from Withrow High School in 1953. In the fall, he entered the University of Cincinnati College of Pharmacy and in 1957 received the bachelor of science degree, just one year after marrying his childhood sweetheart, Vivian. They have twin sons, Pierce and Pierre. Following three years as a practicing registered pharmacist in Dayton, Ohio, he enrolled in Meharry Medical College, from which he received the medical degree in 1964. Dr. Leavell did his postgraduate medical education at St. Joseph's Hospital and at SUNY-Upstate Medical Center, both located in Syracuse, New York. Attaining the rank of major, Dr. Leavell had a ten-year military career in the United States Air Force Reserve as commander of the 426th Medical Service Flight.

Walter F. Leavell, M.D., in 1993, while serving as Howard University's interim vice president for health affairs. Courtesy of HUCM Department of Biomedical Communications.

Dr. Leavell's pioneering efforts are mainly in the area of medical education administration. He originated and developed the Upstate Medical Education Development (UMED) program at SUNY-Upstate. One of the first programs of its kind, the primary purpose of UMED was to enhance the medical center's minority enrollment. Under his medical education administrative leadership as associate dean of the medical school and his leadership position on the admission committee, Dr. Leavell's concept, which incorporated the academic, financial and sociological support of minority students, served as a model for enrollment and retention programs at majority medical schools throughout the United States. Each of these components working together increased minority graduation significantly. At the program's inception at the Upstate Medical Center, there were only two minority students enrolled, one male and one female. He saw that number increase to 15 and then to 30 minority students. While at Upstate, he wrote and distributed several thousand copies of the *Minority Medical School Admission Guide*.

Dr. Leavell was in 1975 a founding member of the National Association of Minority Medical Educators (NAMME). He was also primarily responsible for establishing the Minority Affairs Section (MAS) in the AAMC and was elected its president in 1969. From 1987 to 1991, he served as the first full-time president of the Charles R. Drew College of Medicine and Science in Los Angeles. As of 1993, he is the senior associate vice president for health affairs at Howard University.

Personal Observations

Dr. Leavell stated that several obstacles were present along the way to achieving professional success. Particularly problematic was the chronic lack of finances. He stated that while in college, it was necessary to work three jobs concurrently. He noted that as an administrator who worked with students over the years, it was frequently difficult to get them to differentiate between programmatic elements and their own inadequate class preparation.

Acknowledging help that he received while pursuing his medical career, Dr. Leavell stated, "It does not matter who you are, you did not make it alone; you have had to stand on the shoulders of others." He gives credit to African Americans such as: Dr. Charles W. Johnson, whose father, a former president of Fisk University, provided financial assistance and good advice while Dr. Leavell was still a medical student; and Mrs. Martha Johnson, Charles' mother, who took Dr. Leavell under her wing and also helped him with his young family. Others, not African Americans, who offered assistance to Dr. Leavell included Dr. Joseph Kowalewski, dean of the College of Pharmacy, University of Cincinnati.

When asked how he would inspire others to be pioneers or "firsts" in the medical profession, Dr. Leavell acknowledged that it is important to have role models who are examples of what can be achieved. He added, "Don't let anyone rain on your parade. If someone tells you that you do not have the necessary background to achieve your goal, do not let that limit you; see it as opportunity for self-improvement. It is your responsibility to go out and acquire that background."

Finally, underscoring this advice to those aspiring to be medical pioneers, he said, "Don't ever let anyone tell you that you cannot do something. Have confidence in yourself." He concluded, saying, "In contemplating a potential obstacle, I think I would ask myself—if someone were to put me in the middle of a desert—what can I make with sand?" Dr. Leavell's message to our young people is to employ this same kind of thinking and not view circumstances as obstacles but as opportunities to do something constructive.

LaSalle Doheny Leffall, Jr., M.D., F.A.C.S.

Chronological History

LaSalle D. Leffall, Jr., the first African-American president of the American Cancer Society, was born on May 22, 1930, in Quincy, Florida, a small town near Tallahassee. His parents were both schoolteachers who brought him up to believe that "with a good education and hard work, there are no boundaries."

Although LaSalle was an excellent student who graduated from high school at age 15, he knew that his race would prevent him from being accepted at the University of Florida or other predominantly white schools in his area. Instead, he attended Florida

A&M University where he majored in biology, minored in English, and graduated with highest honors in 1948.

In spite of his outstanding academic record and his goal of becoming a physician, he realized it would probably be a waste of time and money to seek admission to predominantly white medical schools. When he applied to Howard and Meharry, he was not immediately accepted, probably because his scores on the Medical College Admission Test were not as outstanding as his college grades. Eventually, however, he was admitted to the Howard University College of Medicine from which he graduated as the ranking student in 1952.

Thanks to Dr. W. Montague Cobb's having obtained practice privileges for blacks in Washington, D.C., hospitals, Dr. Leffall was able to spend part of his residency taking care of black patients at D.C. General Hospital even though most of the physicians there at the time were white. In 1957, he was one of the first blacks to become a surgical fellow at the Memorial Sloan-Kettering Cancer Center, where patients were mostly white.

After serving in the U.S. Army as the chief of general surgery at a hospital in Munich, Germany, Dr. Leffall entered full-time academic medicine at HUCM and rose through the ranks to become professor and chairman of its Department of Surgery in 1970. His pioneering honors include being the first African-American president of the American Cancer Society, of the Society of Surgical Oncology, and of the Society of Surgical Chairmen (of the 126 U.S. medical schools). He subsequently also became the first black officer of the American College of Surgeons, serving as its Secretary. In 1992, he was named the first Charles R. Drew Professor of Surgery at HUCM.

Personal Observations

When asked about the help he had received along the way, Dr. Leffall gave great credit to his parents, his wife, and his teachers in Florida and elsewhere. He also singled out Mr. Walter Beinecke of S&H Green Stamps, a white man who had made it financially possible for him to complete medical school after LaSalle's father had died at the beginning of his senior year.

Professionally, he credited a half dozen black physicians (including Charles Drew, Robert Jason, Jack White, and Burke Syphax) with teaching him surgery, helping him obtain the appointment at Sloan-Kettering, and encouraging him to become active in the American Cancer Society. Similarly, he appreciated a number of white physicians (including W.

Gerald Austen, Oliver Beahrs, Paul Ebert, C. Rollins Hanlon, Arthur Holleb, Dean Warren, and Robert Zeppa) for helping him achieve prominence in the American Cancer Society and the American College of Surgeons.

Dr. Leffall's philosophy is to recognize the reality of racism but not to be paranoid about it. One story he likes to tell his students is about a professional meeting he attended in Chicago. When he went to a diner for

Lasalle D. Leffall, Jr., M.D., becomes the first Charles R. Drew Professor of Surgery at HUCM on March 8, 1992. Courtesy of HUCM Department of Biomedical Communications.

a morning meal with several black colleagues, the elderly white waitress asked, "What will you boys have for breakfast?" Although their immediate reaction was that of anger, it changed to laughter when the waitress asked the identical question in the identical tone of voice of the three white physicians who had just sat down at the next table.

Dr. Leffall strongly encourages other black physicians to consider academic medicine as a career and believes the challenging role of a medical school teacher is to "instruct, inspire, stimulate, develop talent, raise aspirations, and stretch the imagination." He advises his students (and African Americans in general) always to strive for excellence and to avoid using race as an excuse for any lack of success. He has attempted to impart this philosophy to the approximately 3,500 medical students and the more than 150 residents in general surgery whom he has helped train.

Dr. Leffall has consistently tried to promote self-esteem among blacks and harmony among the races. He recalls his father telling him, "No one is better than you are, but if you think of yourself as second-class then you will be second-class." He tries to accept invitations to speak and to operate at predominantly white institutions and tells the story of how the white residents "helped him to look good" when he was the first black to perform a surgical operation at a white hospital in Florida. In 1989, the citizens of his home town of Quincy, Florida, named a street and a surgical wing in the Gadsden Memorial Hospital in his honor.

Ruth Smith Lloyd, Ph.D.

Chronological History

Ruth S. Lloyd, the first African-American woman to earn a Ph.D. degree in anatomy, was born on January 17, 1917, in Washington, D.C. Her father, Bradley Donald Smith, was a pullman porter who prided himself on his work with some of America's most prominent white citizens and developed respect and affection for many of them. Her mother, Mary Elizabeth Morris Smith, was a homemaker for her husband and three daughters and also worked for 30 years as a first grade clerk in the U.S Department of the Treasury.

Ruth attended D.C.'s famous Dunbar High School where she achieved a straight-A record. Partly because her brother-in-law, Dr. W. Montague Cobb, had attended Amherst College, she enrolled at nearby Mt. Holyoke. Again, she earned an excellent academic record, graduating magna cum laude in 1937 with a major in zoology. During 1937–38, she obtained a fellowship for graduate study and earned a master of science degree in zoology at Howard University under Dr. Ernest Everett Just, the eminent zoologist who had received the first Spingarn Medal in 1915 for his research in cell biology.

With encouragement from both Drs. Cobb and Just, she then became from 1938–40 a Rosenwald Fellow in anatomy at Western Reserve University in Ohio, where she coauthored several publications with her major advisor, Dr. Boris Rubenstein. On December 30, 1939, she married Dr. Sterling M. Lloyd, a physician graduate of Howard University. In 1941, Dr. Ruth Lloyd was the first African-American woman to earn a Ph.D. in anatomy.

After serving during 1941–42 as an instructor in zoology at Hampton Institute, Dr. Lloyd returned to Howard as an assistant in physiology at its

College of Medicine (HUCM). She also became an instructor in anatomy in 1942 and rose through the ranks to assistant professor in 1947 and associate professor in 1955. In addition to her duties in anatomy, Dr. Lloyd served as chairperson of HUCM's Committee on Student Guidance and director of its Academic Reinforcement Program. Since her retirement in 1977, Dr. Lloyd has continued to be very active in the Washington, D.C., community, including integrated All Souls Unitarian Church and the National Museum of Women in the Arts, which she helped found in 1987.

Personal Observations

When asked about obstacles she had encountered along the way, Dr. Lloyd replied that there had been very few. Because of her excellent education at Dunbar, she had no academic problems at Mt. Holyoke. And her college classmates apparently went out of their way to make her feel welcome and to include her in their social activities. Dr. Lloyd reported that she was the only African American in her entering class at Mt. Holyoke but that another (Mabel Murphy) transferred there from Spelman

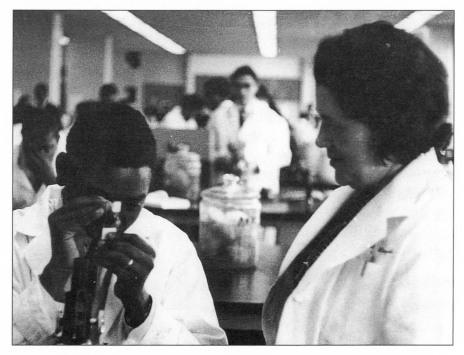

Ruth S. Lloyd, Ph.D., instructs a student during the 1940s in the HUCM microscopic anatomy laboratory.

College for her senior year. (One reason for the transfer was that the president of Spelman was a Mt. Holyoke graduate and the two schools considered themselves to be sister institutions).

Similarly, Dr. Lloyd apparently had very pleasant experiences at both

predominantly black Howard and predominantly white Case Western universities. She speaks very fondly of both Dr. Just at Howard and Dr. Rubenstein at Case Western. Her fellowships at these two institutions helped her overcome any financial obstacles she might otherwise have encountered. While at Mt. Holyoke, she met her financial needs by living in a cooperative house, and by working as a dormitory helper and as a laboratory assistant in the zoology department.

In response to questions about African Americans who had helped in her growth and development, Dr. Lloyd mentioned not only her parents' emphasis on excellence and on the importance of a good education but also the encouragement she had received from many of her teachers. She particularly appreciated Dr. Clyde McDuffy, a Williams College graduate and Latin teacher at Dunbar, who strongly encouraged her (and other Dunbar graduates) to attend the best colleges. Similarly, Dr. Just vigorously encouraged her to continue her studies toward a Ph.D. degree, and Dr. Cobb helped her gain admission at Case Western (where he earned his own doctorate in anatomy and physical anthropology).

Among the whites she especially appreciated were the science faculty at Mt. Holyoke, who gave her a solid academic background and encouraged her to pursue graduate study. She also cited Dr. Rubenstein and the other white faculty at Case Western Reserve, who not only provided her with an excellent advanced education but also encouraged her to complete her studies even though married. Finally, she noted the inspiring white ministers she had in her early days at All Souls Church.

Regarding advice to young blacks considering careers in medicine, Dr. Lloyd said, "There is no better way to serve your fellowman and to bring happiness to yourself and your family." Although she never aspired to become a physician, she said she had gained similar satisfactions from teaching medical students and from providing them with academic reinforcement and guidance. Thus she implies that academic medicine is one aspect of the medical profession worthy of particular consideration. Her life also is a reminder that one can share the satisfactions of academic medicine without necessarily being a physician.

Audrey Forbes Manley, M.D., M.P.H.

Chronological History

Audrey F. Manley, the first female deputy assistant secretary for health in the U.S. Department of Health and Human Services, was born on March 25, 1934, in Jackson, Mississippi. In 1955, she received her bachelor of arts degree from Spelman College, Atlanta, Georgia, and in 1959, a medical degree from Meharry Medical College. She took her residency in pediatrics at Cook County Children's Hospital in Chicago from 1961 to 1963 and received additional training in neonatology at the University of Illinois Abraham Lincoln School of Medicine. In 1987, she received a master's degree in public health from the Johns Hopkins University School of Public Health and Hygiene.

Dr. Manley's "firsts" began as an undergraduate student at Spelman, a women's college. She realized that the chemistry offered at Spelman would not adequately prepare her for medical school. In 1953, she was one of the first Spelman women permitted "to go across the street" to take chemistry at Morehouse, an all-men's college.

In 1962, Dr. Manley was the first African-American woman to be named chief resident of Cook County's 500-bed Children's Hospital in Chicago, a facility treating over 1,000 patients a day. In 1966, she became the first African American to hold a faculty appointment at the University of Chicago School of Medicine. In 1988, she was the first woman to become assistant surgeon general (rear admiral) in the U.S. Public Health Service. In May of 1989, Dr. Manley was appointed as deputy assistant secretary for health, U.S. Department of Health and Human Services. As the first woman to be named to this post, she became the number two ranking person in the Public Health Service.

Personal Observations

Dr. Manley stated that coming from a poor family in rural Mississippi and being a woman, especially a minority woman, were obstacles she needed to overcome to achieve professional success. She received her elementary and junior high education in Tougaloo, Mississippi, at the Laboratory School of Tougaloo College. Dr. Manley indicated that her junior high school mathematics and science teachers in Mississippi were encouraging and nurturing and gave her a good start. After her family moved to Chicago, however, the situation was quite different. When she entered high school there, many of its teachers were white. Their counseling discouraged her ambitions to pursue a medical education. To them, it was inconceivable that a poor black girl from Mississippi would want to go to medical school. Consequently, Audrey spent three years in senior high school trying to convince them that it could be done. Completing high school, she returned to the South because she realized this was the place to find the support necessary to fulfill her educational goals.

Dr. Manley was able to overcome the hurdle of poverty by means of scholarships that financed her undergraduate and medical education. She stated that she never paid any college tuition. This is especially significant because at the time she was a student, federal loan and financial aid programs were not available. Once she entered Meharry Medical College, being accepted socially was a problem since the classes were unaccustomed to having a woman present. Dr. Manley stated that there were not such problems after she completed medical school. She said, "The doors were really open. My intern and house officer experiences were really challenging and rewarding." She added, "You simply had to do what everyone else did, with no excuses."

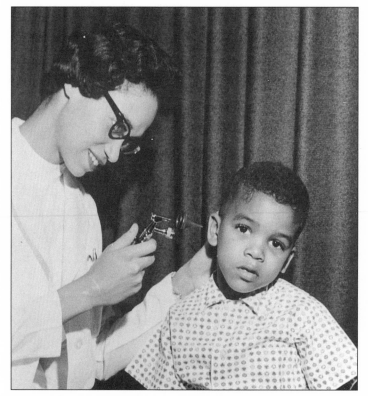

Audrey F. Manley, M.D., as a young pediatrician in the 1960s, examines a young patient.

There were many African Americans instrumental in Dr. Manley's professional accomplishments. She remembers especially Mr. Charles Caldwell, her junior high school mathematics and science teacher, who always told her she could "do better." These words had a significant effect on her life. They challenged her early to make "better equal best." She also remembered Drs. Henry McBay, who taught chemistry at Morehouse, and Helen Albro, head of the biology department at Spelman. She noted, too, that then Spelman College president, Dr. Albert E. Manley, now her husband, was key to her success. It was he who gave her permission to take chemistry at Morehouse.

Dr. Manley stated there were three white professionals who influenced the direction of her career. Drs. Joseph Greengard, chief of service, and Rowine Brown, administrator of the hospital, both at Cook County; and Dr. Ira Rosenthal, chairman, Department of Pediatrics, University of Illinois. They encouraged her to pursue a broader-based career than she had initially considered.

To those aspiring to make a contribution in any field, Dr. Manley strongly urges, "First, prepare yourself." Further, she advises, "Develop your talents. Take whatever God has given you and use it to its maximum. Then you are able to help someone else." She added, "I encourage young people to take it one test at a time, one day at a time, and one year at a time. Get all the experience and training that you need; travel if you can; become a person. By doing this, opportunities will find you and you will make a contribution."

Marion Mann, M.D., Ph.D.

Chronological History

Marion Mann, the first African-American physician brigadier general in the U.S. Army Medical Reserve Corps, was born in Atlanta, Georgia, on March 29, 1920. His father "left the house early on" and he was raised, along with his five brothers, by his mother who was a musician. She is remembered as "a tremendous lady" who lived to be 92. Marion graduated in 1940 (at age 20) from Tuskegee Institute (now Tuskegee University).

He then taught at a small school in Alabama for a year and held miscellaneous jobs in New York until 1942 when he was inducted into the Army as a private. Following Medical Administrative Corps Officer Candidate School at Carlisle Barracks in Pennsylvania, he was assigned as a second lieutenant to administrative duty at Tuskegee Army Air Base. Among his memories of that tour was "learning respect for authority" when then Colonel Vance Marchbanks told mess officer Mann to report to his office "immediately" rather than at Marion's convenience.

Following eight years of active military service, Marion entered HUCM in 1950 at age 30 and graduated in 1954 at age 34. One of the older members of his class, he served as their president during his senior year. While in medical school, he became interested in the field of pathology, largely through the influence of Dr. Robert Jason, who chaired that department and who subsequently became dean of HUCM.

After completing his internship at Staten Island Public Health Service Hospital, Dr. Mann conferred with Dr. Jason about the possibility of a career in pathology and Dr. Jason helped arrange for Dr. Mann to obtain a residency in pathology at Georgetown University School of Medicine. As one of the first black residents at Georgetown, Marion performed so well that he became senior resident during the last year of his training. He also earned a Ph.D. in pathology in 1961 and served as an instructor during his last year at Georgetown.

An Army captain in 1950, Dr. Mann rose to become on March 1, 1975, the first African-American physician to attain the rank of brigadier general in the U.S. Army Medical Reserve Corps. In that capacity, he was

Marion Mann, M.D., Ph.D., graduates in 1954 from HUCM, where he served as president of his senior class.

in active command of a major military hospital (the 2290th U.S. Army Hospital in Rockville, Maryland). While in the service he also graduated from the U.S. Army Command and General Staff College, the Industrial College of the Armed Forces, and the Army War College.

As a civilian, Dr. Mann was a part-time assistant in pathology at HUCM from 1957–60, became a full-time assistant professor in 1961, and rose through the ranks to be a full professor in 1970. That same year, when HUCM was looking for a new dean in the turbulent atmosphere of student activism, Dr. Mann was selected. His selection is attributed not only to his unique combinations of academic and military careers but to his reputation for positive relations with students—both individually and as groups.

While dean, Dr. Mann was credited with raising the academic standards of the school, in part by getting the faculty to require the passage of the National Board Examinations for advancement to the third year and for graduation. He retired as dean in 1979 and from full-time teaching at the medical school in 1983. In 1988 he was recalled to Howard to serve as vice president for research for the entire university.

Personal Observations

When asked about whether there were still opportunities to become a medical pioneer, Dr. Mann replied that "technology and science are moving so far and so rapidly that it is almost impossible to predict where the frontiers will be—and where there will be new worlds to conquer. Therefore, anyone who wants to get his or her name on the map will have to get a good education and to take active initiative to get into new situations."

Marion Mann, M.D., Ph.D., commander of the 2290th U.S. Army General Hospital, receives his brigadier general's stars on February 25, 1975, from Major General Benjamin L. Hunton, commander of the 97th Army Reserve Command. Courtesy of TASO Army Photo Facility, Fort Meade, Md.

(In addition to the above personal observations by Dr. Mann, the individual who prepared this biographical sketch [DGJ] would like to express his personal gratitude for all the courtesies and support that Dean Mann extended to him as a white person working in a predominantly black educational institution. When the writer started his part-time consulting at HUCM in 1972, Dean Mann personally escorted him to the offices of most of the department chairmen and introduced him as a friend of medical education for minorities. And at the first faculty meeting he attended, Dr. Mann extended his personal welcome and made him feel at home. These thoughtful courtesies, plus the pleasure of coauthoring several publications with Dr. Mann, strengthened the writer's intrinsic belief in working toward greater racial cooperation and harmony.)

Maxie Clarence Maultsby, Jr., M.D.

Chronological History

Maxie C. Maultsby, Jr., the first African-American M.D. author of books on rational behavioral therapy, was born in Pensacola, Florida, on April 24, 1932. He was the eldest of three children, with the younger two being a twin brother and sister. Maxie's mother was an elementary school teacher in a segregated, one-room, first-through-eighth grade Florida school located on a turpentine plantation where his father was the master turpentine stiller. For the first seven years of his school life, Maxie's mother was his only teacher. Maxie completed his education in the public schools of Orlando, Florida, graduating from Jones High School in 1949.

In the fall of 1949, Maxie entered Talladega College, a small, predominantly African-American liberal arts college in Talladega, Alabama. He received a bachelor's degree in 1953 and entered the medical school of Case Western Reserve University in Cleveland, Ohio. The tuition then was only $800 a year. Although his parents could have afforded to pay it, they did not have to. Due to Maxie's academic success at Talladega College, he received a full medical school scholarship, good at any U.S. medical college that would accept African-American students. In 1957, Dr. Maultsby received a medical degree from Case Western Reserve University and in 1958 completed his internship at Philadelphia General Hospital.

From 1958 to 1962, Dr. Maultsby was a family practitioner in Cocoa, Florida. From 1962 to 1966, he served as a captain in the United States Air Force stationed in the Philippines and Japan. During his military career, he developed an interest in mental health. He then decided to become a psychiatrist who focused on assisting psychiatrically well people to help themselves attain as much happiness as possible. In 1970, Dr. Maultsby completed psychiatric residency training in adult and child psychiatry at the University of Wisconsin Hospitals, Madison, Wisconsin. He received additional training in cognitive behavioral therapy at the Eastern Psychiatric Institute, Philadelphia; the Institute for Rational Living, New York; and the Center for Marital and Sexual Studies, Long Beach, California.

Dr. Maultsby's unique contributions include making emotional self-help a legitimate focus of scientific research and clinical use. He is also the first to formulate a comprehensive system of cognitive-behavioral psychotherapy and counseling that incorporated, in a clinically useful way, the most recent neuropsychological facts about how the brain works in relation to emotional and behavioral self-control. The technique of cognitive-behavioral therapy and counseling that Dr. Maultsby created is called Rational Behavior Therapy, and it is the first comprehensive, yet short-term, culture and drug-free technique of psychotherapy that produces long-term therapeutic results. In addition to authoring books for health professional therapists and counselors, Dr. Maultsby has written four pioneering books that describe his method of emotional self-help, called Rational Self-Counseling.

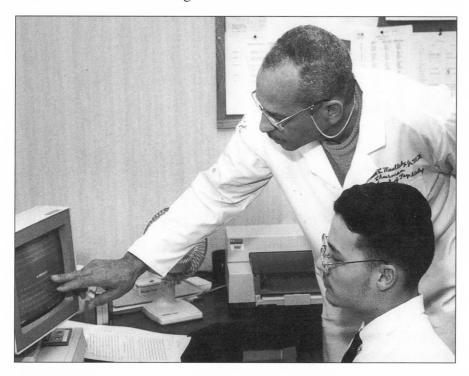

Maxie C. Maultsby, Jr., M.D., reviews a psychiatric case during the 1990s with HUCM student Douglas S. Wilson.

Personal Observations

When asked what obstacles he encountered and had to overcome to achieve his professional goals, Dr. Maultsby responded, "The only obstacle that I had to overcome was oppressive, rigidly enforced rules of segregation and the consequential, inferior educational experiences that African-American children were forced to endure." He began compensating for this when he enrolled in Talladega College. Since its founding, Talladega College was integrated. Its small but nurturing campus gave students a healthy, cosmopolitan environment. Talladega's motto was, "We take what we have and make what we want." Dr. Maultsby is a product of that motto.

Unlike many African-American medical pioneers, poverty was never an obstacle to Dr. Maultsby's success. On the contrary, he said that he had never heard the words "poor" or "poverty" used to describe any member of his family. Despite growing up during the Great Depression of the 1930s, the only comments about their economic state that he remembers were his father's and uncle's repeated proclamation, "No Maultsby has every been on a soup line or on welfare and never will be as long as I live."

The most important African Americans who had a significantly positive influence on Dr. Maultsby's professional development were his parents, a high school mathematics teacher, Mrs. Brayboy, and a high school athletic coach, Mr. Reddick. At Talladega College, the most important person was Nurse Parker, an early graduate of its nursing school who managed the infirmary. She was well informed on various subjects and taught him an important educational fact: "Teachers only teach; becoming educated is the personal achievement that only the individual can complete." Nurse Parker was the only person on campus who had information on the foundation that funded Dr. Maultsby's medical school education.

Several white people positively influenced Dr. Maultsby's life. Ms. Montgomery, the communications teacher at Talledega, recognized Maxie's writing talent and encouraged him to develop it. The white president of Talladega College and his family took a personal interest in Dr. Maultsby's educational development and suggested that he attend Case Western Reserve.

The single most important influence in Dr. Maultsby's developing Rational Behavior Therapy was the white psychologist Dr. Albert Ellis, considered by many to be the father of cognitive behavior therapy. In Dr. Maultsby's first year of psychiatric residency, he discovered Dr. Ellis' books. According to Dr. Maultsby, they were the most scientifically interesting and clinically useful of all the books he had studied during his residency. Dr. Maultsby became one of Dr. Ellis' first psychiatric protégés.

Dr. Maultsby advises young people pursuing career goals and aspiring to become pioneers to do what makes the most logical sense to them regardless of whoever else disagrees with their view. He believes that ability is the key to becoming a pioneer. Reflecting further, Dr. Maultsby added, "Forget about trying to become a pioneer. Do what you are most capable of and enjoy doing; if you happen to be living at the time when no one else has done what you are doing, and there is a need for it, then you will become a pioneer."

Russell Loyd Miller, Jr., M.D.

Chronological History

Russell L. Miller, Jr., the first African-American internal medicine resident at the University of Michigan Medical School, was born in Harvey, West Virginia, on June 30, 1939. He grew up, however, in Washington, D.C. His parents were very loving and supportive but both had to work outside the home to maintain their lower middle-class income. Accordingly, his teachers assumed major importance and some are described as being like second parents to young Russell.

He enjoyed classwork and did very well throughout his schooling, which included one year at Washington's famous Dunbar High School. When the D.C. schools were desegregated, he was transferred to Roosevelt where he discovered that he could more than hold his own academically with the predominantly white student body.

In spite of being accepted by a number of prestigious predominantly white colleges, he decided to attend Howard University—partly for financial reasons and partly because he believed its environment would be more supportive. Similarly, after receiving his bachelor of science degree with honors in 1961, he attended its College of Medicine and graduated with high honors in 1965.

While in medical school, he was a summer fellow at the National Institutes of Health and found that he was attracted to the challenges, independence, and intellectual stimulation of basic research. He was encouraged by his supervisors to consider research as a career and they became his friends and mentors. However, they warned him that his African-American race might keep him from receiving grants to support his work. Accordingly, rather than forgo an internship to embark immediately on a research career, he applied for one in internal medicine.

Although he was not aware of it until several years later, Dr. Miller became in 1965 the first African-American internal medicine intern at the University of Michigan Medical School. He performed so well there that, as a third-year resident, he was put in charge of medical education at the University Hospital. In that capacity, he participated in the grading process and became aware that, in borderline cases, the benefit of the doubt was given to the white but not to the black students. When Dr. Miller called this to the attention of his colleagues, they admitted this was true and tried to be more objective and fair. Dr. Miller was favorably impressed that they "owned up" to the problem and that they sincerely attempted to correct it.

During 1968–69 and 1971–73, Dr. Miller was a fellow at the Cardiovascular Research Institute of the University of California at San Francisco, where he participated in an increased effort to provide mentoring and other support to the University's African-American medical students.

Dr. Miller was on active duty with the U.S. Army from 1969–71 and served as chief of professional services and acting hospital commander of the Third Surgical Hospital in Vietnam where he attained the rank of major. During 1973–74, he was a visiting scientist in the Department of Cellular Biology at the Roche Institute of Molecular Biology. He returned to HUCM in 1974 as a faculty member in the Department of Internal Medicine. In 1977, he became the first African-American Burroughs-Wellcome Scholar in Clinical Pharmacology.

He was for five years professor of internal medicine and pharmacology and director of the Section of Clinical Pharmacology. On July 1, 1979, Dr. Miller became dean of the College of Medicine at the relatively young age of 40. In 1988 he was elevated to the position of vice president for health affairs at Howard University. In 1990, Dr. Miller was also appointed to the position of senior vice president of the entire university.

Personal Observations

When asked about obstacles he had encountered along the way, he said the main ones were financial. Although he received a substantial amount of financial aid from National Medical Fellowships, Inc., and other sources, his concern for the financial welfare of his parents and other family members somewhat curtailed his freedom of choice. Without such monetary concerns, Dr. Miller indicated he might have devoted even more of his career to basic research.

In reply to questions about others who had helped him along the way, he expressed great appreciation to his parents and teachers, including those at the elementary and junior high school levels. Many of these early teachers helped him and others realize that, with their teachers' generous help, "they could learn hard material" even though it might take considerable joint time and effort to master difficult concepts in mathematics, for example. He also cited the white professionals who had encouraged him when he was a summer fellow at NIH and the white chairmen of medicine at Michigan and at UCSF. Among the black men and women who made a great impact on his career, he particularly appreciated Dr. W. Lester Henry, former chair of medicine at HUCM, and Dr. Edward Hawthorne, one of HUCM's top scientists with whom Dr. Miller collaborated on at least one project.

Relative to his philosophy of life, Dr. Miller emphasized the importance of developing positive relationships with others and of being of service to humankind. He also encourages himself and others to "aspire to reach one's full potential, and to explore and take advantage of one's opportunities." That he has lived this philosophy is demonstrated by his substantial amount of volunteer work with such organizations as the Association of American Medical Colleges, the National Resident Matching Program, the National Board of Medical Examiners, National Medical Fellowships, Inc., the Educational Commission for Foreign Medical Graduates, and Physicians for Social Responsibility. He has received many significant research grants from NIH, among others, and was named the "man of the sixties decade" by National Medical Fellowships, Inc.

(An informal photograph of Dr. Miller at a Howard University building dedication ceremony appears at the beginning of this chapter with the biography of Dr. W. Montague Cobb.)

Claude H. Organ, Jr., M.D., F.A.C.S.

Chronological History

Claude H. Organ, Jr., the first African American to chair a department of surgery at a predominantly white medical school, was born on October 16, 1928, in Marshall, Texas. He was the second of three children of Claude Organ, Sr., and Ottolena Pemberton Organ. His father was a graduate of Lincoln University (Missouri) and his mother had a bachelor of arts degree from Wiley College. Both his parents placed a high premium on education. Claude Jr. attended public segregated schools in Denison, Texas, and was valedictorian of the 1943 graduating class of Terrell High School.

In part because his sister was a student there, Claude attended college at Xavier University in New Orleans, Louisiana. His uncle, Ralph

Metcalfe, of Olympic fame, had also been a track coach at that institution. Since two other uncles, Charles and Dogan Pemberton, were physicians, Claude was encouraged to take courses that would qualify him to enter medical school. Although he originally applied only to Howard and Meharry medical schools, he was invited to have a Xavier campus interview with the dean of Creighton and was promptly accepted—undoubtedly because of his strong academic record, favorable recommendations of his faculty, and the positive impression he made in the interview.

After receiving his bachelor of science degree cum laude in 1948, Claude moved to Omaha and enrolled as the only black student in his Creighton University medical school class. He performed so well in medical school and was so highly thought of that following his graduation in 1952 he was selected to remain as a surgical intern from 1952–53. Dr. Organ was so successful in that role that he was asked to remain as an assistant resident from 1953–56, and was appointed as chief resident in surgery from 1956–57.

Dr. Organ then served in the U.S. Navy from 1957–59 where he was a lieutenant commander at the 1000-bed U.S. Naval Hospital at Camp Pendleton, California. While there he passed the qualifying examinations for the American Board of Surgery and became the only board-certified surgeon at the camp. Although he had several opportunities to remain in California, Dr. Organ decided to accept the invitation he received to return to Creighton.

Starting as an instructor in surgery from 1960–63, Dr. Organ was promoted to assistant professor in 1963 and to associate professor in 1966. In 1971, he was appointed as professor and chairman of surgery at Creighton, which made him the first African American to chair a department of surgery at a predominantly white medical school. Dr. Organ served as chairman until 1982, at which time he became professor of surgery at the University of Oklahoma Health Sciences Center. As of 1991, he was still active in academic medicine in Oakland, California. He came to Oakland as professor of surgery at the University of California, Davis, and as chairman of the UCD-East Bay Surgery Program, in which there are 70 residents.

In addition to his distinguished career in academic medicine, Dr. Organ has been an outstanding leader in organized medicine. His "African-American firsts" in that area include being elected as both chairman of the Southwestern Surgical Congress (1984–85) and as chairman of the American Board of Surgery (1984–86). He was also the first black member of the Surgery Residency Review Committee and the first black editor (since 1989) of the *Archives of Surgery,* which is the largest surgical journal in the English-speaking world. In 1986, he became the first black fellow in the Royal College of Surgeons of South Africa, and he received a similar honor in 1989 from the Royal Australian College. During the 1980s, Dr. Organ was the senior author of the highly acclaimed two-volume work entitled *A Century of Black Surgeons: The U.S.A. Experience,* which was published in 1987.

Claude H. Organ, Jr., M.D., is shown in 1993 conferring with (L to R) surgery residents Francis Duhaylongsod, M.D., and Andrea Hayes-Jordan, M.D., at the University of California Davis-East Bay Hospital in Oakland.

Personal Observations

From Dr. LaSalle Leffall's chapter about Dr. Organ in that book, it is apparent that Dr. Organ encountered a number of racial obstacles along the way but that he was able to cope with them without too much difficulty. It is reported that "at first, he found the atmosphere at Xavier quite uncomfortable and some of its white teachers somewhat condescending." He also experienced some hard-core racism in the city of New Orleans, but his "parents had instilled in their three children a sense of dignity and self-worth that did not allow them to think of themselves as less than any other person."

Going to Omaha and medical school was also a fairly difficult transition, both because Claude was the only black student in his class and because he was only 20 years old and single while most of his classmates were older married veterans of World War II. Claude made a number of close friends among his classmates and became a member of a national medical fraternity. He did not marry until his internship, but he and his wife, Elizabeth Mays Organ, eventually had a strong family of seven children.

Relative to help received along the way, Dr. Leffall's chapter cites not only Dr. Organ's parents, physician uncles, and wife, but also several of his white college and medical school teachers. These included Dr. Phillip Hornung at Xavier, who arranged for him to receive an Audubon summer fellowship to study birds in Louisiana, and Dr. Arnold Dowell, one of the radiologists at Creighton. Dr. Organ was also very appreciative of Dean Joseph Holthaus who appointed him as chairman of surgery at Creighton.

Among the words of advice in this chapter that might be helpful to black youth aspiring to careers in academic and organized medicine is Dr. Organ's favorite saying that "attitude, not just aptitude, determines altitude." Another of his memorable quotations is that "mastery of fundamentals is the key to self-confidence in the student."

(This sketch was prepared from chapter 23 of <u>A Century of Black Surgeons</u> *[Organ and Kosiba, 1987]).*

Vivian Winona Pinn, M.D.

Chronological History

Vivian W. Pinn, the first director of the NIH Office of Research on Women's Health, was born on April 21, 1941, in Halifax, Virginia. She received her early education in Lynchburg, Virginia, and graduated as the valedictorian of Dunbar High School's class of 1958. In 1963, she earned a bachelor of arts degree from Wellesley College in Massachusetts and in 1967, a medical degree from the University of Virginia School of Medicine. Dr. Pinn was the only African American and the only woman in her medical school class. In 1970 she completed her postgraduate training in pathology at Massachusetts General Hospital while also serving as a teaching fellow at the Harvard Medical School.

Dr. Pinn was the first African-American female to complete an internship in pathology at Massachusetts General Hospital. She was also among the first African Americans to serve as assistant dean for student affairs at Tufts University School of Medicine (1974–82).

In September 1982, Dr. Pinn assumed the position of professor and chair in the department of pathology at Howard University College of Medicine. With this appointment, she became the first African-American woman in the United States to chair a department of pathology, only the third woman to do so. Dr. Pinn served as the 88th president of the National Medical Association (1989–90). She was this organization's second woman president.

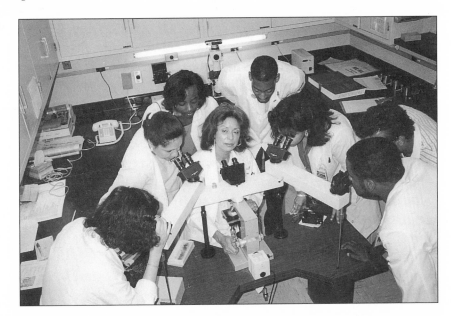

Vivian W. Pinn, M.D., instructs HUCM graduate physicians (residents) in the 1980s on the proper interpretation of pathology slides.

In the summer of 1991, then NIH Director Dr. Bernadine Healy offered Dr. Pinn the position of director in the Office of Research on Women's Health. Accepting this offer, Dr. Pinn became the first permanent director of this office, whose mission is to represent women's issues and to promote their interests within NIH and the biomedical community.

Personal Observations

Most of the female medical pioneers we interviewed recalled that being a woman and African American were among the obstacles to overcome while pursuing professional careers. Dr. Pinn, however, stated that these were not obstacles to successful performances in either her internship or other training programs in pathology. She holds and has held leadership positions in numerous professional organizations; gender or race never deterred her advancement in any of them. Dr. Pinn said, "I never thought my abilities or qualifications were different or less than my peers. If anything, being African American and female provided me with special sensitivities and understanding to make me, perhaps uniquely, more qualified for academic positions in majority institutions."

She indicated, however, that once she assumed higher levels of responsibility in academic medicine, obstacles did occur. She remembered learning that the perception of others about women in power was a unique experience. She thinks that this knowledge can be an obstacle when it affects opportunities to make those creative changes that characterize an effective leader. "Having the support and understanding of others, being competent at what you do, together with firmly believing that being African American and a woman must not be a deterrent, is my way of addressing obstacles," she said.

Dr. Pinn stated that she had several mentors, both African American and white, who supported her professional goals. Among them, she credits her father's liberal thinking for encouraging her early aspirations to become a physician. Other family members also provided positive support. Additionally, Pauline Weeden Maloney, a high school guidance counselor and a leader of several African-American women's organizations, guided Dr. Pinn's educational and career choices.

Dr. Martin A. Flax, professor and chairman, Department of Pathology at Tufts University, was instrumental to Dr. Pinn's internship at Massachusetts General Hospital and her position at Harvard Medical School. Providing continuous career and professional advice, Dr. Flax has been an ongoing mentor.

When asked how she would advise young people who have professional aspirations, Dr. Pinn stated, "Doors, previously closed, are now open to you; opportunities are there, do not be afraid to explore them." She recalled that when she came along, no one was ever given anything simply because he or she was black. "This has not changed," she said. "This means," she concluded, "you will have to work a little harder, be a little stronger, and have confidence in yourselves to achieve." She added, "Be proud of your heritage, know your history, and be familiar with the struggle of those before you. Only then can you appreciate what was undertaken to get us where we are today."

Dr. Pinn also pointed out that racism is a detriment, but it does not have to keep a person from achieving. She added that it helps if one can eliminate hostility. Concluding, she advised, "Be honest and loyal to yourself; respect yourself and have respect for others. Recognize diversity and difference in others, but realize we are all a part of the same human race."

Deborah Boutin Prothrow-Stith, M.D.

Chronological History

Deborah B. Prothrow-Stith, the first African-American woman commissioner of public health for the state of Massachusetts, was born in Marshall, Texas, on February 6, 1954. Majoring in mathematics at Spelman College, Atlanta, Georgia, she received the bachelor of arts degree in 1975. In 1979, she received the medical degree from Harvard University Medical School, and in 1982 became a diplomate in internal medicine. Subsequently she received an honorary doctorate in public service in 1988 from North Adams State College, North Adams, Massachusetts, and one in education from Wheelock College, Boston, in 1992.

From 1985 to 1987, Dr. Prothrow-Stith was codirector of Boston's Health Promotion Center for Urban Youth, Department of Health and Hospitals. As of 1993, she is assistant dean for government and community programs at Harvard University's School of Public Health.

While working as a staff physician at Boston City Hospital and the Harvard Street Neighborhood Health Center, Dr. Prothrow-Stith developed an interest in adolescent violence. She has recommended strategies to stem the tide of violence among society's youth in many publications, in major print media, and on national television, including "CBS Evening News," "Good Morning America," and "Today" on NBC.

In 1987, Dr. Prothrow-Stith implemented a violence prevention program at Boston City Hospital that was the nation's first public health program to address violence. For pioneer work in violence, she was the 1989 recipient of the Secretary of Health and Human Services Award. From 1987–89, Dr. Prothrow-Stith was the first woman and youngest person to serve as commissioner of public health of the Commonwealth of Massachusetts. In that position, she established the first state office of violence prevention and expanded treatment programs on AIDS, drug rehabilitation, and other urban issues. She is the author of the book *Deadly Consequences,* published in 1991. The first book to present a public health perspective on violence to a mass audience, it analyzes this problem and offers revolutionary ways of preventing the continued deaths of African-American youth.

Personal Observations

The path to prominence and recognition has not always been smooth, according to Dr. Prothrow-Stith. She recalls that her first prolonged experience in an integrated setting was during medical school. It was there that she struggled with a racially and sexually biased system where fellow students and professors offered constant challenges to her self-esteem. She proved by her accomplishments that she had earned a place and could offer invaluable, fresh perspectives to many problems.

Dr. Prothrow-Stith stated, "Too many people worked too hard and too long so that I could gain a place at the table. I couldn't give up when I felt people disrespected me or distrusted my intellectual talents or abilities. I knew deep inside, there was nothing wrong with me but with society."

Among the many African Americans who either encouraged, supported or inspired her career are: Dr. Audrey Manley, wife of the former president of Spelman College and from 1989–92 deputy assistant secretary for the U.S. Department of Health and Human Services; Dr. Alvin F. Poussaint, psychiatrist and associate dean of students at Harvard

Deborah B. Prothrow-Stith, M.D., with a copy of her 1991 book, Deadly Consequences, *that deals with violence as a public health issue.*

Medical School; and Mrs. Sandra Graham, health career counselor, who worked tirelessly to get women from Spelman College admitted to Harvard University Medical School; Dr. Etta Falconer, who chairs a national science department; and Dr. Van Dunn, who was President John F. Kennedy's chief of medical affairs. She gratefully acknowledges the tremendous support of her family, countless friends, and, of course, her husband, the Reverend Charles Stith.

Dr. Prothrow-Stith also recognized the support she received from individuals who were not African Americans, including Drs. Gladys Boise of Spelman College; John Noble, chief of internal medicine at Boston City Hospital; Mark Rosenberg, director of the Division of Injury Control at the U.S. Centers for Disease Control; Howard Spivak, chief of the Department of Pediatrics at the New England Medical Center; and Harvey Fineberg, dean of Harvard University Medical School. Each, in his or her unique way, had an encouraging role to play in Dr. Prothrow-Stith's career.

To young people who want to be a positive force in today's society, Dr. Prothrow-Stith offers this advice: "True service is the essence of achieving. If you are working passionately to solve a collective problem, then, undoubtedly, you will make a major contribution." She concluded: "All that you need is your perspective on the problem. Keep that perspective and work to serve."

Calvin Coolidge Sampson, M.D.

Chronological History

Calvin C. Sampson, the first African-American resident at Philadelphia's Episcopal Hospital, was born on February 1, 1928, on the Eastern shore of Maryland in the small farming town of Linkwood. As the tenth of 12 children, he was named by his Republican parents after the president of the United States. Although Calvin said that his family was "very poor," the children were not particularly aware of it because of the strong emotional bonds with their family and neighbors. His parents also taught him such basic values as "believing in other people and helping them believe in you." His father emphasized that "one's word is one's bond" and should always be heeded.

Calvin's mother especially placed a high value on education and he excelled in school from an early age. Starting first grade a year ahead of schedule in a one-room schoolhouse, Calvin skipped the seventh grade and finished high school at age 15 as the second ranking student in his class. He speaks very highly of his public school teachers and says "they taught not only subject matter but how to cope with life through hard work and realistic but positive attitudes."

Partly for financial reasons, Calvin attended Hampton Institute (now Hampton University) in Virginia where he could participate in what was originally intended to be a five-year work-study program. (His father had died during the spring of his senior year of high school.) Even though Calvin was majoring in chemistry and minoring in biology and mathematics, he also worked at the school's experimental farm, which

Calvin C. Sampson, M.D. (far right), as a resident in June 1956 with the other pathology staff members at Philadelphia's Episcopal Hospital.

required him to milk cows and do chores from 4:30 to around 8:30 a.m. He learned the value of "time" and used it so well that he graduated in only four years with high honors and with more than the required number of credits.

Deciding to become a physician, he applied only to Meharry because in 1947 its tuition was less than Howard's and other U.S. medical schools were essentially closed to black applicants. For a while he did not know how he could afford Meharry, but one of his sisters discovered that since the Maryland medical schools did not accept black students, he could receive money for travel, tuition, and books at an out-of-state school. With that backing and with fairly high-paying summer jobs, he was able to devote enough time and effort to his demanding studies to earn his medical degree with honors in 1951.

After completing an internship at the traditionally black Mercy-Douglass Hospital in Philadelphia, he decided to seek a career in pathology, even though warned by white friends that the job market might not be good for one of his race. Although he was quickly approved by the director of pathology at Philadelphia's Episcopal Hospital, other staff members were hesitant to appoint a black and referred him to a psychiatrist for screening. The psychiatrist's first question was, "What do you think of interracial marriages?" Apparently Calvin gave an acceptable answer for he became the first black resident at Philadelphia's Episcopal Hospital. He performed so well that he became senior resident and headed the program when the director was on vacation.

Dr. Sampson's residency was interrupted by two years of military service during the Korean War, where he served as chief of the laboratory service at Fort Lee, Virginia, and as a general medical officer. He reports no racial problems on the Army base but implies that the situation was not as favorable in town. Although he had married a nurse (Corrine D. Pannell) when he entered the service, they decided that she should remain in Philadelphia until he returned there. (Incidentally, Dr. Sampson remained in the army reserves until 1988 and retired with the rank of full colonel.)

While completing his residency, Dr. Sampson became in 1957 one of the first black physicians to be certified in clinical pathology. In 1958 he started a long career in academic medicine at Howard University when he became director of laboratories and hospital pathologist at Freedmen's Hospital. In 1963 he became the first pathologist director of Howard's new Department of Medical Technology and in 1971 was named the first acting chairman of its newly established Department of Allied Health Professions. He rose through the academic ranks to become full professor and vice chairman of the Department of Pathology before retiring from HUCM in 1990. Dr. Sampson has also been editor since 1978 of the *JNMA* and is the author of over 100 publications. He and his wife have two daughters and two grandchildren.

Personal Observations

When asked about obstacles he had encountered, and overcome, the major one appeared to be financial, which he overcame by extensive part-time work and by discovering the financial resources available to him through the state of Maryland. He, along with many others of his era, also experienced fear of failure while in medical school, but overcame it by studying diligently.

Replying to questions about help received along the way, Dr. Sampson mentioned not only his family and early teachers, but also Dr. Anita Hall, a biology teacher at Hampton who encouraged him to do graduate work, and Dr. George Washington Hunter, a college chemistry teacher and role model. Other black supporters included Dr. W. Montague Cobb, who was a mentor about life in general and writing and editing in particular. He also cited William Coleman, Sr., who hired him to work at a boys camp during his medical school summers and allowed him to shift from counseling to the higher paid job of washing pots and pans! Finally, he appreciated his many fine colleagues in the Howard University Department of Pathology, including Drs. Robert Jason, Marvin Jackson, R. Frank Jones, Marion Mann, and Vivian Pinn.

Dr. Sampson also cited several white persons who had been very helpful to him in his life and professional career. Both Dr. William Beck, director, and Dr. Alan Wallis, deputy director, of pathology at Episcopal Hospital were always very supportive and the latter even helped him out financially through gifts of books. Rev. Arthur Azlein was also appreciated as a white minister in the District of Columbia who remained with his church when most of his white parishioners fled to the suburbs.

Regarding advice to prospective minority physicians, Dr. Sampson stressed the importance of hard work and the satisfactions of serving and teaching others. He reminds us that "if we do something right on the first try, we will save valuable time in the long run." He encourages young blacks to consider "the enjoyable colleagues and students one has in *academic medicine*" and "the advantages of being able to broaden one's influence through participation in *organized medicine*."

Roland Boyd Scott, M.D., D.Sc.

Chronological History

Roland B. Scott, one of the first African-American diplomates of the American Board of Pediatrics, was born in Houston, Texas, on April 18, 1909. Life for African Americans in Texas at that time was strictly segregated. Although his parents were not college graduates, they were hard-working, energetic, and anxious to have their children acquire a college education. After graduating from high school in Kansas City, Missouri, he came to Washington, D.C., to attend Howard University. Majoring in chemistry, a subject he learned to like while in high school, he received the bachelor of science degree in 1931. Roland applied to medical school at the end of his junior year in college, and graduated from the Howard University College of Medicine in 1934. He completed his postgraduate pediatric training in Chicago.

Dr. Scott accepted a full-time position as assistant professor of pediatrics at Howard University in 1939; his annual salary was only $3,000. At that time, he was married and had an infant son. Since that salary was not sufficient to meet their needs, the university made a special arrangement permitting him to do part-time pediatric consultations at Freedmen's Hospital to supplement his income. In 1945 he became chief of the Division of Pediatrics; from 1949 to 1973 he was chairman of the Department of Pediatrics.

Shortly after his appointment at Howard University, Dr. Scott became seriously involved in the care of children with sickle cell disease. Over the years, Dr. Scott's research findings, publications and exhibits documenting the nature of sickle cell disease have been presented at medical meetings throughout the country and occasionally abroad. In 1971, Dr. Scott established the Howard University Center for Sickle Cell Disease. He served as its director until he retired in 1990. For his leadership and pioneering efforts in directing national and international attention to sickle cell disease, Dr. Scott has received numerous honors and awards,

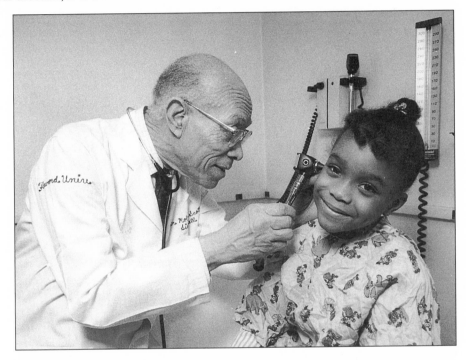

Roland B. Scott, M.D., is shown in 1987 examining a young patient at the HUCM Center for Sickle Cell Disease which he established in 1971.

including the Jacobi Award of the American Academy of Pediatrics and awards from the Advisory Board of the Comprehensive Center for Sickle Cell Disease, College of Physicians and Surgeons of Columbia University; and the National Institutes of Health's National Sickle Cell Disease Program. Dr. Scott is recognized world-wide as an outstanding author, educator, and researcher.

With his dedication to medicine in general and sickle cell disease and pediatrics in particular, Dr. Scott blazed a trail for many to follow in these fields. In 1939, Dr. Scott, along with Dr. Alonzo Smith, became the first African-American physician admitted to membership in the American Academy of Pediatrics. That same year he became the second African-American diplomate of the American Board of Pediatrics. In 1952, Dr. Scott was the first African-American physician admitted to membership in the American Pediatric Society and the Society for Pediatric Research. He was a leader in the area of sickle cell disease long before the significance of this disease was recognized.

Personal Observations

When asked to comment on the obstacles he encountered in achieving his illustrious medical career, Dr. Scott responded, "I feel that my biggest lifelong problem has been coping with racism and discrimination in America." He stated that mentors encouraged him and that he received support from many friends and professional organizations. He added, "Their help enabled me to deal with racism in a responsible, tactful way, and I continued working to help African-American children and their families."

Since there were so few African Americans who were in a position to help at the time he was making his medical journey, Dr. Scott remembers very little assistance coming from this group. However, Drs. Robert Crawford, Angella Ferguson, and Melvin Jenkins assisted some of his early research on sickle cell disease in infants. Also, African-American organizations such as Alpha Kappa Alpha Sorority and similar groups assisted his work with small grants.

Dr. Scott stated that he received some assistance from white persons. They were in a position and had the necessary contacts to give help. Too, neither he nor his work was a threat to them. He acknowledged support from Dr. Frederick W. Schultz, chairman of the Department of Pediatrics at Provident Hospital, which is affiliated with the University of Chicago, who was his mentor. In 1971, the National Institutes of Health awarded sufficient funds to allow Dr. Scott to establish the Center for Sickle Cell Disease at Howard. He was then able to increase research productivity and plan an interdisciplinary approach to treat the disease. He acknowledged NIH's support.

In closing, Dr. Scott recognized that today's children are tomorrow's leaders. He offered several pieces of advice to prepare them for these future roles. He advises, "Don't dodge difficult subjects; keep contacts broad, including African Americans and white people; don't expect promotions without hard work; and keep in mind the importance of being scholarly." Dr. Scott concluded by reminding today's professionals of their obligation to do as much as possible to provide for our children's current and future needs.

Jeanne Spurlock, M.D.

Chronological History

Jeanne Spurlock, the first female to head a psychiatry department at an American medical school, was born in Sandusky, Ohio, on July 19, 1921. She was educated in the public schools of metropolitan Detroit, and began her college education at Spelman College in Atlanta, Georgia, where she completed her sophomore year in 1942. To continue her education, it was necessary to seek full-time employment; thus a transfer to Roosevelt University, Chicago, in the fall of 1942. She received the medical degree from Howard University in 1947.

Dr. Spurlock completed an internship at Provident Hospital, Chicago, in 1948 and residency training in general psychiatry, Cook County Psychopathic Hospital, also in Chicago, in 1950. That same year, she accepted a two-year fellowship in child psychiatry at the Institute for Juvenile Research, Chicago. Part-time postgraduate training continued from 1953 to 1962 at the Chicago Institute for Psychoanalysis. Dr. Spurlock earned a certificate in adult and child psychoanalysis from this institute. She was also chief of child psychiatry and director of child psychiatry training at Michael Reese Hospital in Chicago.

Reportedly, there have only been four females in this country heading departments of psychiatry. When Dr. Spurlock joined the faculty at Meharry Medical College in 1968, and headed its psychiatry department, she became one of them. Accepting this position at Meharry, she became the first woman to head a psychiatry department at an American medical school. In 1971, she was the first African American and the first woman to receive the Edward A. Strecker, M.D., Award from the Institute of Pennsylvania for outstanding contributions in psychiatric care and treatment. In 1974, Dr. Spurlock joined the staff of the American Psychiatric Association as the deputy medical director and director of the Office of Minority National Affairs. She retired from this position in 1991.

Personal Observations

Dr. Spurlock recalled a number of obstacles that had to be overcome while pursuing a career in psychiatry. Being African American and female were among them. Many residency training programs were closed to African Americans in the 1950s. A popular opinion during this decade was that since African Americans were such a "happy-go-lucky people" they did not suffer many psychiatric disorders. She stated, "During my clinical years at Howard, I became aware that there was a psychological overlay to the physical difficulties experienced by most of my patients. I was persistent and pursued psychiatry." Sometimes this pursuit was arduous. Her application to a veterans hospital training program was ostensibly rejected because there were no living arrangements on the grounds for female residents. Years later, she was told, with an apology, that she was rejected because she was black. Dr. Spurlock also indicated that the racist attitudes of policy makers in organized medicine continue to be obstacles. She said, "Often it is necessary to set aside some of the racial assaults if one is to accomplish his or her goals."

Dr. Spurlock reported that among the African Americans who had helped her reach her professional goals were her parents. She said that although they were poor, they always had middle-class aspirations and clung to the belief that "you can be anything you want to be." They said it often enough to instill the message in her. Another was Dr. Mary McLeod Bethune. During her sophomore year in medical school, Dr. Spurlock

Jeanne Spurlock, M.D., making a presentation at the 1969 scientific session of the American Psychiatric Association in Miami, Fla.

turned to Dr. Bethune for help in obtaining a loan. Dr. Bethune cosigned a promissory note that enabled Dr. Spurlock to continue her education.

Dr. Spurlock also indicated that some white colleagues had provided psychological support and encouragement. An early mentor was the late Dr. Charlotte Babcock. She also identified Drs. Viola Bernard and Mary Jane Jensen as key supporters.

Advising young people regarding their career aspirations, Dr. Spurlock suggests that they identify several alternative goals to avoid disappointment. She noted that goals change as experiences and circumstances change; it is important to be flexible and to be willing to modify goals to avoid missing an opportunity.

Louis W. Sullivan, M.D.

Chronological History

Louis W. Sullivan, the first African-American physician to be appointed secretary of the U.S. Department of Health and Human Services, was born on November 3, 1933, in Atlanta, Georgia. At an early age, he moved to rural Blakely, Georgia, where his father had a funeral home and his mother was a teacher. Because the local segregated public schools for blacks were thought by his parents to be inadequate, they sent Louis and his brother to Atlanta from the fifth grade on. There also, Louis attended Morehouse College from which he graduated as a premedical major in 1954.

He was the first Morehouse alumnus to attend Boston University Medical School and earned his medical degree with honors in 1958. He then became the first black house staff officer at Cornell Medical School's New York Hospital; and subsequently (from 1961–64) was the first black fellow on the Harvard service of the Thorndike Laboratory at Boston City Hospital. This was followed by a distinguished career in academic internal medicine at Harvard, the College of Medicine and Dentistry of New Jersey, and the Boston University School of Medicine. In 1975, Dr. Sullivan was appointed as the first dean of the new Morehouse Medical Education Program, and in 1981 became the first president of the Morehouse School of Medicine.

In 1982, Dr. Sullivan was one of three black leaders on then Vice President Bush's 12-member team to visit seven African countries, and in 1989 he was appointed as the first black physician secretary of the U.S. Department of Health and Human Services. Another of Dr. Sullivan's "firsts" is that of being the founding president in 1978 of the Association of Minority Health Professions Schools.

Personal Observations

When asked about obstacles encountered and overcome, Dr. Sullivan mentioned the racism of his small town in Georgia and said there were still lynchings in that area when he was young. As already mentioned, the problem of inadequate education for blacks in his area was overcome by living with friends in Atlanta while attending public schools there. (It is ironic that a few days before our June, 1991, interview, Dr. Sullivan was the invited speaker at the annual dinner of the same high school he could not attend as a youth because it was segregated.)

His other major obstacles were financial, and they were overcome by part-time jobs and financial aid. While at Morehouse, Louis worked for one of the deans; while in medical school, he helped support himself as a busboy in the hospital cafeteria and as an aide in the medical school library. He also received financial aid from such sources as the Jessie Smith Noyes and the Leopold Schepp foundations.

Regarding help received from specific individuals, Dr. Sullivan expressed appreciation for a substantial number of persons, most of them black. In addition to his parents, his early mentors included Dr. John Griffin, the first black physician he ever met and the only one near his hometown. (Louis saw him fairly frequently because his father provided an ambulance as well as a funeral service and used to take Louis with him on some of his trips to Dr. Griffin's.)

Teachers who were particularly appreciated by Dr. Sullivan included Miss Laura Woods, an eighth grade biology treacher, and Mr. R.E. Cureton, who taught at the Booker T. Washington High School in Atlanta and was a neighbor to Louis and his brother when they lived there. Dr. Sullivan also made special note of the positive influence of his scoutmaster, Mr. Arthur Richardson.

Cited as most influential of all was Dr. Benjamin Mays, president of Morehouse during Sullivan's student days. Dr. Mays encouraged all of the Morehouse students to "set high standards, have confidence in themselves, be willing to take risks, and contribute to society." Other mentors at Morehouse included Dean B.R. Brazeal, for whom Louis worked, and Dr. James Birnie, who was professor of biology and an extremely effective premedical advisor. Dr. Birnie was a Morehouse graduate who returned there from Syracuse University and spent lots of time advising his preprofessional students. His success is indicated by 17 of the 18 premedical students in Louis's class being admitted to medical school, five of them to predominantly white schools.

Foremost among the nonblacks appreciated by Dr. Sullivan was Dr. E. Hugh Luckey, chief of internal medicine at Cornell, who appointed him as the first black member of Cornell's house staff. Dr. Sullivan knew that Dr. Luckey was from Tennessee and expected him to be racially prejudiced. To his pleasant surprise, Dr. Luckey not only admitted him to his service but went out of his way to let Dr. Sullivan know that he was "in his corner." On the only occasion when a white patient refused to be treated by Dr. Sullivan, Dr. Luckey promptly had the patient discharged from the hospital (even though his admitting physician was very influential). By coincidence, Dr. Luckey later became a member of the Josiah Macy Foundation Board that was instrumental in awarding funds to the new medical school at Morehouse.

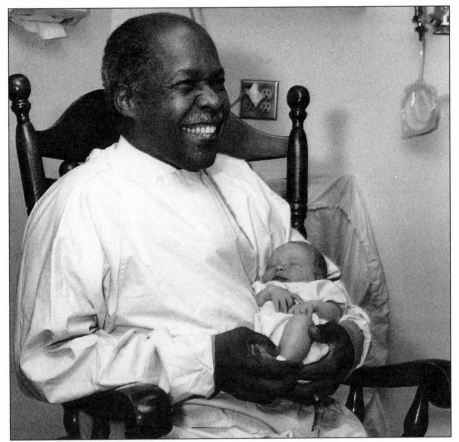

Louis W. Sullivan, M.D., relaxes from duties as secretary of the U.S. Department of Health and Human Services by holding a young patient at St. Rita's Medical Center in June 1992. Dr. Sullivan embodies the spirit of "a physician enjoying his work."

The other white person whom Dr. Sullivan cited by name was Dr. William E. Cassell, who was chief of the Harvard Unit when Dr. Sullivan was a fellow at the previously mentioned Thorndike Laboratory. In addition, although not specifically mentioned in the interview, other sources have noted the support that Dr. Sullivan has received from both former President George Bush and his wife, Barbara. (Mrs. Bush was a Morehouse Medical School board member from 1983–89 and an honorary trustee thereafter).

Finally, Dr. Sullivan's advice to other African Americans interested in becoming leaders in medicine is to "be sure of your values and stick to them; strive to excel in whatever you do; be willing to take prudent risks and be guided by a vision of what ought to be rather than being held back by the reality of what exists today."

Burke Syphax, M.D., F.A.C.S.

Chronological History

Burke (Mickey) Syphax, one of the first African Americans certified by the American Board of Surgery, was born in Washington, D.C., on December 18, 1910. His father had only six years of formal education, but through self-learning and hard work rose from being a dining car waiter, to head waiter at Washington, D.C.'s distinguished Raleigh Hotel, to chief file clerk for the U.S. Supreme Court. Burke's mother was a teacher in Washington, but regulations forced her to stop when she married. After that, she shifted her occupation to that of government clerk.

Burke attended D.C. public schools and graduated from Dunbar High School in 1928. He then attended Howard University, where he was a member of its undefeated 1929 championship basketball team, received a bachelor of science degree in 1932, and the medical degree in 1936. Following his internship at Freedmen's Hospital, Dr. Syphax entered Freedmen's newly established surgical residency program as the second general surgery resident under Dr. Edward Howes. He remained in that program from 1937–40 and was an assistant in surgery from 1940–41.

From 1941–42, Dr. Syphax was the first Rockefeller Fellow in surgery at the Strong Memorial Hospital of the University of Rochester in Rochester, New York. (He was recommended for that fellowship by Dr. Howes, the white chief of surgery at HUCM, who had come to HUCM with funding from Rockefeller to build up the surgery department over a five-year period). In 1943 Dr. Syphax also became one of the first black physicians certified by the American Board of Surgery.

Dr. Syphax returned to Freedmen's in 1942 as an instructor in surgery under Dr. Charles R. Drew, who had succeeded Dr. Howes as head of the department. When Dr. Drew was killed in an auto accident in 1950, Dr. Syphax was appointed as the first chief of general surgery at HUCM (previously general surgery had been handled by the department head). In 1957 Dr. Syphax became acting head of surgery and from 1958–70 was professor and head of the department. Since 1970 he has been the senior professor in the department and in 1974 he received the first Howard University Department of Surgery Distinguished Surgeon's Award. In 1985, Howard University awarded him an honorary doctor of science degree.

Personal Observations

When asked about obstacles he had encountered along the way, Dr. Syphax indicated that his year at Rochester had been quite difficult. Professionally, as a black physician he was only allowed to observe and was not permitted even to assist at surgery. When he raised questions about the appropriateness of various procedures, he was virtually ignored, and he had to educate some of the white physicians about the ailments of black patients. In Dr. Syphax's words, "Perhaps the main thing I learned at Rochester was that they had the same problems as those we had at Howard."

As one of only two black physicians at Strong Memorial, he was not made to feel welcome by anyone, and one white colleague from Mississippi consistently left his cafeteria table when Dr. Syphax sat down there. When he tried to eat at a white restaurant in the Rochester area, Dr.

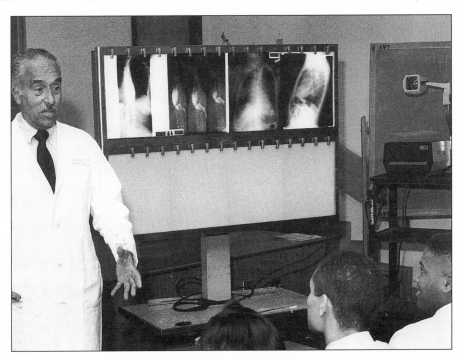

Burke Syphax, M.D., while in his 80s, teaching surgery part-time to residents at HUCM.

Syphax was refused service until the state police were called to intervene and enforce the relatively new antidiscrimination laws. These professional and personal experiences made him appreciate Howard more than ever.

Dr. Syphax may also have been delayed in becoming certified by the American Board of Surgery because one of their requirements was to be a member of the local medical society; and for a long time the D.C. society admitted no blacks. (Those first certified lived in New York City and Chicago where these segregated policies were abolished earlier.)

In working with George Washington and Georgetown universities to improve the educational and patient services at D.C. General Hospital, Dr. Syphax felt that too much emphasis was put on arrangements that would benefit the two white universities and not enough on what would benefit the hospital and its patients. He indicated, however, that his relationships were generally cordial with his counterpart chiefs of surgery at those institutions.

Regarding African Americans who helped him along the way, Dr. Syphax cited not only his parents (who emphasized education, honesty, and hard work), but also some of his high school and college teachers and coaches. Specifically, he noted high school coach Frank Perkins and Howard University chemistry professor Dr. Percy Julian. He gave major credit for his professional success, however, to such HUCM individuals as W. Montague Cobb (who integrated the D.C. medical society), Charles Drew (who was a role model at both Dunbar and in surgery), faculty members Paul Cornely (public health), Robert Jason (pathology) and Moses Young (anatomy), and Dean Joseph Johnson.

The only white person that Dr. Syphax appreciated with any enthusiasm during our interview was Dr. Edward L. Howes, who trained him at HUCM and recommended him for the fellowship at Rochester. One thing Dr. Syphax said he liked about Dr. Howes was that he received no special consideration from him because he was black. Dr. Howes would criticize him when he needed it, but would also ask him to fill in as a lecturer when Dr. Howes had an emergency elsewhere. Although he appreciated the fact that Dr. Morton, chief of surgery at Rochester, had accepted him for the fellowship, he was disappointed with the professional and personal experience he had at that institution.

Finally, Dr. Syphax indicated that one of the attractions of medicine was that it could lead in so many directions. He noted that his original intention was to become a private practioner where he could help others directly and "be his own boss." He specifically did not want to become a teacher because he had observed the thanklessness of the dedicated work his sister had done in that capacity. Due to a combination of circumstances, however, he became a distinguished teacher and administrator. Dr. Syphax was credited at a 1978 testimonial dinner as having trained over 60 surgeons, including "90 percent of the black surgeons practicing in the Washington metropolitan area."

Pauline Yvonne Titus-Dillon, M.D.

Chronological History

Pauline Y. Titus-Dillon, the first African-American woman M.D. administrator in the dean's office of the Howard University College of Medicine, was born on January 1, 1938, in Jamaica, West Indies. She graduated from Manning's High School in Jamaica at the age of 14 and shortly thereafter moved to New York City to live with her aunt, Hilma A. Titus. Because she was a foreign student and so young, Columbia University officials encouraged her to enroll in college preparatory courses as a condition for admission but she declined. As a teenager, Pauline never doubted her abilities, even when others had doubts. She enrolled in Pratt Institute and in 1957 transferred to Howard University, where she received a bachelor of science degree in chemistry summa cum laude in 1960.

In 1964 she received the medical degree from Howard University College of Medicine where she ranked first in her class. She completed a rotating internship and an internal medicine residency at Freedmen's Hospital in Washington, D.C. In 1966 she received the Daniel Hale Williams Award for outstanding performance during internship. Two years later she received the same award for outstanding performance during residency.

From 1977 to 1980, Dr. Titus-Dillon was the first female chief of the Howard University medical service at the District of Columbia General Hospital. She was also the first female director of an accredited training program in internal medicine. While serving there in 1979 she received the HUCM Student Council Award for Inspirational Leadership, and upon leaving in October 1980 was given the Howard University Department of Medicine Award for superior performance as the chief medical officer.

Since 1980, Dr. Titus-Dillon has been the first female physician to serve as associate dean for academic affairs at HUCM. In this position, she has taken a personal interest in developing support programs to retain more students. Recognizing that the four-year medical curriculum, which was designed for all students, was not meeting the needs of some students, she formulated a five-year curriculum which was approved by the dean, the faculty, and the Board of Trustees in 1988.

Personal Observations

Commenting on the obstacles encountered on the way to becoming a physician, Dr. Titus-Dillon stated that she realized that some were present, but she never let them serve as hindrances. Throughout her life she has been motivated to excel. Educated in a predominantly black setting, she stated that she was comfortable excelling and receiving recognition just as a person, not as a "different" person. Reflecting, she said, "At Howard University, during my undergraduate and medical education I was protected from racism." After finishing her residency she pursued fellowship training in a majority setting, where she encountered racism. The discomforts created by racist situations were short-lived, however, because her preceptor always had confidence in her abilities. Dr. Titus-

Pauline Y. Titus-Dillon, M.D., practicing general internal medicine in 1969 at the veterans hospital in Columbia, S.C.

Dillon said, "Obstacles are there, but students should never let them stand in the way because when obstacles are overcome character is strengthened."

African Americans who have influenced Dr. Titus-Dillon's career choice include her aunt, a registered nurse, who helped her finance her education; her cousin, Patrick A. Titus, an obstetrician and gynecologist who is an HUCM graduate, and her mentor, Dr. W. Lester Henry, Jr. Her admiration for Dr. Henry influenced her to choose an internal medicine specialty, and an endocrinology and metabolism subspecialty, and to embark on a career in academic medicine.

For those aspiring to make contributions in medicine or in other professional fields, Dr. Titus-Dillon advises, "Set a goal for yourself and never be satisfied with less than the best." Concluding, she added, "You may not be the first to do a particular deed, but you just might be the first to do the best job there is to be done."

Levi Watkins, Jr., M.D., F.A.C.S.

Chronological History

Levi Watkins, Jr., the first African-American full professor at the Johns Hopkins University School of Medicine, was born the third of six children on June 13, 1944, in Parsons, Kansas. He was raised, however, in Montgomery, Alabama, and received his elementary and secondary education at the Alabama State Laboratory School. He was valedictorian of his high school and a member of the Montgomery all-star basketball team.

He attended Tennessee State University in Nashville, Tennessee, where he majored in biology, was president of the student body, and graduated with highest honors in 1966. Although Vanderbilt had never had any black medical students, Levi decided to apply there because of its excellent academic reputation and convenient location (and because he believed in integration of the races). His mother advised him to attend Meharry to avoid the types of problems that James Lawson, the first black student at Vanderbilt divinity school, had encountered a few years earlier, but Levi persisted and became Vanderbilt's first African-American medical student.

While he had been the top scholar in almost all of his courses at college, he placed near the bottom of his medical school class on its first biochemistry test. This experience motivated him to study more diligently throughout the remainder of his medical school training. Due to a change in the grading system, he never learned his exact standing at Vanderbilt, but he was advised by Dean John Chapman and others to aim for a highly competitive internship and residency. That advice implied that he was probably in the top 5–10 percent of his graduating class. He was also elected to the Alpha Omega Alpha honor society.

With this encouragement, Levi applied for an internship at the Johns Hopkins University School of Medicine and eventually (in 1977–78) became Hopkins' first black chief resident (in surgery and cardiac surgery). In 1980, Dr. Watkins became internationally known as the first surgeon to implant in man the life-saving automatic implantable cardiac defibrillator (AICD). In July of 1991 he was promoted to be the first black full professor at the Johns Hopkins School of Medicine and in September of that year he also became their first black assistant dean with responsibilities for 58 accredited postdoctoral programs and faculty development.

Personal Observations

When asked about obstacles he had encountered in attaining these "black firsts," Dr. Watkins said he had experienced "individual and societal racism in all its grotesque forms." As a child, he was not allowed to use the white parks or theaters or to shop at the local Dairy Queen.

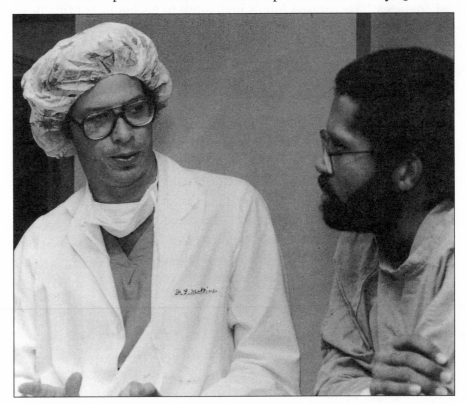

Levi Watkins, Jr., M.D., shown in 1993 explaining a cardiac operation to medical student Howard Jackson at the Johns Hopkins University School of Medicine.

Later, partly because his pastors included Drs. Ralph Abernathy and Martin Luther King., Jr., Dr. Watkins understandably became very active in the civil rights movement. While in medical school, he had Dr. King's picture outside the door of his dormitory room. When King was assassinated, he was hurt to be greeted by many with sarcasm rather than sympathy. The words "coon" and "nigger" were also commonly used at Vanderbilt by patients, technicians, and even by some faculty.

Perhaps the most extreme incident of racism encountered by Dr. Watkins occurred during his medical school years when he was on his way to buy some food for the "Poor Peoples' Campaign" marchers who were passing through Nashville on their way to Washington, D.C. As he was leaving his dormitory, someone threw a bucket of feces at him. While at Hopkins, Dr. Watkins did not encounter much overt prejudice, but he was aware that he was left out of some activities because of his race, and he lacked the family and social network in Baltimore that he had enjoyed in Nashville.

On the other hand, he made a few close white friends while in medical school, including John Tarpley whom he first thought of as a typical "redneck." He refused John's invitations to his home, but finally accepted an invitation to attend his church, even though it was a segregated institution. In Dr. Watkins' words, "This was the beginning of a profound relationship that made me rethink my own stereotypes about white people."

Perhaps in part because of this positive relationship with this classmate (and with some medical school faculty and administrators), Dr. Watkins has channeled his feelings about negative racial experiences along very positive lines. An outstanding example is a speech he delivered in the late '70s to the several hundred people who attended the annual Halstead Residents Party. He told the group about his personal experiences, particularly during his years at Hopkins, and made a number of constructive recommendations on how things could be improved for African-American students, house staff, and faculty.

In 1979 Dr. Watkins became an active member of the Hopkins admissions committee, and he was instrumental in increasing the black proportions of students to about 10 percent and the number of black house staff and faculty to approximately 50 each. Dr. Watkins also initiated an annual Martin Luther King commemoration at Hopkins which has featured such world leaders as Nobel Laureate Bishop Desmond Tutu, Coretta Scott King, and Mayor Andrew Young. Similarly, he started an annual reception for blacks at Hopkins and their families. Their theme in 1991 was "One Family."

In response to questions about help he had received from black men and women, Dr. Watkins cited his parents and several other close relatives, as well as the previously mentioned civil rights leaders. Among the whites he noted were not only John Tarpley and Dean Chapman but also Vanderbilt's chairman of surgery (William H. Scott), and the former head of physiology at Harvard Medical School (Dr. Cliff Burger).

For young blacks considering a medical career, Dr. Watkins advises, "Believe in yourself and your abilities. Pursue excellence to the fullest extent possible. Treat people as individuals rather than stereotypes. Embrace all races with open arms, but never try to 'Uncle Tom' your way to the top." (At one time, Dr. Watkins was afraid that his outspokenness about race might be an impediment to his career, but he decided to be open about his beliefs and apparently was constructive and tactful enough so that it worked out to be the best both for him and for other African Americans—as well as Hopkins and the medical profession. He has contributed greatly to medical education, medical technology, and racial harmony!)

Donald E. Wilson, M.D.

Chronological History

Donald E. Wilson, the first African-American dean of a predominantly white medical school, was born on August 28, 1936, in Worcester, Massachusetts. Although his father was uneducated, both of his parents placed a high premium on learning and Donald was the ranking male student of his high school. He was one of only six blacks out of 1,160 students in the class that graduated in 1958 from Harvard college. Donald did well enough there to be admitted to Tufts medical school, where he was one of only three black students in the class that graduated in 1962. Subsequently, he was elected to the Alpha Omega Alpha Medical Honorary Society.

Dr. Wilson served his internship at St. Elizabeth's Hospital in Boston but, probably because of his race, was not invited to return as a resident. Fortuitously, he ended up at the Boston veterans hospital and received excellent training in internal medicine and gastroenterology. Similarly, he was not accepted by Tufts as a research fellow in gastroenterology, but he found a fellowship at Boston's Lemuel Shattuck Hospital where he also became chief resident. In addition, he was a teaching fellow in medicine at Tufts from 1964–66.

Upon completing his postgraduate training in 1966, Dr. Wilson served as an air force physician in Nebraska for two years and concurrently instructed in medicine at the University of Nebraska. Returning to civilian life, he was an attending physician and instructor in medicine at SUNY-Downstate (Brooklyn, New York) from 1968–71. Dr. Wilson then moved to become chief of gastroenterology at the University of Illinois School of Medicine in Chicago. There he rose from assistant professor of medicine in 1971 to associate professor in 1973 and to full professor in 1975. From 1976 to 1977 he served as acting chairman of Illinois's Department of Medicine and during 1977–78 was a visiting professor at King's College Medical School in England.

In 1980 Dr. Wilson returned to SUNY-Downstate as the first African-American professor and chairman of its Department of Medicine. After serving in that capacity for a decade, he was appointed in 1991 as dean of the University of Maryland Medical School. This made him the first African-American dean of a predominantly white college of medicine. Dr. Wilson's other "firsts" include being the first African-American officer elected to the Association of Professors of Medicine (he became secretary-treasurer in 1990) and being one of several founders (in 1986) of the Association for Academic Minority Physicians. He has also been a very productive researcher and has written alone or jointly over 100 journal articles.

Donald E. Wilson, M.D., dean of the University of Maryland School of Medicine, shown in 1993 conferring with one of his medical students.

Personal Observations

When asked about obstacles he had encountered and overcome, Dr. Wilson said he faced the usual obstacles of being black, but ended up taking them for granted and dealing with them as best he could. He did admit that "it was not too great" being one of only six African Americans in his college class and noted that the year before he entered, a cross had been burned in Harvard Yard. He also reported that after graduating from Harvard, he was unable to rent a desirable apartment in the Boston area because of being African American. As already indicated, race may have also been a problem in his not being asked to return to St. Elizabeth's or to Tufts, but these temporary disappointments turned out to have been, in Dr. Wilson's words, "blessings in disguise."

Although he was the only full-time African-American faculty member in SUNY-Downstate's Department of Medicine when he was there from 1968–71, there were 18 percent black faculty in that department by the time he left the chairmanship in 1991. Dr. Wilson believes that his race was also an obstacle to his becoming dean of a predominantly white medical school and cited some of the difficulties he had in making sure that he was adequately considered by the University of Maryland search committee that reviewed over 140 candidates. One of the reasons he cofounded the Association for Academic Minority Physicians was to help create an "old boy's network" for current and future African Americans in medicine.

Regarding help he received from other African Americans, Dr. Wilson particularly appreciated his father, who was a model of the self-made man and who emphasized that "education is one thing that no one can take away from you." Another role model and powerful influence in Dr. Wilson's life was Dr. Carroll Leevy, who was the first African-American chair of medicine at a predominantly white medical school (New Jersey at Newark) and whose advice was sought frequently regarding choices in academic and organized medicine. He also appreciated the support received from his wife and children.

Among the nonblacks cited as being helpful were Dr. Maurice Strauss, chief of medicine at the Boston veterans hospital; Dr. Morton Bogdonoff, who recruited him as chief of gastroenterology at Illinois; and Dr. Roger Bulger, president of the Association of Academic Health Centers. He also acknowledged having been recruited to Downstate by Dr. Stanley Lee and selected as dean at Maryland by Dr. Errol Reese.

Relative to advice for young African Americans aspiring to careers in academic and organized medicine, Dr. Wilson said one should never expect advancement because you deserve it but rather you should expect to have to earn it. He also strongly recommended becoming board certified in a specialty and finding people who care about you as an individual. In that connection, he emphasized the importance of having a supportive spouse and of being willing to sacrifice today for future rewards. Finally, he reminds us that "nothing worthwhile comes easily!"

Asa G. Yancey, Sr., M.D., F.A.C.S.

Chronological History

Asa G. Yancey, Sr., the first African-American associate dean at the Emory University School of Medicine, was born on August 19, 1916, in Atlanta, Georgia, as one of seven children of Arthur H. and Daisy Sherard Yancey. Although Asa's father had been trained as a carpenter at Tuskegee Institute, he worked as a letter carrier. His mother was a full-time homemaker. Asa attended the Atlanta public schools and was valedictorian at Booker T. Washington High School. He then attended Morehouse College from which he graduated with high honors in 1937.

He considered becoming an engineer but soon learned that the job prospects for black engineers were so bad that Edward, son of Morehouse's president John Hope, had to go to South America for employment. Partly because Asa's older brother, Bernise, had earned a medical degree in 1930 from the University of Michigan (and was tragically executed by a poorly insulated wire to an x-ray machine shortly after graduation), Asa took the Medical College Aptitude Test and also decided to apply to Michigan.

Asa visited the University of Michigan medical school during July 1937 and told Dean A.C. Furstenberg of his desire to enter that fall. Although the dean advised him to "forget it," Asa proceeded to have his excellent transcript sent from Morehouse, reminded the dean that his brother was one of their alumni, and made another trip to the school. This time, the dean said that "one more place had opened up" and admitted Asa on the spot as one of four black students in a class of 144.

In the past, no more than three black students had graduated in any one class, but in Asa's class all four received their medical degrees and eventually became board certified. The three men were all certified in general surgery and the one woman in pediatrics. In Dr. Yancey's words, "All four were treated absolutely fairly by the university." After his graduation in 1941, Dr. Yancey served a general rotating internship at City Hospital in Cleveland, Ohio, and then took a very meaningful three-year residency in surgery under Dr. Charles R. Drew at Howard University's Freedmen's Hospital.

This was followed by a year as a surgical fellow at the U.S. Marine Hospital in Boston, Massachusetts, and two years with Dr. Matthew Walker as instructor in surgery while studying gynecological and general surgery at Meharry. In 1948, he became chief of surgery at the Tuskegee veterans hospital and, with others, established the first accredited training program for black surgeons in Alabama. While there, he also did research at the Tuskegee Veterinary School which modified the Swenson Technique for Congenital Megacolon. (His 1952 report of this research appeared 10 years before a similar publication about the operation which bears Soave's name.) In 1958, Dr. Yancey became the first chief of surgery at the Hughes Spalding Pavilion of Grady Memorial Hospital (a black private hospital within a hospital) and administered the first accredited surgical training program for black surgeons in Georgia.

Other of Dr. Yancey's "African-American firsts" include being the first board-certified surgeon in Georgia (1958), first member of the Southern Surgical Association (1985), first medical director of Grady Memorial Hospital and associate dean at Emory University School of Medicine (1972), and first full professor of surgery at Emory (1975). In addition to his medical activities, Dr. Yancey also made time to serve from 1967–77 on the Atlanta Board of Education where he chaired its "Atlanta Plan" committee that helped desegregate Atlanta's public schools.

Personal Observations

When asked about obstacles encountered, Dr. Yancey indicated that these had been the usual ones experienced by an African American, such as denial of access to Georgia educational institutions and restaurants. However, such difficulties were greatly reduced by the massive work of Martin Luther King, Jr., and by the positive attitudes Asa had learned from his parents, the fair treatment he had received in medical school, and realistic advice from his mentors. For example, he cited Dr. Drew's belief that "excellence of performance will transcend segregation," and a letter he received from Drew forewarning him that, in his new role in Atlanta, his work would not always be appreciated. He deeply regrets, however, the time when, because of segregation, one of his black patients with a bullet in his head was originally sent to a hospital without a neurosurgeon.

Dr. Yancey is highly appreciative of the numerous individuals—both black and white—who nurtured and supported him along the way. Among the blacks, he spoke particularly of his parents who instilled in him the need for hard work, the pleasure that can be derived from a job well done, and a sincere respect for all people, including those of low income, minimal education, and inhibited opportunities. He also noted the important example of his older brothers, who also became physicians, and of Dr. Drew, who inspired him to enter medical education and to train other blacks. Finally, he cited Mrs. Grace Towns Hamilton, a black social worker, director of the Atlanta Urban League and member of the Georgia House of Representatives, who urged Mr. Hughes Spalding to establish a medical pavilion of Grady Memorial Hospital and who encouraged the specialty education of African-American physicians. Much was also learned from Matthew Walker, M.D., of Meharry Medical College, and from Benjamin E. Mays, Ph.D., with whom Dr. Yancey served on the Atlanta Board of Education.

Among nonblacks, individuals he appreciated not only include the previously mentioned Dr. Furstenberg and Mr. Spalding, but also Ira A. Ferguson, M.D., who supported the Tuskegee veterans hospital surgical

(L to R) Asa G. Yancey, Sr., M.D., and classmates Martin R. Sutler, M.D., C. Waldo Scott, M.D., and Maggie Laura Walker, M.D., celebrate as the four African-American graduates of the University of Michigan Medical School class of 1941.

training program; John D. Martin, Jr., M.D., chair of surgery at Emory and at Grady, who sponsored Dr. Yancey as a partner in the Emory University Clinic; W. Dean Warren, M.D., chair of surgery at Emory, who appointed him as professor of surgery and recommended him for membership in both the American and the Southern Surgical Associations; and Arthur P. Richardson, M.D., dean at Emory, and Mr. J.W. Pinkston, Jr., executive director of Grady, who concurrently invited him to become associate dean and medical director of their respective institutions. In Dr. Yancey's words, the people at Emory and Grady during his active years there from 1972–89 "couldn't have been more cooperative!"

Regarding advice to young blacks considering careers in medicine, Dr. Yancey encourages "pursuing excellence from kindergarten on," "carrying oneself at all times as a gentleman (or lady)," and "recognizing that all worthy talents (whether in science, mathematics, music, or art, for example) can be used in medicine." Finally, he cited his mother's useful advice that "whenever you see a discussion degenerating into an argument, just walk away in dignity." Dr. Yancey has obviously put these words of advice to good use in his own life and has contributed significantly not only to academic and organized medicine, but also to public education and improved harmony among the races. Dr. Yancey has also served as a role model for his four children, three of whom are certified by medical specialty boards and one who is a teacher in the Atlanta public school system.

5

Voices and Patterns

Analysis of the contents of the biographical sketches in the previous chapter reveals that these 33 African-American pioneers in academic and organized medicine were the first of their race to achieve prominence in no less than 91 different aspects of medical education, medical organizations, and/or closely related activities. Almost all encountered significant obstacles (including racism and sexism) but were able to overcome them through positive attitudes, hard work, and help from both blacks and nonblacks. Their advice to minority young people—especially African Americans interested in the health professions—is to set the lofty goal of becoming a physician and to consider careers in academic medicine and participation in organized medicine.

Of the 33 individuals whose biographical sketches appear in this book, a total of 21 are male and 12 are female (Table 5). Those born first (both in 1904) were Drs. Cobb and Drew; while the youngest is Dr. Prothrow-Stith, born in 1954.

Fourteen are graduates of Howard University College of Medicine (HUCM), four are alumni of Meharry Medical College, and the remaining 15 received their doctorates from other institutions (Table 5). Of this number, two each graduated from the University of Michigan and Western Reserve; and one each graduated from Boston University, Creighton, Harvard, McGill, Tufts, Vanderbilt, and Wayne State, and from the universities of Illinois, Kansas, Virginia, and Wisconsin. Relative to undergraduate education, a total of 20 (61 percent) attended traditionally black institutions such as Howard and Spelman, and 13 (39 percent) attended predominantly white schools such as Amherst and Harvard.

The most frequent specialties of the 33 individuals in these sketches were internal medicine (7), pediatrics (7), and general surgery (6). Others were pathology (3), psychiatry (3), anatomy (2), and one each in cardiovascular surgery, endocrinology, obstetrics and gynecology, orthopaedic surgery, and public health.

This chapter summarizes both the chronological histories and the personal observation portions of the biographical sketches. Following the summary table below, the remainder of this chapter presents the findings under the major headings of achievements, attitudes, and advice.

Finally, sketches for Drs. Cobb, Drew, and Organ are based on written materials rather than interviews. Of the 30 interviews, 17 were conducted by Dr. Johnson, 11 by Ms. Vaughan, and two by Dr. Epps. Of the 33 biographical sketches, 21 were prepared by Johnson and 12 by Vaughan.

Table 5—Summary Information about 33 Individuals with Biographical Sketches

Name	Life Span	Education Undergraduate/Graduate	Specialty
Callender, Clive O.	1936–	Hunter/Meharry	Surgery
Cobb, W. Montague	1904–90	Amherst/Howard	Anatomy
Comer, James P.	1934–	Indiana/Howard	Psychiatry
Cornely, Paul B.	1906–	U. Michigan	Public Health
Dickens, Helen O.	1909–	U. Illinois	Ob./Gyn.
Drew, Charles R.	1904–50	Amherst/McGill	Surgery
Epps, Charles H., Jr.	1930–	Howard	Ortho. Surg.
Epps, Roselyn P.	1930–	Howard	Pediatrics
Ferguson, Angella D.	1925–	Howard	Pediatrics
Franklin, Eleanor L.	1929–	Spelman/Wisconsin	Endocrinology
Henry, W. Lester, Jr.	1915–	Temple/Howard	Internal Medicine
Hunter, Gertrude C.T.	1926	Howard	Pediatrics
Jenkins, Melvin E., Jr.	1923–	U. Kansas	Pediatrics
Jenkins, Renee R.	1947–	Wayne State	Pediatrics
Leavell, Walter F.	1934–	Cincinnatti/Meharry	Internal Medicine
Leffall, LaSalle D., Jr.	1930–	Fla. A&M/Howard	Surgery
Lloyd, Ruth S.	1917–	Mt. Holyoke/W. Reserve	Anatomy
Manley, Audrey F.	1934–	Spelman/Meharry	Pediatrics
Mann, Marion	1920–	Tuskegee/Howard	Pathology
Maultsby, Maxie C., Jr.	1932–	Talladega/ W. Reserve	Psychiatry
Miller, Russell L., Jr.	1939–	Howard	Internal Medicine
Organ, Claude H., Jr.	1927–	Xavier/Creighton	Surgery
Pinn, Vivian W.	1941–	Wellesley/U. Va.	Pathology
Prothrow-Stith, Deborah B.	1954–	Spelman/Harvard	Internal Medicine
Sampson, Calvin C.	1928–	Hampton/Meharry	Pathology
Scott, Roland B.	1909–	Howard	Pediatrics
Spurlock, Jeanne	1921–	Roosevelt/Howard	Psychiatry
Sullivan, Louis W.	1933–	Morehouse/Boston U.	Internal Medicine
Syphax, Burke	1910–	Howard	Surgery
Titus-Dillon, Pauline Y.	1938–	Howard	Internal Medicine
Watkins, Levi, Jr.	1945–	Tenn. State/Vanderbilt	Cardiac Surgery
Wilson, Donald E.	1937–	Harvard/Tufts	Internal Medicine
Yancey, Asa G., Sr.	1916–	Morehouse/Michigan	Surgery

Achievements

As indicated in Table 6, the individuals in this analysis had a wide range of "black first" achievements in various aspects of academic and/or organized medicine. The 33 representative achievements selected for this table are equally divided between black "firsts" in academic medicine (dean of a predominantly white medical school), in organized medicine (president of the American Orthopaedic Association), and in activities closely related to academic or organized medicine (president of the American Cancer Society).

Table 6—Representative "Firsts" from the 33 Biographical Sketches

Name	Pioneering Achievements as African Americans	No. of Listed Firsts[1]
Callender, Clive O.	Member, National Task Force on Organ Procurement and Transplantation	2
Cobb, W. Montague	Principal historian of African Americans in medicine	4
Comer, James P.	Cofounder, Black Psychiatrists of America	2
Cornely, Paul B.	President, American Public Health Association	3
Dickens, Helen O.	Woman member, American College of Surgeons	2
Drew, Charles R.	Director, American Red Cross Blood Bank	2
Epps, Charles H., Jr.	President, American Orthopaedic Association	4
Epps, Roselyn P.	President, American Medical Women's Association	2
Ferguson, Angella D.	Woman associate vice president for health affairs, Howard University	1
Franklin, Eleanor L.	Woman major administrative officer, Howard University College of Medicine	1
Henry, W. Lester, Jr.	Governor, American Board of Internal Medicine	6
Hunter, Gertrude C.T.	Director of Health Services, Head Start Program	3
Jenkins, Melvin E., Jr.	Governor, American Board of Pediatrics	4
Jenkins, Renee R.	President, Society of Adolescent Medicine	1
Leavell, Walter F.	President, Minority Affairs Section of AAMC's Group on Student Affairs	3
Leffall, LaSalle D., Jr.	President, American Cancer Society	3
Lloyd, Ruth S.	Woman Ph.D. in anatomy	1
Manley, Audrey F.	Woman deputy assistant secretary for health	3
Mann, Marion	M.D. brigadier general in U.S. Army Medical Reserve Corps	1
Maultsby, Maxie C., Jr.	Author, books on rational behavioral therapy	1
Miller, Russell L., Jr.	Internal medicine resident, University of Michigan Medical School	2
Organ, Claude H., Jr.	Chair of surgery, predominantly white medical school (Creighton)	5
Pinn, Vivian W.	Director, NIH Office of Research on Women's Health	5
Prothrow-Stith, Deborah B.	Woman commissioner of public health, state of Massachusetts	1
Sampson, Calvin C.	Resident, Philadelphia's Episcopal Hospital	3
Scott, Roland B.	One of first diplomates, American Board of Pediatrics	3
Spurlock, Jeanne	Woman chair, U.S. medical school department of psychiatry (Meharry)	3

Table 6, *continued*

Name	Pioneering Achievements as African Americans	No. of Listed Firsts
Sullivan, Louis W.	M.D. Secretary, U.S. Department of Health and Human Services	6
Syphax, Burke	One of first certified, American Board of Surgery	2
Titus-Dillon, Pauline Y.	Woman M.D. major administrative officer, Howard University College of Medicine	2
Watkins, Levi, Jr.	Full professor, Johns Hopkins University School of Medicine	2
Wilson, Donald E.	Dean of a predominantly white medical school (University of Maryland)	2
Yancey, Asa G., Sr.	Associate dean, Emory University School of Medicine	2
		Total: 91

[1] These numbers are limited to the "pioneering achievements as African Americans" that are listed in tables 12, 13, and 14.

In addition to the representative "firsts" listed in this table, most of the 33 individuals had several other pioneering achievements. According to their entries in tables12–14, a total of 11 had at least two "black firsts"; 10 had at least three; three had at least four; two had at least five; and two more had at least six. For example, Dr. Roselyn Epps was not only the first African-American president of the American Medical Women's Association, but also the first African-American female president of the D.C. Medical Society. Similarly, Dr. Louis Sullivan was not only the first African-American physician secretary of the U.S. Department of Health and Human Services, but also the first African-American house officer at the Cornell Medical Center, fellow at the Thorndike laboratory, president of the Morehouse Medical Education Program, president of the Association of Minority Health Professions Schools, and president of the Morehouse School of Medicine.

One reason that the qualifying term of "at least" is used in the preceding paragraph is that not all of their pioneering achievements as African Americans in academic and organized medicine are listed in tables 12–14. For example, Dr. Charles Epps has only four such achievements listed in Table 12, but his biographical sketch includes a total of eight "black firsts."

Another reason for qualifying the total of "firsts" is that they emphasize the "black firsts" that were volunteered at the time of the interviews, most of which were conducted during 1991 and 1992. In addition to some "black firsts" that may have been overlooked or forgotten, other "black firsts" may have occurred since the interviews were held, for it is a truism that "success breeds success." It can be conservatively reported, therefore, that the 33 individuals in this analysis achieved at least 91 "black firsts" in academic medicine, organized medicine, or closely related activities. This figures out to an average of 2.76 "firsts" per individual.

It should also be noted that a number of these 33 individuals had other major achievements in these areas even though they were not the *first* of their race to do so. For example, Drs. Charles Epps, Marion Mann, and Russell Miller have also been deans of the Howard University College of Medicine (HUCM) but were not the *first* African Americans to achieve that status. Dr. Numa P. G. Adams was the first African-American dean of HUCM from 1929 to 1940.

Family Background

One of the surprising findings of the analysis of the backgrounds of these 33 high achievers in academic and organized medicine was that none of them had parents who were physicians. This is in contrast to the published fact that between 12 and 15 percent of all enrolled medical students from the 1950s through the 1970s (when most of these pioneers were in medical school) had fathers who were physicians (Johnson, 1983, 107–8). A few of the individuals, however, had close relatives in the medical profession.

The family backgrounds of these 33 pioneers ranged from one who was raised by foster parents and low-income relatives to one whose father was president of a traditionally black college and whose mother was a college professor. More typical occupations of their fathers, however, were farmer, letter carrier, postal clerk, pullman porter, and public school teacher; while those of their mothers more typically were government clerk, homemaker, household worker, and public school teacher. Several of the pioneers came from not only poor but very large families, with one individual being the tenth of 12 children.

It is clearly evident, therefore, that the impressive "black firsts" of most of these 33 individuals were achieved not as a result of having come from privileged family backgrounds but rather through their own diligent efforts and positive attitudes.

Attitudes

Dr. Claude Organ, who has achieved at least five "black firsts" in academic and organized medicine, had a favorite saying: "Attitude, not just aptitude, determines altitude" (Organ and Kosiba, 1987, 805). This observation is affirmed by our analysis of these biographical sketches.

Obstacles Encountered

The philosopher J.C. Bell stated, "When you are looking for obstacles, you can't find opportunities." Even though most of the individuals we interviewed emphasized taking advantage of available opportunities, all but one of the 33 medical pioneers indicated that they had still encountered significant obstacles achieving their "black firsts." Not surprisingly, the most frequently encountered obstacles were racial. As children, these racial obstacles ranged from restrictions on where they could attend school, play, eat, and travel, to verbal insults and even physical assaults. When in public school, some of these future "pioneers" were told by white teachers and counselors that they had only limited ability and opportunity and should not even consider going on to college or attending professional school.

Racial obstacles followed many of our pioneers from public school to college. Those who attended predominantly white colleges and/or medical schools often encountered racially prejudiced remarks from both faculty and fellow students. Many believed that it would be futile to apply for medical school or graduate medical education in other than a predominantly black institution.

After achieving the M.D. degree, many were rejected for residency training in white institutions and were still subject to other forms of racial discrimination. For example, one individual reported being unable to obtain adequate housing. Another was insulted during his postgraduate fellowship when a white colleague consistently moved to another cafeteria table so they would not have to eat together. Still another reported that he and his wife were excluded from the Christmas parties and other social events to which all of their white colleagues were invited. Several individuals complained that their board certifications and memberships in state and national medical organizations were delayed because they were not members of a local medical society, whose by-laws prohibited admitting African-American members.

Of the 12 females in this analysis, seven reported that they had also encountered obstacles related to gender bias. These obstacles included being turned down for graduate training and for employment because of their gender. One outstanding female pioneer also reported that she encountered little sexism in the early stages of her career, but as she achieved increasing levels of power she encountered increased resistance and lack of cooperation from her male colleagues.

The other major obstacle reported by both males and females in this analysis was financial. In addition to financial problems related to their generally modest socioeconomic backgrounds, seven of the 33 pioneers cited significant problems that were based in part on the early illness and/ or death of one or both of their parents. Two of the individuals also reported having had serious health problems of their own.

How Obstacles Were Overcome

When asked how they overcame obstacles of racism, sexism, and finances, it became obvious that much of their success came from their underlying psychological attitudes. For example, common answers to how they overcame racism included using racism as an extra source of motivation to succeed rather than as an excuse for lack of achievement and seeing others as individuals rather than as stereotypes. Similarly, the obstacles of gender bias were commonly overcome by striving exceptionally hard for excellence, and avoiding attitudes of hostility toward males

Means of overcoming financial obstacles included attending no-tuition or low-tuition schools, working at multiple part-time jobs including driving a taxi at night while studying medicine, and by aggressively seeking out financial aid in the form of scholarships, loans and fellowships. Several of the individuals reported that the segregation laws of their states prevented them from attending their own state colleges or medical schools. However, they discovered that their states would pay tuition, for example, for them to attend such schools in other states.

Although it is clear that the ultimate credit for overcoming these obstacles is due to these individuals themselves, all 33 enthusiastically acknowledged the help they had received from their fellow African Americans. All but two also reported the help they had received from individuals who were not African American.

Help Received From Blacks

Almost all of these pioneers gave major credit to their parents for instilling in them the attitudes and values that contributed to their achievements. For example, one individual appreciated having parents who "emphasized the importance of education, honesty, and hard work."

Another was taught from childhood "to believe in other people and to help them believe in you." Similarly, another's parents impressed on him "the need for hard work, the satisfaction derived from a job well-done, and the importance of respecting all people regardless of background."

Other family members who played key roles in the achievements of these 33 individuals included brothers, sisters, aunts, uncles, and cousins. A few of these close relatives were physicians who served as role models. Nine individuals specifically appreciated the substantial help they had received from their spouses, and one noted similar help from his children. Several also mentioned neighbors who had played a significant role in their development. For example, one reported that a neighbor had encouraged him and other local boys to form a debating team. This experience eventually helped him win a state oratorical contest and a college scholarship.

Black teachers also received significant credit from most of these pioneers. One individual noted that, since both of his parents worked outside the home, some of his early teachers were "like second parents" Another pioneer appreciatively reported that his black public school teachers "taught not only subject matter, but how to cope with life through hard work and realistic but positive attitudes."

These black teachers, many of whom were cited by name after all these years, ranged from elementary school through medical school. One pioneer indicated that his public school and college teachers were held in such respect that they were known only by their last names. A number of high school mathematics and science teachers received particular plaudits. Several high school and college counselors were also appreciated for encouraging individuals to set and achieve ambitious educational and professional goals.

Four individuals specifically appreciated the career help they had received from their African-American medical school deans and a substantial number cited the names of their African-American role models, mentors, and/or sponsors. Finally, several individuals noted the importance of their African-American athletic coaches, church youth leaders, and camp counselors in helping them develop positive attitudes and self-confidence.

Help Received From People of Other Races

All but two of the 33 pioneers also volunteered appreciation for the help they had received from individuals who were not black. Several reported having received specific aid and support from white public school teachers and college faculty members (including white faculty at traditionally black Spelman College). Those who attended predominantly white medical (or graduate) schools cited white faculty members and deans who were particularly supportive, with one individual being told by four white male faculty that they would assure her graduate school finances.

A large number appreciated their white residency program directors and a significant number appreciated the white leaders who had hired, promoted, and/or sponsored them for membership and for leadership positions in their medical organizations and professional societies. Several indicated that they had white mentors and role models.

Contributions to Racial Harmony

One characteristic of almost all of these 33 pioneers is that they have made positive contributions to harmony between the races. In addition to the close association with whites afforded by many of their professional "firsts," some have participated in integrated lay organizations. For example, a few have belonged to integrated churches while others have been active in such integrated organizations as local boards of education and national boards of youth groups. A few also noted that they had purposely sent their children to predominantly white schools and summer camps.

A large number of these 33 pioneers attended predominantly white institutions of higher education. Specifically, 64 percent of the 33 attended a predominantly white undergraduate college and/or medical school. Many of the pioneers also attended integrated public schools.

Over half of the 21 males had served in the military. They were represented in the army, navy, and air force and saw both combat and non-combat duty. Their military ranks ranged from captain to general. Although none of the 12 female pioneers was in the military, several served in the federal government and most worked with nonblacks in their professional roles.

The demonstrated competence and positive attitudes of these 33 pioneers should certainly have helped dispel negative racial stereotypes. This is consistent with the frequently quoted saying of Dr. Charles Drew, "Excellence of performance will transcend the barriers of racial discrimination and segregation."

Most of the 33 have also contributed to racial harmony by their personal example and by their advice to younger blacks.

Advice

In addition to advice given to individuals already committed to a medical career, all 31 of the living black pioneers in this analysis offered valuable advice to young minority individuals—especially African Americans—who might be good prospects for the field of medicine. The two deceased pioneers, Drs. Cobb and Drew, provided equally valuable advice through their writings and personal example.

Primarily, minority youth were advised to obtain the best education possible and to strive for excellence in all areas. Specific admonitions included: "Strive for excellence from kindergarten on;" "Don't dodge difficult subjects;" "Have confidence that, with help, you can learn hard material;" "Seek understanding rather than just rote memorization;" and "Remember that one of the underpinnings of slavery was the prohibition of learning to read and write."

A second major emphasis to minority young people was the need for and satisfaction of hard work. One pioneer said he was taught by his parents, "With a good education and hard work, there are no boundaries." Another noted, "Nothing worthwhile comes easy." Still another said that at an early age he was helped to recognize that "life is not fair and that in a white man's world, a black person has to work twice as hard to succeed." Several pioneers also noted that achievement and recognition are the result not of what one "deserves" but of what one "earns."

Closely related to these emphases on education, excellence, and hard work were reminders of the importance of such basic virtues as honesty, discipline, determination, patience, and persistence. Over a third of the pioneers also stressed the importance of developing self-confidence and self-esteem. One pioneer recalls his father saying, "No one is better than you; but if you think of yourself as second-class, you will be second-class." Another advised young minority persons to "be proud of your heritage, know your history, and be familiar with the struggles of those who came before you."

Similarly, several of the pioneers emphasized the importance of respecting others—regardless of their backgrounds. In addition to the previously reported advice about believing in and respecting other people, one pioneer, who had himself experienced extreme racism, went so far as to advise young African Americans to "embrace all races with open arms."

Other advice to young minorities encouraged them to set lofty goals, to establish a broad vision, and not to be deterred by those who lack confidence in your ability to succeed. Several noted the need to recognize and develop one's unique gifts and talents and encouraged young people to "do what you are capable of and what you enjoy." As one means of setting and staying with such lofty goals, it was recommended that young people should seek out role models and mentors who "care about you as an individual."

A third of the pioneers also offered specific recommendations to the young about eventually repaying society for the benefits they receive. They pointed out that this can be accomplished through teaching, mentoring, and community service and can result in great personal satisfaction. One of the pioneers offered the interesting observation that an African-American physician can often make an even greater contribution in a nonmedical setting (for example, as a board member of a lay organization) than in a medical setting.

Relative to future opportunities of becoming a pioneer in academic and/or organized medicine, the consensus was that there were still a number of good possibilities. For example, one pioneer stated, "While there may already be black 'firsts' on a few certification and editorial boards, the barriers have not yet been broken for many others." A second pioneer noted, "Doors previously closed are now open to you, opportunities are there, and don't be afraid to explore them." Another thought-provoking observation was, "You might not be the first to do a particular deed, but you just might be the first to do the best job there is to be done."

Finally, several of the pioneers pointed out the special advantages of taking part in academic and organized medicine. For example, one individual encouraged prospective minority group physicians to consider "the colleagues and students one enjoys in academic medicine and the advantages of being able to broaden one's influence through participation in organized medicine."

Summary and Conclusion

In spite of major obstacles (including racism, sexism, and finances), most of the 33 individuals in this analysis were able to overcome them through intellectual curiosity, hard work, lofty goals, respect for themselves and others, and motivation to serve society and promote racial harmony. In this way, they achieved almost 100 examples of African-American "firsts" in academic medicine, organized medicine, and closely related activities.

Both the personal examples and the practical advice of these 33 individuals should encourage an increasing number of minority group members—especially African Americans—to consider seeking careers in medicine. Further, the example and advice of these pioneers should encourage those who enter medicine to consider becoming medical school teachers and/or administrators and to consider taking leadership roles in their local, state, and national medical societies and in professional organizations.

PART III

THE PIONEERING "FIRSTS" OF 556 AFRICAN AMERICANS IN MEDICINE

This section provides key information about each of the 556 black medical pioneers who were identified in the study. In addition to facts about the first 290 male and female African-American graduates of the 126 existing U.S. medical schools, this part provides both individual and group information about 75 pioneering graduates of Howard University College of Medicine, 50 of Meharry Medical College, and 164 of other U.S. medical schools. Although there are a total of 579 entries, 23 people are included in both the "first graduate" and the "pioneering graduate" categories, for a total of 556 different individuals.

6

First African-American Graduates
of U.S. Medical Schools

Whereas chapters 4 and 5 dealt with the entire lives of 33 selected pioneers, this chapter focuses on only two points in time for 290 individuals and 126 medical schools. Specifically, it reports the dates that these schools were organized (or founded) and the dates that their first male and female African Americans were graduated (Table 7).

In almost every case, this chapter also documents the full names, gender, home states, and undergraduate colleges of these pioneering African-American graduates. (For each medical school, the names of these graduates are listed chronologically by year of graduation). In addition, this chapter includes four summary tables and accompanying commentaries.

Gender and Number of First African-American Graduates

A total of 110 (87 percent) of the 126 medical schools reported having both male and female identifiable African-American graduates. Six schools reported having identified only their first male graduates and four schools identified only their first female African-American graduates. Four schools (North Dakota, South Dakota, Ponce, and Puerto Rico) said they had no known African-American graduates, and two schools (Loyola-Stritch and the Medical College of Wisconsin) indicated that despite considerable effort they were unable to provide the requested information from their records. One school (Dartmouth) indicated that it had earlier African-American graduates but had no record of their names until 1974. Two schools (UCSF and USC) reported having graduated male African Americans in 1896 and 1955 respectively but were unable to provide their names.

A total of 290 individuals are listed in Table 7, with all but two of them identified by name. By coincidence, an equal number (145) were male and female. Although 74 of the schools reported having had a maximum of only one male and one female first African-American graduate, 32 schools reported having multiple males and/or females in their first graduating classes containing African Americans. For example,

Morehouse had 15 and Drew had 7 in their respective first graduating classes. More typically, schools with multiple first African-American graduates had two of one gender and one of the other graduating in their respective years. Nineteen of the medical schools were unsure as to the number and gender of their first African-American graduates.

The organization of Table 7 is based on the alphabetical listing of medical schools seen in column one. (See Appendix C for full names and addresses, or refer to AAMC's *Directory of American Medical Education.)* Named graduates are listed chronologically by year of graduation; both "first black males" and "first black females" are included. The "Medical School" column includes name, location, and year organized, and the "Home State" column lists the student's legal state of residence at the time of admission to medical school ("Unk." indicates an unknown and a question mark [?] indicates birthplace which is also presumed to be the legal state of residence when admitted to medical school.)

Table 7—First Male and Female African-American Graduates of U.S. Medical Schools[1]

MEDICAL SCHOOL	NAME	GENDER	YEAR	HOME STATE	UNDERGRADUATE COLLEGE
Alabama AL 1859	Richard Charles Dales	M	1970	AL	Howard University
	Samuel William Sullivan, Jr.	M	1970	AL	Howard University
	Patience Hodges Claybon	F	1974	AL	Tuskegee University
Alabama, South AL, 1967	John Henry Wagner, III	M	1977	AL	Oakwood College
	Patricia Ann Sanders	F	1977	AL	University of Alabama
Albany NY, 1838	George Clay Carter	M	1914	NY	Unknown
	Ann V. Als	F	1970	MA	Boston University
Albert Einstein NY, 1955	Carol E. Burnett	F	1960	NY	Hunter College
	Edwin Markham Jallah	M	1961	PA	University of Pennsylvania
	Ernest Preston Porter	M	1961	OH	Ohio State University
Arizona AZ, 1962	Ruth Louise Smothers	F	1975	AZ	University of Arizona
	Sherard York Morgan	M	1977	AX	University of Arizona
Arkansas AR 1879	Edith Irby Jones	F	1952	AR	Knoxville College
	Morris Jackson	M	1954	AR	Philander Smith College
	Truman B. Tollette	M	1954	AR	Philander Smith College
Baylor TX 1900	Leo Earsel Orr, Jr.	M	1969	TX	Prairie View A&M University
	Judith Berwick Carven	F	1974	TX	Bowling Green State University

Table 7, *continued*

MEDICAL SCHOOL	NAME	GENDER	YEAR	HOME STATE	UNDERGRADUATE COLLEGE
Boston MA, 1873	Rebecca Lee Crumpler[2]	F	1864	MA	Unknown
	Edward Thomas St. John	M	1888	BWI	Unknown
Bowman Gray NC 1902	William Thomas Grimes, Jr.	M	1972	NC	Clark College
	Yvonne Jackson Weaver	F	1974	AL	Howard University
Brown RI, 1963	Janice G. Allen	F	1976	PA	Brown University
	Clarence L. Wiley	M	1977	OK	Brown University
California (Southern) CA, 1885	Name unknown	M	1955	Unk	Unknown
	Rebecca Wills	F	1973	Unk	Howard University
California (UC Davis) CA, 1963	Otis Gladdis, Jr.	M	1973	CA	Sacramento State College
	Sandra Dian Battis	F	1975	CA	Fisk University
	Diane Lorene Pemberton	F	1975	CA	Drexel University
California (UC Irvine) CA, 1962	John Richard Crear, Jr.	M	1968	TX	University of Texas
	Female not reported				
California (UCLA) CA, 1951	Lawrence W. Scott	M	1961	CA	University of California, Berkeley
	Augua Andrews	M	1975	TX	Lamar University
California (UCSD) CA, 1962	Rodney Grant Hood	M	1973	CA	Northeastern University
	Betty Louise Cox	F	1974	CA	Spelman College
California (UCSF) CA, 1864	Name unknown	M	1896	CA	University of California
	Female not reported				
Caribe PR, 1976	Roy De la Coates-Johnson	M	1988	CA	Los Angeles Community College
	Female not reported				
Case Western OH, 1843	Charles B. Purvis	M	1865	PA?	Oberlin College
	Doris A. Evans	F	1968	OH	University of Chicago
	Loma K. Brown Flowers	F	1968	CA	Western Reserve University
Chicago Medical, IL 1912	Green G. Johnson	M	1925	Unk	Unknown
	Agnes Lattimer Bethel	F	1954	TN	Unknown
Chicago-Pritzker IL 1924	James L. Hall, Sr.	M	1925	TX	University of Chicago
	Ruth Aaron	F	1937	IL	University of Wisconsin

Table 7, *continued*

MEDICAL SCHOOL	NAME	GENDER	YEAR	HOME STATE	UNDERGRADUATE COLLEGE
Cincinnati OH, 1819	Lucy Oxley	F	1935	OH	University of Cincinnati
	Emmett Campbell	M	1953	OH	University of Dayton
Colorado CO, 1883	Samuel L. Raines	M	1907	MS	Unknown
	Deborah Green	F	1975	CO	Grinnell College
	LaRae H. Washington	F	1975	CA	University of Colorado
Columbia NY, 1767	Travis J. A. Johnson	M	1904	Unk	Unknown
	Agnes O. Griffin Levy	F	1923	NY	Unknown
Connecticut CT, 1961	John Richard Nailor	M	1973	NY	Hunter College
	Marja Marie Hurley	F	1976	CT	University of Connecticut
Cornell NY, 1898	Roscoe Conkling Giles	M	1915	NY	Cornell University
	Marie Metoyer	F	1951	NJ	Fordham University
Creighton NE, 1892	William Gordon	M	1901	NE	Creighton University
	Jewel Irvin Smith	F	1975	MI	Roosevelt University
Dartmouth[3] NH, 1797	Joseph Travernier	M	1974	MA	University of Massachusetts
	Sydney Claye Bush	F	1976	MO	Spelman College
Drew CA 1978[4]	Delilah Dukes	F	1985	NY	York College
	Marco Fabrega	M	1985	CA	University of Southern California
	Alan Garvin	M	1985	SC	South Carolina State College
	Kimberly Gregory	F	1985	CA	University of California, Los Angeles
	Zyn Seabron	M	1985	WA	University of Washington
	James Shaw	M	1985	CA	Stanford University
	Adelaide Willis	F	1985	CA	California State University, Long Beach
Duke NC 1925	Wilhelm Delano Meriwether	M	1967	SC	Michigan State University
	Jean Gaillard Spaulding	F	1973	NC	Columbia University
	Joanne Antoinette Peebles Wilson	F	1973	NC	University of North Carolina, Chapel Hill
East Carolina NC 1967	Natalear R. Collins	F	1981	NC	University of North Carolina, Chapel Hill
	Brenda Mills Kluttz	F	1981	NC	North Carolina A&T State University
	Julius Q. Mallette	M	1982	NC	North Carolina State University
	James Reid	M	1982	NC	East Carolina University
Emory GA, 1854	Hamilton Earl Holmes	M	1967	GA	University of Georgia
	Marshalyn Yeargin-Allsopp	F	1972	SC	Sweet Briar College

Table 7, *continued*

MEDICAL SCHOOL	NAME	GENDER	YEAR	HOME STATE	UNDERGRADUATE COLLEGE
Florida	Reuben Earl Brigety	M	1970	FL	Morehouse College
FL	Henry Earl Cotman	M	1970	FL	Florida A&M University
1956	Cassandra J. Ndiforchu	F	1972	FL	Fisk University
Florida, So.	John Irison Hughes	M	1975	FL	Florida A&M University
FL, 1965	Jacqueline Blutcher Gollman	F	1976	FL	Florida Tech University
George	James Edwin Jackson	M	1959	GA	Morehouse College
Washington	Joan R. Sealy	F	1968	PA	University of Chicago
DC, 1825					
Georgetown	Mary Louise Gardner	F	1964	DC	Catholic University
DC, 1851	Ifeanyi A.O. Zissi	M	1968	Nigeria	Fordham University
Georgia,	John Harper	M	1971	GA	Morehouse College
Med. College	Frank Rumph	M	1971	GA	Ft. Valley State College
of, GA	Angelica Valencia Sims	F	1975	GA	Morris Brown College
1828	Elizabeth Hawkins Woods	F	1975	GA	Clark College
Hahnemann	Thomas C. Imes	M	1884	PA	Unknown
PA, 1848	Eunice Stanfield	F	1973	TX	Macalester College
Harvard	Edwin Clarence J.T. Howard	M	1869	KS	Unknown
MA, 1782	Mildred F. Jefferson	F	1951	TX	Texas College
Hawaii	Lori Margaret Campbell	F	1983	HI	University of Hawaii
HI, 1967	Paul Jeffrey Smith	M	1983	HI	Howard University
Howard	James L.N. Bowen	M	1871	DC	Unknown
DC	George W. Brooks	M	1871	DC	Unknown
1868	Eunice P. Shadd	F	1877	CAN	Howard University
Illinois,	Levester Thompson	F	1975	IL	Southern Illinois University, Carbondale
Southern					
IL, 1969	Elizabeth Bertram	F	1977	IL	Southern Illinois University, Carbondale
Illinois,	Rivers Frederick	M	1897	LA	Dillard University
University	Elizabeth Webb Hill	F	1933	IL?	Unknown
of, IL 1881					
Indiana	Clarence A. Lucas, Sr.	M	1908	OH	None
IN	Deborah Lynne McCullough	F	1975	IN	Howard University
1903	Beverly J. Perkins	F	1975	IN	Butler University
Iowa	Edward Albert Carter	M	1907	IA	University of Iowa
IA 1869	Florence Battle Shafiq	F	1976	GA	Coe College

Table 7, *continued*

Medical School	Name	Gender	Year	Home State	Undergraduate College
Jefferson PA, 1824	Algernon B. Jackson	M	1901	IN	Indiana University
	Cora LeEthel Christian	F	1971	WI	Marquette University
Johns Hopkins MD 1893	James Nabwangu	M	1967	Kenya	Johns Hopkins University
	Robert Lee Gamble[5]	M	1967	WV	Howard University
	Margaret Edwina Barnett	F	1973	NY	Ohio State University
	Patricia Ann Jenkins	F	1973	MD	Morgan State University
Kansas KS, 1905	Edward V. Williams	M	1941	KS	University of Kansas
	Marjorie Ransome Cates	F	1958	KS	Kansas State University
Kentucky KY 1956	Carl Weber Watson	M	1964	KY	University of Kentucky
	Doris L. Clowney	F	1978	SC	South Carolina State College
	Marsha C. Miller	F	1978	KY	Kentucky State University
Loma Linda CA, 1909	Clayton L. Scuka	M	1939	CT	Pacific Union College
	Hughenna L. Gauntlett	F	1951	NY	New York University
Louisiana, New Orleans LA, 1931	Claude Jenkins Tellis	M	1970	LA	Michigan State University
	Charleta Guillory	F	1974	LA	Southern University, Baton Rouge
	Critty Lillette Hymes	F	1974	LA	Xavier University of Louisiana
Louisiana, Shreveport LA, 1966	George Cortez Henderson, Jr.	M	1975	LA	Southern University and A&M College
	Jamesetta Ward Tate	F	1979	LA	Southern University and A&M College
Louisville KY, 1837	Sarah Helen Fitzbutler	F	1892	KY	Unknown
	Male not reported				
Loyola-Stritch IL, 1915	Information not reported				
Marshall WV, 1974	Kevin S. Smith	M	1986	WV	Marshall University
	Tyshawn M. James	F	1989	WV	Marshall University
Maryland MD, 1807	Roderick Edward Charles	M	1955	MD	Howard University
	Donald Wallace Stewart	M	1955	MD	Morgan State University
	Lois Adelaide Young	F	1960	MD	Howard University
Massachusetts MA 1962	Marcia Clair Bowling	F	1978	MA	Brandeis University
	Vernette Jones Bee	F	1978	MA	Radcliffe College
	George Chidi Njoku	M	1979	MA	Worcester State College
	Harold F. Tate	M	1979	MA	Cornell University
Mayo MN, 1971	Joyce Jones	F	1976	TN	Memphis State University
	Alrundus Hart	M	1978	NC	Carleton College

Table 7, *continued*

MEDICAL SCHOOL	NAME	GENDER	YEAR	HOME STATE	UNDERGRADUATE COLLEGE
Meharry	James Monroe Jamison	M	1877	TN	Central Tennessee College
TN	Anna D. Gregg	F	1893	Unk	Unknown
1876	Georgia Esther Lee Patton	F	1893	TN	Central Tennessee College
Mercer	Sharon Renee Moses	F	1986	GA	Spelman College
GA, 1973	Redney Mark Jackson	M	1987	GA	Emory University
Miami	George Sanders	M	1969	FL	Morehouse College
FL, 1952	Jacqueline Simmons	F	1980	FL	Tennessee State University
Michigan	Janice Marie Fox	F	1973	MI	Michigan State University
State	Judith Ann Ingram	F	1973	MI	Eastern Michigan University
MI	Donald Gregory Weathers	M	1973	NC	St. Augustine's College
1964	Rogers O'Neil Whitmire	M	1973	TX	Prairie View A&M University
Michigan, University of, MI, 1850	William H. Fitzbutler[6] Female not reported	M	1872	CAN	None
Minnesota, Minneapolis MN, 1883	Paul Bowell	M	1940	MN	Unknown
	Regina Lee Williams	F	1972	MN	University of Minnesota
Mississippi	James Oliver	M	1972	MS	Miss. Valley State University
MS, 1903	Peggy Jean Johnson Wells	F	1974	MS	Tougaloo College
Missouri, Columbia MO, 1841	Freddie Lee Hayes	M	1958	MO	Lincoln University (Mo.)
	Rita Ann Ellsworth	F	1977	MO	University of Missouri-Kansas City
Missouri, Kansas	Karen Baucom	F	1975	MO	University of Missouri, Kansas City
City MO	Sharon Baucom	F	1975	MO	University of Missouri, Kansas City
1968	Michael Weaver	M	1977	MO	University of Missouri, Kansas City
Morehouse	Tanya L. Brown	F	1985	NY	Boston University
GA	Rogers Cain	M	1985	FL	Florida A&M University
1978	Linda Jean Cannon	F	1985	MS	Mississippi State University
	Lemsuel Leon Dent	M	1985	GA	University of Georgia
	Patricia Pelhem Harris	F	1985	FL	Florida State University
	Alise M. Jones	F	1985	NY	Spelman College
	Wendell E. Jones	M	1985	MI	Morehouse College

Entry continues

Table 7, *continued*

MEDICAL SCHOOL	NAME	GENDER	YEAR	HOME STATE	UNDERGRADUATE COLLEGE
Morehouse, *continued*	Hariette E. Lewis	F	1985	CA	University of California Berkeley
	Constance G. Madison	F	1985	OH	University of Colorado
	James F. Moorhead	M	1985	FL	Morehouse College
	David Garth Walters	M	1985	BWI	Florida Memorial College
	Robin Trudy Watt	F	1985	NY	Oberlin College
	Kim Maria Willard	F	1985	PA	St. Joseph University
	Evelyn Wilson	F	1985	GA	Emory University
	William L. Yarde	M	1985	Guyana	Long Island University
Mount Sinai NY, 1963	Miriam Senhouse	F	1970	NY	Simmons College
	Samuel Bruce	M	1971	DC	University of Bridgeport
Nebraska NE, 1881	W. H. C. Stephenson	M	1882	NE	Not required
	Female not reported				
Nevada NV 1969	Abigail L. Pennington[7]	F	1976	NV	University of Nevada– Reno
	Carl Demardrian Virgil	M	1991	NV	University of Nevada– Las Vegas
New Jersey (Newark) NJ 1956	Marjorie Earline Jones	F	1960	NY	St. John's University
	Albert Paul Knott	M	1960	PA	Yale University
	David Roland Snead	M	1960	NJ	Seton Hall University
New Jersey (RWJ) NJ 1966	Davill Armstrong	M	1974	NJ	Blackburn College
	Sharon Jones Warren	F	1975	NJ	Rutgers University Douglass College
New Mexico NM, 1961	Franklin D. Perry	M	1973	NM	University of New Mexico
	Judy M. Stubbs	F	1977	NM	University of New Mexico
New York Medical NY, 1858	Susan Smith McKinney Steward	F	1870	NY	None
	Male not reported				
New York University NY, 1841	Neville C. Whiteman	M	1925	NY	City College of New York
	Arthur M. Williams	M	1925	Unk	Pomona College
	Vivian L. Williams	M	1925	Unk	Pomona College
	Jean Beasley	F	1948	NY	Hunter College
No. Carolina NC 1879	Edward Oscar Diggs	M	1955	NC	Winston-Salem State University
	Venita Carol Newby Thweatt Allen	F	1973	NC	Howard University
No. Dakota ND, 1905	No known African-American graduates				

Table 7, *continued*

MEDICAL SCHOOL	NAME	GENDER	YEAR	HOME STATE	UNDERGRADUATE COLLEGE
Northwestern IL, 1859	Daniel Hale Williams	M	1883	PA	Hare's Classical Academy
	Emma Reynolds	F	1895	Unk	Unknown
Ohio, Med. College of OH, 1964	Jack Lewis Clark	M	1972	OH	Case Western Reserve University
	Mary Helen Robinson	F	1975	OH	University of Kansas
Ohio, North-eastern OH 1973	Rochelle A. Broome	F	1983	OH	Kent State University
	Joseph D. Lewis	M	1983	OH	University of Akron
	Yvonne A. Patterson	F	1983	OH	University of Akron
	Margo Shamberger Prade	F	1983	OH	Kent State University
Ohio State OH, 1907	William Frederick Ebert[8]	M	1893	Unk	Unknown
	Clotilde Dent Bowen	F	1947	OH	Ohio State University
Oklahoma OK, 1900	Daniel W. Lee	M	1955	OK	Langston University
	Vivian Moon Sanford Lewis	F	1959	OK	Oklahoma City University
Oregon OR, 1887	Walter Reynolds	M	1949	OR	University of Oregon
	Marva Graham	F	1977	OR	Howard University
Pa., Medical College of PA, 1850	Rebecca J. Cole	F	1867	PA	Institute for Colored Youth
	Wayne L. Gibbons	M	1979	PA	Fairfield University
	Virgil Thompson	M	1979	PA	Temple University
Pennsylvania State PA 1963	James F. Byers	M	1974	NY	State University of New York at Buffalo
	Theodore R. Densley	M	1974	MI	Michigan State University
	Wade A. Johnson	M	1974	NJ	Morgan State University
	Janiece C. McIntosh	F	1974	MD	University of California
	Lewis E. Mitchell	M	1974	VA	Muskingum College
Pennsylvania, University of PA, 1765	Nathan Francis Mossell	M	1882	PA	Lincoln University (Pa.)
	Arlene Bennett	F	1964	Unk	Unknown
Pittsburgh PA, 1886	J.C.G. Fowler	M	1906	PA	Unknown
	Elaine W. Morris-Grooms	F	1975	PA	Unknown
Ponce PR, 1977	No known African–American graduates				
Puerto Rico PR, 1977	No known African–American graduates				
Rochester NY 1920	Edwin Arzel Robinson	M	1943	NY	Cornell University
	Ruby Lavonzelle Sturgis Belton	F	1972	MS	Jackson State University

Table 7, *continued*

MEDICAL SCHOOL	NAME	GENDER	YEAR	HOME STATE	UNDERGRADUATE COLLEGE
Rush, IL 1837	David Jones Peck	M	1847	PA	None
	Doris Jean Young McCulley	F	1974	IL	Gustavus Adolphus College
Saint Louis MO, 1901	Harry Revels, III	M	1956	MO	St. Louis University
	Maceola L. Cole	F	1958	MO	St. Louis University
So. Carolina, Medical University of, SC, 1823	Bernard W. Deas	M	1971	SC	Iowa State University
	Rose Delores Gibbs	F	1973	SC	Fisk University
So. Carolina, University of SC, 1974	Everlyn Lilease Hall	F	1981	SC	Howard University
	Floyd Earl Scott, Jr.	M	1985	SC	Wofford College
South Dakota SD, 1907	No African–American graduates				
Stanford CA, 1908	Augustus Aaron White, III	M	1961	TN	Brown University
	Sharon Ann Bogerty	F	1973	MI	Bryn Mawr College
SUNY– Brooklyn NY, 1858	Lawrence Calvert Arnett	M	1950	Unk	Howard University
	Frances Justina Cherot	F	1954	Unk	New York University
SUNY– Buffalo NY, 1846	Joseph Robert Love	M	1880	BWI	Christ Church Grammar School
	Joan E. Clemmons	F	1966	NY	State University of New York at Buffalo
SUNY– Stony Brook, NY 1962	Paul J. Fox	M	1975	NY	City College of New York
	Janice C. Lark	F	1975	NY	Howard University
	Mitchelene J. Morgan	F	1975	NY	Denison University
	Johnson B. Murray	M	1975	NY	New York University
SUNY– Syracuse NY, 1864	Sarah Lougen Fraser	F	1876	NY	Unknown
	Male not reported				
Temple, PA 1901	Agnes Berry Montier	F	1912	PA?	Philadelphia Normal School
	William Beverly Carter	M	1916	Unk	Unknown
Tennessee State, East TN, 1978	Gregory Patterson	M	1983	TN	Fisk University
	Emma Ruthlyne Thompson	F	1984	TN	University of Tennessee at Nashville
Tennesse, University of, TN, 1851	Alvin H. Crawford	M	1964	TN	Tennessee State University
	Earline Houston	F	1967	TN	Lemoyne–Owen College

Table 7, *continued*

MEDICAL SCHOOL	NAME	GENDER	YEAR	HOME STATE	UNDERGRADUATE COLLEGE
Texas A&M TX, 1971	Phillip Wayne Jones	M	1983	TX	Texas A&M University
	Gayle Smith-Blair	F	1987	TX	Texas A&M University
Texas Tech TX 1969	Stella Pinkney Jones	F	1976	TX	Texas Southern University
	Johnnie Paris Frazier	F	1976	TX	Texas Southern University
	Charles Edward Mathis, III	M	1976	TX	Texas Tech University
Texas, University of, Dallas TX, 1943	Charles Douglas Foutz	M	1973	TX	Lamar University
	Johnny Lee Henry	M	1973	TX	University of Texas, Austin
	Kathryn Haley Flangin	F	1974	TX	North Texas State University
Texas, University of, Galveston TX, 1890	Herman Aladdin Barnett	M	1953	TX	Huston-Tillitson College
	Virginia Elizabeth Stull	F	1966	TX	Texas Southern University
Texas, University of, Houston TX, 1969	Estella Louise Bryant	F	1974	TX	Our Lady of the Lake University
	Ronald Wayne Jones	M	1976	TX	Texas A&M University
Texas, University of, San Antonio TX, 1966	Richard A. Mosby	M	1970	TX	Prairie View A&M University
	Carol L. Gray	F	1972	TX	University of Texas, Austin
Tufts MA, 1893	Ruth Marguerite Easterling	F	1921	MA	Tufts University
	Male not reported				
Tulane LA, 1834	Alvin Joseph Aubry, Jr.	M	1972	LA	Tulane University
	Henrynne Ann Louden	F	1974	LA	University of New Orleans
Uniformed Services University MD, 1972	Maceo Braxton	M	1980	CA	U.S. Military Academy
	Sabrina Ann Benjamin	F	1981	MD	Howard University
Utah UT 1905	William Anthony Robinson	M	1974	NY	Hunter–Lehman College
	Denise L. Capel	F	1979	NY	University of Utah
	Marjorie S. Coleman	F	1979	UT	University of Utah
Vanderbilt TN 1874	Levi Watkins, Jr.	M	1970	AL	Tennessee State University
	Darlene Dailey	F	1978	OH	Ohio State University
	Janis Adelaide Jones	F	1978	FL	Smith College
Vermont VT, 1822	Mark Smythe Yerby	M	1976	MA	University of New Hampshire
	No black female graduate				

Table 7, *continued*

MEDICAL SCHOOL	NAME	GENDER	YEAR	HOME STATE	UNDERGRADUATE COLLEGE
Virginia, Eastern, VA 1973	Marcus Lewis Martin	M	1976	VA	North Carolina State University
	Johnett Peyton George-LaBrie	F	1978	VA	Hampton University
Virginia, Med. College of, VA, 1838	Jean Louise Harris	F	1955	VA	Virginia Union University
	Paulus Clayton Taylor	M	1956	VA	Hampton University
Virginia, University of, VA, 1827	Edward B. Nash	M	1957	VA	Virginia Union University
	Edward T. Wood	M	1957	VA	Dartmouth College
	Barbara Starks Favazza	F	1966	VA	Beaver College
Washington University, St. Louis MO, 1885	James Leonard Sweatt, III	M	1962	TX	Middlebury College
	Karen LaFrance Scruggs	F	1973	NC	Macalester College
Washington, University of, Seattle, WA 1945	Lloyd Charles Elam	M	1957	WA	Roosevelt University
	Blanche Marie Chavers	F	1975	MS	University of Washington
	Robin Eleanor Wragg	F	1975	NY	Stanford University
Wayne State MI, 1885	Robert J. Boland[9]	M	1883	Unk	Unknown
	Helen Peebles-Meyers	F	1943	NY	Hunter College
West Virginia WV, 1902	Thomas Carter	M	1965	WV	West Virginia State College
	Jenee Barber Walker	F	1984	CA	Loma Linda University
Wisconsin, Medical College of WI, 1912	No information available				
Wisconsin, University of, WI, 1907	Walter J. Tardy, Jr.	M	1967	MI	Tennessee State University
	Ada M. Fisher	F	1975	VA	University of North Carolina, Greensboro
Wright State OH, 1973	Thomas Matthew Travis	M	1980	OH	Southern Illinois University
	Carol Jean Hubbard	F	1982	OH	University of Cincinnati
Yale CT 1812	Courtland Van Rensselaer Creed	M	1857	CT	None
	Beatrix Ann McCleary	F	1948	Unk	Unknown

[1] The year of organization given for each medical school is taken from the annual medical education issues of the *Journal of the American Medical Association.* Names of colleges are shown as they appear in *World Almanac* (1986) and/or *Comparative Guide to American Colleges* (1987). If college name has been changed, latest name is used.

²Graduate of predecessor school, N.E. Female Medical College.

³Had earlier graduates but didn't keep records until 1974.

⁴The Charles R. Drew Postgraduate Medical School was incorporated in 1966 and became part of the King-Drew Medical Center when the Martin Luther King, Jr., General Hospital was opened in 1972. An expanded affiliation agreement was signed with UCLA in 1978 to develop an undergraduate program for the third and fourth years leading to a joint M.D. degree. The charter class graduated in 1985 and the school's name was changed in 1987 to the Charles R. Drew University of Medicine and Science.

⁵Changed name.

⁶Information is from *Blacks in Science and Medicine* (Sammons, 1990).

⁷Completed Nevada's 2-year program in 1974 before the school offered the M.D. degree.

⁸Graduate of predecessor school, Staring-Ohio Medical College.

⁹Graduate of predecessor school, Detroit Medical College.

Year of Graduation

As shown in Table 8, the graduation years of these pioneering students ranged from the 1840s to the 1990s. The earliest reported African-American male graduate of a U.S. medical school was David Peck, who graduated from Rush Medical College in 1847; and the latest in this study was Carl Virgil, who graduated from the University of Nevada School of Medicine in 1991. The earliest reported first female African-American graduate was Rebecca Lee Crumpler, who graduated in 1864 from the New England Female Medical College (now the Boston University School of Medicine); and the latest was Tyshawn James, who graduated from the Marshall University School of Medicine in 1989.

Table 8—Year of Graduation of First Male and Female African-American Graduates of U.S. Medical Schools

YEAR OF GRADUATION	MALE	FEMALE	TOTAL	PERCENT
1840–49	1	0	1	0.3
1850–59	1	0	1	0.3
1860–69	2	2	4	1.4
1870–79	4	3	7	2.4
1880–89	6	0	6	2.1
1890–99	3	4	7	2.4
1900–09	7	0	7	2.4
1910–19	3	1	4	1.4
1920–29	5	2	7	2.4
1930–39	1	3	4	1.4
1940–49	4	4	8	2.8
1950–59	18	11	27	9.3
1960–69	19	11	29	10.0
1970–79	49	78	127	43.1
1980–89	23	27	50	17.2
1990–99	1	0	1	0.3
Total:	145	145	290	99.9
Median graduation year:	1970	1977	1973	

In general, the male pioneers completed the M.D. earlier than female pioneers. The most common decade in which the schools graduated their first African Americans was the 1970s. That decade accounted for over a third of the males, more than half of the females, and 43 percent of the total first graduates. The median graduation year for all these pioneers was 1973 (1970 for males compared with 1977 for females).

At a total of 87 (69 percent) of the 126 AAMC-member schools, the first African-American graduates were male. At 22 schools (17 percent), the first African-American graduates were female, and at 11 (9 percent), the pioneering men and women graduated in the same year. Comparative information was unavailable for the remaining six schools.

Years from Organization to Graduation

It is interesting to compare the number of years that transpired from the time that each medical school was organized (or founded) to the time that it graduated its first known male and/or female African-American student(s). As shown in Table 9, the median time lapse for the 117 known cohorts of males was 19 years, that for the 113 known cohorts of females was 45 years, and that for the 230 known cohorts of both sexes was 27 years. (The term "cohort" designates the group of individuals, who, regardless of their number, graduated from a given medical school in a given year.) Although it should be emphasized that it ordinarily takes 5 to 10 years for anyone to graduate from a newly organized medical school, it is obvious that there was a significant time lapse before African-American students were graduated from most U.S. medical schools. Note that the three cohorts in the "Less than 0" category graduated from "predecessor" schools. Some of the eight cohorts in the "150 or more" category graduated from schools that had earlier African-American graduates but no records to document them.

**Table 9—Number of Years from Medical School Organization to
Graduation of First Male and Female African-American
Students**

| Number of Years[1] | Cohorts of Known Graduates | | | |
	Male	Female	Total	Percent
Less than 0	2	1	3	1.3
0–9	26	20	46	20.0
0–19	31	27	58	25.2
20–29	7	4	11	4.8
30–39	9	2	11	4.8
40–49	3	5	8	3.5
50–59	4	8	12	5.2
60–69	7	2	9	3.9
70–79	8	7	15	6.5
80–89	1	7	8	3.5
90–99	2	4	6	2.6
100–109	1	3	4	1.7
110–119	5	4	9	3.9
120–129	2	4	6	2.6
130–139	4	5	9	3.9
140–149	3	4	7	3.0
150 or more	2	6	8	3.5
Total known cohorts:	17	113	230	99.9
Median years:	19	45	27	

[1]Discrepancy between the 230 cohorts in this table and the 290 individuals in Table 8 is due to calculations here being made without regard to the number of individuals from a given school who graduated in a given year.

Table 9 also shows, however, that there was a great deal of variability in the timing of these graduations. For example, 46 (or 20 percent) of the first graduating cohorts received their M.D. degree less than 10 years from the time their schools were organized. These schools included not only the four predominantly black institutions (Howard, Meharry, Morehouse, and Drew) but also schools organized during the 1950s, 1960s, and 1970s, decades of growing demands for social justice and civil rights.

Another group of medical schools with early African-American graduates (but not necessarily a short time lapse from organization to graduation) were those institutions organized in the 1700s and 1800s. These schools (and the years they were organized) include Boston (1873), Cornell (1898), Creighton (1892), Hahnemann (1848), Harvard (1782), University of Illinois (1881), University of Michigan (1850), Nebraska

(1881), New York Medical (1858), Northwestern (1859), Medical College of Pennsylvania (1850), University of Pennsylvania (1765), Rush (1837), SUNY-Syracuse (1864), Wayne State (1885), and Yale (1812).

The longest time lapse from organization to graduation tended to occur at medical schools that were founded prior to 1900, located in the south, or located in states with small black populations. As shown in Table 9, there were 43 cohorts of first African-American graduates for whom there was a time lapse of 100 years or more from the date their medical schools were organized to the date of their graduation. All 43 of these cohorts attended medical schools founded between 1765 and 1892, fifteen attended schools in the south, and at least four attended schools in states with only a small population of African Americans, such as Iowa, New Hampshire, and Vermont.

Residence of First Graduates

As summarized in Table 10, the 275 first U.S. medical school African-American graduates with known residences applied to that school from 39 different states and from the District of Columbia. None came from 11 smaller or less populated states or from Puerto Rico. Eight were from foreign countries.

It is not surprising that the largest number of first African-American graduates came from the states with the largest number of medical schools. For example, the 28 first African-American graduates from New York State applied from a state with 12 medical schools. Similarly, the 23 graduates from Texas came from a state with seven schools, and the 17 from California from a state with nine. Other states that provided 10 or more first African-American graduates were Florida, Georgia, North Carolina, Ohio, Pennsylvania, and Virginia.

In general, the first African-American graduates of U.S. medical schools tended to matriculate at medical schools in their states of residence. This was particularly true of students attending state-supported medical schools that gave preferential admission to residents of their home state.

Note in the table below that while most of the "home states are those in which students resided at the time of admission to medical school, a few are states in which they were born. There were no "first African-American graduates" from Alaska, Delaware, Idaho, Maine, Montana, New Hampshire, North Dakota, Puerto Rico, Rhode Island, South Dakota, Vermont, or Wyoming.

Table 10—Home States of First African-American Graduates of U.S. Medical Schools

HOME STATE	ABBREV.	MALES	FEMALES	TOTAL No.	PERCENT
Alabama	AL	4	3	7	2.5
Arizona	AZ	1	1	2	0.7
Arkansas	AR	2	1	3	1.1
California	CA	8	9	17	6.2
Colorado	CO	0	1	1	0.4
Connecticut	CT	2	1	3	1.1
District of Columbia	DC	3	0	3	1.1
Florida	FL	6	5	11	4.0
Georgia	GA	6	6	12	4.4
Hawaii	HI	1	1	2	0.7
Illinois	IL	1	4	5	1.8
Indiana	IN	1	2	3	1.1
Iowa	IA	1	0	1	0.4
Kansas	KS	2	1	3	1.1
Kentucky	KY	1	2	3	1.1
Louisiana	LA	4	4	8	2.9
Maryland	MD	2	4	6	2.2
Massachusetts	MA	4	5	9	3.3
Michigan	MI	3	4	7	2.5
Minnesota	MN	1	1	2	0.7
Mississippi	MS	2	4	6	2.2
Missouri	MO	3	5	8	2.9
Nebraska	NE	2	0	2	0.7
Nevada	NV	1	1	2	0.7
New Jersey	NJ	3	2	5	1.8
New Mexico	NM	1	1	2	0.7
New York	NY	9	19	28	10.2
North Carolina	NC	6	6	12	4.4
Ohio	OH	6	10	16	5.8
Oklahoma	OK	2	1	3	1.1
Oregon	OR	1	1	2	0.7
Pennsylvania	PA	10	6	16	5.8
South Carolina	SC	4	4	8	2.9
Tennessee	TN	4	5	9	3.3
Texas	TX	12	11	23	8.4
Utah	UT	0	1	1	0.4
Virginia	VA	6	4	10	3.6
Washington	WA	2	0	2	0.7
West Virginia	WV	3	1	4	1.5
Wisconsin	WI	0	1	1	0.4
Total U.S.		129	133	268	97.5
Total foreign[1]		6	1	7	2.5
Total known home states		135	140	275	100.0
Unknown home states		10	5	15	
Total first graduates		145	145	290	

[1] Three were from the British West Indies, two (including the one female) were from Canada, and one each were from Guyana and Kenya.

Undergraduate College of First Graduates

Table 11 lists the undergraduate colleges (or other premedical educational institutions) attended by the first African-American graduates of U.S. medical schools and indicates the number of these individuals who attended each of these institutions. Information about such premedical education was obtained for 264 (or 91 percent) of these 290 pioneering graduates.

Table 11—Undergraduate Colleges[1] of First African-American Graduates of U.S. Medical Schools

UNDERGRADUATE COLLEGE	STATE	GRADUATES
Beaver College	PA	1
Blackburn College	IL	1
Boston University	MA	2
Bowling Green State University	OH	1
Brandeis University	MA	1
Brown University	RI	3
Bryn Mawr College	PA	1
Butler University	IN	1
California State University, Long Beach	CA	1
Carleton College	MN	1
Case Western Reserve University	OH	1
Central Tennessee College	TN	2
Christ Church (Grammar School)	BWI	1
City College of New York	NY	2
Clark College	GA	2
Coe College	IA	1
Colmbia University	NY	1
Cornell University	NY	3
Creighton University	NE	1
Dartmouth College	NH	1
Denison University	OH	1
Dillard University	LA	1
Drexel University	PA	1
East Carolina University	NC	1
Eastern Michigan University	MI	1
Emory University	GA	2
Fairfield University	CT	1
Fisk University	TN	4
Florida A&M University	FL	3
Florida Memorial College	FL	1
Florida State University	FL	1
Florida Technological University	FL	1
Fordham University	NY	1
Fort Valley State College	GA	1

Table 11, *continued*

UNDERGRADUATE COLLEGE	STATE	GRADUATES
Grinnell College	IA	1
Gustavus Adolphus College	MN	1
Hampton University	VA	2
Hare's Classical Academy	PA?	1
Howard University	DC	16
Hunter College	NY	4
Hunter-Lehman College	NY	1
Huston-Tillotson College	TX	1
Indiana University	IN	1
Institute for Colored Youth	PA	1
Iowa State University	IA	1
Jackson State University	MS	1
Kansas State University	KS	1
Kent State University	OH	2
Kentucky State University	KY	1
Knoxville College	TN	1
Lamar University	TX	2
Langston University	OK	1
LeMoyne-Owen College	TN	1
Lincoln University	MO	1
Lincoln University	PA	1
Loma Linda University	CA	1
Long Island University	NY	1
Los Angeles Community College	CA	1
Macalester College	MN	2
Marquette University	WI	1
Marshall University	WV	2
Memphis State University	TN	1
Michigan State University	MI	4
Middlebury College	VT	1
Mississippi Valley State University	MS	1
Mississippi State University	MS	1
Morehouse College	GA	6
Morgan State University	MD	3
Morris Brown College	GA	1
Muskingum College	OH	1
New York University	NY	3
North Carolina A&T State University	NC	1
North Carolina State University	NC	2
Northeastern University	MA	1
North Texas State University	TX	1
Oakwood College	AL	1
Oberlin College	OH	2
Ohio State University	OH	4

Table 11, *continued*

UNDERGRADUATE COLLEGE	STATE	GRADUATES
Oklahoma City University	OK	1
Our Lady of the Lake University	TX	1
Pacific Union College	CA	1
Philadelphia Normal School	PA	1
Philander Smith College	AR	2
Pomona College	CA	2
Prairie View A&M University	TX	3
Radcliffe College	MA	1
Roosevelt University	IL	2
Rutgers University, Douglass College	NJ	1
Sacramento State College	CA	1
St. Augustine's College	NC	1
St. John's University	NY	1
St. Joseph University	PA	1
St. Louis University	MO	2
Seton Hall University	NJ	1
Simmons College	MA	1
Smith College	MA	1
South Carolina State College	SC	2
Southern Illinois University	IL	1
Southern Illinois University at Carbondale	IL	2
Southern University and A&M College	LA	2
Southern University in Baton Rouge	LA	1
Spelman College	GA	4
Stanford University	CA	2
State University of New York at Buffalo	NY	2
Sweet Briar College	VA	1
Temple University	PA	1
Tennessee State University	TN	4
Texas A&M University	TX	3
Texas College	TX	1
Texas Southern University	TX	3
Texas Tech University	TX	1
The Johns Hopkins University	MD	1
Tougaloo College	MS	1
Tufts University	MA	1
Tulane University	LA	1
Tuskegee University	AL	1
University of Akron	OH	2
University of Alabama	AL	1
University of Arizona	AZ	2
University of Bridgeport	CT	1
University of California	CA	2
University of California, Berkeley	CA	2
University of California, Los Angeles	CA	1
University of Chicago	IL	3
University of Cincinnatti	OH	2
University of Colorado	CO	2

Table 11, *continued*

UNDERGRADUATE COLLEGE	STATE	GRADUATES
University of Connecticut	CT	1
University of Dayton	OH	1
University of Georgia	GA	2
University of Hawaii	HI	1
University of Iowa	IA	1
University of Kansas	KS	2
University of Kentucky	KY	1
University of Massachusetts	MA	1
University of Minnesota	MN	1
University of Missouri-Kansas City	MO	4
University of Nevada, Las Vegas	NV	1
University of Nevada, Reno	NV	1
University of New Hampshire	NH	1
University of New Mexico	NM	2
University of New Orleans	LA	1
University of North Carolina at Chapel Hill	NC	2
University of North Carolina at Greensboro	NC	1
University of Oregon	OR	1
University of Pennsylvania	PA	1
University of Southern California	CA	1
University of Tennessee at Nashville	TN	1
University of Texas	TX	1
University of Texas at Austin	TX	2
University of Utah	UT	2
University of Washington	WA	2
University of Wisconsin	WI	1
U.S. Military Academy	NY	1
Virginia State College	VA	1
Virginia Union University	VA	2
Western Reserve University	OH	1
West Virginia State College	WV	1
Winston-Salem State University	NC	1
Wofford College	SC	1
Worcester State College	MA	1
Xavier University of Louisiana	LA	2
Yale University	CT	1
York College	PA	1

	Total:	258
No college		6
Total known college information[2]		264
Unknown college information		26
Total number of graduates		290

[1]College names are as they appear in the *1986 World Almanac* and/or *Comparative Guide to American Colleges* (1987). If college name has been changed, latest name is used.

[2] Known college information, total of 264 graduates equals 91 percent of total graduates.

The most striking finding of this analysis is the large number of different undergraduate institutions that contributed to the education of these pioneers. A total of 162 different institutions participated in the premedical education of these individuals. Of these, 109 (67 percent) had only one alumnus who became a first African-American graduate of a U.S. medical school. Thirty-seven (23 percent) had two such alumni, and nine (6 percent) had three such alumni. Leading the group was Howard University, which provided the premedical education for 16 of these pioneers. Other noteworthy providers included Morehouse (6) and Fisk, Hunter, Michigan State, Ohio State, Spelman, Tennessee State, and the University of Missouri-Kansas City (4 each).

In general, these first graduates were distributed randomly by gender among these 162 undergraduate institutions. Major exceptions were for those who attended such schools as all-male Morehouse and all-female Spelman. Of the 16 who did their undergraduate work at Howard, 6 were male and 10 were female. The location of the undergraduate colleges in this analysis tended to be in the same state or region as the medical schools attended.

7

Black Pioneer Graduates of Howard University College of Medicine

In the same way that Howard University was the leading provider of premedical education for the 290 first African-American graduates of all U.S. medical schools, our research indicates that Howard University College of Medicine (HUCM) apparently has produced more black pioneers in medical education and organized medicine than any other medical school in this country. Detailed information about these individuals is summarized in Table 12.

By applying the three fairly strict basic criteria specified in chapter 1, a total of 75 HUCM graduates have been identified as being African-American pioneers in medical education and/or organized medicine. Of these, 65 are male and 10 are female. Their dates of birth range from 1865 (for Drs. Sarah Jones and Edward Williston) to 1939 (for Dr. Russell Miller). Relative to their years of graduation, the earliest individual (Dr. Henry Thompson) earned his M.D. degree in 1892 (24 years after the medical school was founded) and the latest (Dr. Anna Cherrie Epps) earned her Ph.D. from Howard University in 1966.

When Table 12 is analyzed relative to the nature of their "black firsts," 20 are found to be pioneers in medical education only, 17 in organized medicine only, and 16 solely in activities closely related to medical education or organized medicine. An additional 20 were pioneers in two of the above categories and two (Drs. Cobb and Spurlock) were pioneers in all three areas.

Of the 37 individuals who were the first of their race in various aspects of medical education, 16 achieved this prominence because of their activities at HUCM while the other 21 did their educational pioneering elsewhere. It should be noted, however, that many of the individuals listed in Table 12 have also played prominent educational and administrative roles at HUCM even though most of their "official" pioneering may have taken place elsewhere and may have been solely in organized medicine or in closely related activities (rather than in medical education). Examples of this include Drs. Charles Epps, Robert Jason, and

Marion Mann, all of whom have been deans of HUCM, and Drs. W. Montague Cobb, W. Lester Henry, LaSalle Leffall, and Roland Scott, who have been the chairmen of HUCM's departments of anatomy, internal medicine, surgery, and pediatrics, respectively.

Analysis of the states of birth of these 75 individuals reveals that they were born in 28 different states, districts, or territories of the United States plus Liberia, Nigeria, and the British West Indies (BWI). (Those born in the BWI subsequently became citizens of the United States.) The largest number (11) were born in the District of Columbia, where HUCM is located. Six were born in Georgia, five each in New York and the British West Indies, four in Florida, and three each in Illinois, Louisiana, Massachusetts, South Carolina, Tennessee, Virginia, and West Virginia. A more detailed analysis, including a comparison of the birth states of the pioneering graduates of Howard, Meharry, and the other (predominantly white) medical schools, is provided in Table 17 (see chapter 10).

These 75 pioneering graduates of HUCM did their premedical studies at a total of 34 different undergraduate colleges. The largest number (27) completed their undergraduate work at Howard University. Four did their premedical study at Lincoln University in Pennsylvania, three graduated from the City College of New York, and two each graduated from Columbia University, Dillard University, Florida A&M University, Knoxville College, Morehouse College, New York University, and the University of Pennsylvania. A more detailed analysis of undergraduate colleges attended, including comparisons of the HUCM and the other pioneering graduates, is provided in Table 18 (chapter 10).

In Table 12 below, note that names in boldface type are those individuals whose biographical sketches appear in chapter 4. The symbol (#) means date is unknown.

Table 12—Black Pioneer Graduates of Howard University College of Medicine

Name Birthplace Life Span	Pioneering Achievements as African Americans	M.D. Year	Undergrad. College and Year
Alexander, Leslie L. BWI 1917–	President, Brooklyn Radiological Society, 1963–64 Professor of radiology, SUNY-Brooklyn and SUNY-Stony Brook Health Science Centers, 1969–1988 Member, board of chancellors, American College of Radiology, 1980–85; vice president, 1984–85	1952	New York University 1947
Alexis, Carlton P. BWI 1929–	Trained at Walter Reed Hospital, 1957 Vice president for Health Affairs, Howard University, 1969– 88	1957	New York University 1953
Allen, William E., Jr. FL 1903–1982	Diplomate, American Board of Radiologists, 1935	1930	Howard University 1927
Anderson, John A. WV 1937–	Founder, Southwest Medical Association, Inc., 1973	1962	University of Chicago 1958
Atkinson, Whittier C. GA 1893–1991	Founder, interracial hospital in Pennsylvania, 1932 G.P. of the Year, Pennsylvania Medical Society, 1960	1925	Howard University 1922
Barber, Jesse B., Jr. TN 1924–	Third certified in neurosurgery, 1963 Founder/director, HUCM Medical Stroke Project, 1968–70	1948	Lincoln University[1] 1944
Bath, Patricia E. NY 1942–	Student cofounder, SNMA, 1964 Woman president, HUCM chapter, SNMA, 1966 Resident, ophthalmology, New York University School of Medicine, 1970–73 Cofounder, ophthalmology residency program, King/Drew Medical Center, 1974 Woman surgeon, UCLA Medical Center, 1975 Female chair of ophthalmology, King/Drew Medical Center, 1983–1986 Honorary medical staff member, UCLA, 1992	1968	Hunter College 1964
Becker, Leslie E., Jr., MA 1923–	Faculty member, urology, University of Kansas Medical Center, 1958	1946	Columbia University 1943
Cave, Vernal G. Panama 1918–	President, Medical Society of Kings County, New York, 1980–81	1944	City College of New York 1940

Table 12, *continued*

Name Birthplace Life Span	Pioneering Achievements as African Americans	M.D. Year	Undergrad. College and Year
Clement, Kenneth W. VA 1920–1974	Member, Federal Hospital Benefits Advisory Council, 1964–68	1945	Oberlin College 1942

Cobb, W. Montague
DC
1904–1990
	Founder/president, American Association of
	    PhysicalAnthropologists, 1957–59
	Cofounder, Student NMA, 1964
	Distinguished professor, HUCM, 1969–
	Principal historian of African Americans
	    in medicine
		1929	Amherst
			College
			1925

Coleman, Arthur H.
PA
1920–
	President, Golden State Medical
	    Association, 1972–74
	Cofounder, American Health
	    Care Plan, 1973
		1944	Pennsylvania
			State
			University
			1941

Comer, James P. IN 1934–	Cofounder, Black Psychiatrists of America, 1968 Associate dean, Yale Medical School, 1969	1960	Indiana University 1956
Cowan, Claude, Sr. TN 1904–1975	Chair, ophthalmology, HUCM, 1954–1973	1931	Knoxville College 1927
Cross, Edward B. IN 1922–	Deputy assistant secretary, U.S. Department of Health, Education, and Welfare #	1952	Philander- Smith College 1948?

Curry, Charles L.
NC
1934–
	Charter member, Association of Black
	    Cardiologists, 1975
	Founding member, Association of Professors
	    of Cardiology, 1990
	Member, board of trustees, American College of
	    Cardiology, 1992–1997 term
		1959	Johnson
			C. Smith
			University
			1955

Dibble, Eugene H. SC 1893–1968	Second director, Tuskegee VA Hospital, 1936–46 Medical officer commissioned as colonel, 1944	1919	Atlanta University 1915
Edwards, Lena F. DC 1900–1986	Founder, clinic for Mexican migrant workers, 1961 Recipient of Presidential Medal of Freedom, 1964	1924	Howard University 1921
Epps, Anna Cherrie LA 1930–	Founder, MedREP (an academic reinforcement program), Tulane, 1969	1966	Howard University 1951

Table 12, *continued*

Name Birthplace Life Span	Pioneering Achievements as African Americans	M.D. Year	Undergrad. College and Year
Epps, Charles H., Jr. MD 1930–	Member, American Board of Orthopaedic Surgery, 1977–83 President, District of Columbia Medical Society, 1979 Governor, American College of Surgeons, 1982–88 President, American Orthopaedic Association, 1985	1955	Howard University 1951

Epps, Roselyn P.
AR
1930–
	President, American Medical Women's
	    Association, 1990–91
	Woman president, District of Columbia
	    Medical Society, 1992
		1955	Howard
			University
			1951

Ferguson, Angella D. DC 1925–	Woman associate vice president, health affairs, HUCM, 1969	1949	Howard University 1945
Francis, Milton A. DC 1882–1961	Specialist in genitourinary diseases #	1906	None?
Freeman, Harold P. DC 1933–	Founder, Breast Exam Center of Harlem, 1979 Chair, National Advisory Committees on Cancer, 1984–88 Second president, American Cancer Society, 1988	1958	Catholic University 1954
Garnes, Arthur L. NY 1912–?	Director, Plastic Surgery Program, Harlem Hospital, 1977	1937	City College of New York 1933
Garvin, Charles H. FL 1890–1968	Commissioned army officer in World War I, 1917 Urologist, Lakeside Hospital (of Western Reserve University), 1920	1915	Howard University 1911
Gathings, Joseph G. TX 1898–1965	Certified in dermatology and syphilology, 1945	1928	Howard University 1924
Gilbert, Artishia G. KY 1869–19??	Woman M.D. in KY # (1898?)	1897	Louisville State University 1892
Greene, Charles R. NY 1926–	Dean of students, SUNY-Brooklyn Health Sciences Center, 1973–1992	1954	Howard University 1950
Greene, Clarence S. DC 1901–1957	HUCM graduate, certified, surgical board, 1943 Chief, HUCM Division of Neurosurgery, 1949 Diplomate, American Board of Neurosurgery, 1953	1936	University of Pennsylvania 1932

Table 12, *continued*

Name Birthplace Life Span	Pioneering Achievements as African Americans	M.D. Year	Undergrad. College and Year
Hawthorne, Edward W. MS 1921–1986	Eminent researcher in cardiovascular physiology, HUCM Physiology Ph.D., University of Illinois, 1951	1946	Howard University 1941

Henry, W. Lester, Jr.
PA
1915–
	Markle Scholar, 1953–58
	Governor, American Board of Internal Medicine,
	    1971–78
	Member, Resident Review Committee,
	    Internal Medicine, 1971–78
	Representative to American Board of Medical
	    Specialties, 1974–78
	Regent, American College of Physicians, 1974–80
	Master, American College of Physicians, 1987
		1941	Temple
			University
			1936

Higginbotham, Peyton R., VA 1902–	Member, West Virginia State Board of Health, 1948–	1926	Howard University 1923

**Hunter, Gertrude
C.T.,**
MA
1926–
	National director of health services,
	    Project Head Start, 1965–71
	Regional health administrator, Public Health
	    Service, 1972–76
	Chair, community medicine and family
	    practice, HUCM, 1976–80
		1950	Howard
			University
			1946

Ish, George W.S., Jr. AR 1919–1965	Fellow (Memphis, Tenn.), American College of Surgeons, 1963	1944	Talladega College 1939
Jason, Robert S. PR 1901–1984	Ph.D. in pathology (University of Chicago), 1932	1928	Lincoln University[1] 1924
Jones, R. Frank DC 1897–1979	Diplomate, American Board of Urology, 1936 Staff (w/Johnson), Georgetown University Hospital, 1954 Member, American Urological Association, 1965 (1st?)	1922	Howard University 1919
Jones, Sarah G. B. VA 1865–19??	Woman to pass medical board in Virginia #	1893	Richmond Normal Schl., 1889?

Kenney, John A., Jr.
AL
1914–
	Dermatology resident, University of
	    Michigan, 1950–53
	Member, American Dermatology
	    Association, 1970
	Board member, American Academy of Dermatology,
	    1971–73
		1945	Bates
			College
			1942

Entry continues

Table 12, *continued*

Name Birthplace Life Span	Pioneering Achievements as African Americans	M.D. Year	Undergrad. College and Year

Kenney, John A., Jr.
continued
	Board member, Society for Investigative
	  Dermatology, 1974?
	Board member, Dermatology Foundation, 1980?
	Recipient, Finnerwood Award, Dermatology
	  Foundation, 1988		

Lathen, John W. NJ 1916–	Intern, Hackensack, N.J., Hospital, 1949–50 President, Mental Health Association, Bergen Co., N.J., 1955–57	1949	Virginia State College 1938
Leffall, LaSalle D., Jr. FL 1930–	President, Society of Surgical Oncology, 1978 President, American Cancer Society, 1979 President, Society of Surgical Chairmen, 1988–90	1952	Florida A&M University 1948
Lowry, John E. NY 1898–	President, Queens Medical Society, 1954	1923	University of Pennsylvania 1919
Mann, Marion GA 1920–	First physician brigadier general, U.S. Army Medical Reserve Corps, 1975	1954	Tuskegee University 1940
Marchbanks, Vance H. WY 1905–1988	Surgeon, 332nd Fighter Group, Tuskegee Army Air Force Base, 1941	1937	University of Arizona 1931

Matory, William E.
IL
1926–
	Founder, HUCM Trauma Canter, 1963
	Founder, HUCM Hemodialysis Service, 1963
	Founder, Department of Family Practice
	  and its residency program, 1969
	Initiator, HUCM Continuing Medical
	  Education Program, 1976
	Second member, Board of Governors,
	  American College of Surgeons, 1977–83
		1953	Howard
			University
			1949

Miller, Ross M., Jr. MA 1928–	President, Los Angeles Surgical Society, 1991	1951	Howard University 1947

**Miller,
Russell L, Jr.**
WV
1939–
	Medical intern, University of Michigan
	  Medical School, 1965–66
	Burroughs-Wellcome Scholar in Clinical
	  Pharmacology, 1977-82
		1965	Howard
			University
			1961

Morman, William D. GA 1901–1951	One of first two (with Walter A. Younge) in St. Louis Medical Society, 1949 Member, Missouri State Medical Society, 1949	1929	Morehouse College 1925

Table 12, *continued*

NAME BIRTHPLACE LIFE SPAN	PIONEERING ACHIEVEMENTS AS AFRICAN AMERICANS	M.D. YEAR	UNDERGRAD. COLLEGE AND YEAR
Murray, Peter M. LA 1888–1969	Certified, American Board of Obstetrics and Gynecology, 1931 Member, American Medical Association House of Delegates, 1950 President, New York County Medical Society, 1954–55	1914	Dillard University 1910
Odeku, E. Latunde Nigeria 1927–1974	Second certified, neurosurgery, 1961 Pioneer neurosurgeon, Nigeria, 1962–74	1954	Howard University 1950
Payne, Howard M. DC 1907–1961	Vice president, National Tuberculosis Association, 1951–52	1931	Dartmouth College 1928
Porter, Vincent NY 1926–1980	Certified in plastic surgery, 1968	1954	City College of New York 1950
Rimple, Hubert M. BWI 1921–	Director, Norfolk City Health Department # Regional medical director, U.S. Department of Health and Human Services # Director, National Health Service Corps #	1957	Columbia University 1952
Ross, Julian W. GA 1884–1961	Chair, obstetrics and gynecology, HUCM, 1930–57 Certified, both obstetrics and gynecology, 1935 Founding fellow, American College of Obstetrics and Gynecology, 1951	1911	Lincoln University[1] 1907
Rosser, Samuel B. GA 1934–	Certified, pediatric surgery, 1975	1960	Clark College 1954
Scott, Roland B. TX 1909–	Read scientific paper at District of Columbia Medical Society, 1938? Second member, American Board of Pediatrics, 1939 Recipient, Jacobi Award, highest award of AMA and American Academy of Pediatrics #	1934	Howard University 1931
Simmons, Arthur H. DC 1899–	Organizer, first all-Negro Army hospital, 1943	1925	Harvard University 1921
Sinkler, William H. SC 1906–1960	Faculty member, Washington University, St. Louis #	1932	Lincoln University[1] 1928
Smoot, Roland T. DC 1927–	President, Maryland State Medical Society # Dean's office, Johns Hopkins University School of Medicine #	1952	Howard University 1948

Table 12, *continued*

Name Birthplace Life Span	Pioneering Achievements as African Americans	M.D. Year	Undergrad. College and Year
Spellman, Mitchell W. LA 1919–	President/dean, Drew Postgraduate Medical School (and assistant dean, UCLA Medical School), 1969–77 Executive vice president and dean for medical services, Harvard Medical Center, 1978–90	1944	Dillard University 1940
Spurlock, Jeanne OH 1921–	Woman chair, Meharry Department of Psychiatry, 1968–75 Woman and black recipient, Strecker Psychiatric Award, 1971 Member, Committee on Certification in Child Psychiatry, 1972–80 (chair, 1979)	1947	Roosevelt University 1944
Standard, Raymond L. CT 1925–1990	District of Columbia commissioner of public health, 1969–1980	1952	Howard University 1948
Steptoe, Robert C. IL 1920–1994	Professor, obstetrics and gynecology, Rush, 1957–79 Chief, gynecology, University of Chicago, 1979–	1944	Northwestern University 1941
Syphax, Burke DC 1910–	Among first certified, American Board of Surgery, 1943 HUCM Distinguished Professor Award, 1974	1936	Howard University 1932
Thompson, Alvin J. WA 1924–	President, Seattle Academy of Internal Medicine, 1972–73 President, King County (Washington) Medical Society, 1974 Governor (for Washington and Alaska), American College of Physicians, 1974–78 President, Washington State Medical Association, 1978–79	1946	Howard University 1943
Thompson, Solomon H. WV 1870–1950	Cofounder (with Howell and Unthank), Douglas Hospital, Kansas City, Kan., 1899	1892	Storer College 1886
Thomson, Gerald E., NY 1932–	Chairman, American Board of Internal Medicine, 1991	1959	Queens College 1955
Titus-Dillon, Pauline Y. BWI 1938–	Woman director, Internal Medicine Program, D.C. General Hospital, 1977–80 Woman M.D. administrator, HUCM dean's office, 1980	1964	Howard University 1960
Turner, Guthrie IL 1930–	Brigadier general in Army Medical Corps, 1980–83 Hospital commander, Madigan Army Medical Center, 1980–83	1953	Shaw University 1949

Table 12, *continued*

NAME BIRTHPLACE LIFE SPAN	PIONEERING ACHIEVEMENTS AS AFRICAN AMERICANS	M.D. YEAR	UNDERGRAD. COLLEGE AND YEAR
Warfield, William A. MD 1866–1951	Longest surgeon-in chief, Freedmen's Hospital, 1901–1936 Developer, Freedmen's residency programs	1894	Morgan State University 1891

Weddington, Wilburn
GA
1924–
	Southern member, AMA, 1952
	Professor, Ohio State University College
	    of Medicine, 1991
	Associate dean, medical administration, Ohio
	    State University College of Medicine, 1991
		1948	Morehouse
			College
			1944

White, Jack E. FL 1921–1988	Founder/director, HUCM Cancer Center, 1972–88	1944	Florida A&M University 1941
Williams, Ernest Y. BWI 1899–19??	Founder, Psychiatry Service, Freedmen's Hospital, 1939	1930	Howard University 1927
Williston, Edward D. NC 1865–1928	M.D. to pass D.C. medical examination #	1894	Howard University 1890

Young, Moses W.
SC
1904–1986
	Ph.D., anatomy, University of Michigan,
	    1934 (first?)
	Taught anatomy, HUCM, 1934–70
	Taught anatomy, University of Maryland, 1973
	    (first?)
		1930	Howard
			University
			1926

---

[1] In Pennsylvania.

8

Black Pioneer Graduates of Meharry Medical College

In the same way that chapter 7 describes the 75 African-American medical pioneer graduates of Howard University College of Medicine, this chapter provides details about the 50 individuals who were identified as being black medical pioneer graduates of Meharry Medical College School of Medicine.

The difference in the number of identified pioneers from Howard and Meharry is undoubtedly due in part to the fact that the authors of this book are all affiliated with Howard. It is also explained to some degree by Howard having more physician graduates. For example, the AMA's latest official book about medical alumni (Eiler, Pasko, and Max, 1986) indicates that as of 1985, Howard University College of Medicine had 3,723 living alumni as compared with 3,041 for Meharry. That volume also reports that as of 1985, HUCM had 1,438 graduates who were board certified as compared with 909 for Meharry.

Although the total number of identified pioneers from Meharry is only two-thirds as large as the number identified for Howard, their proportion of males and females is almost identical. A total of 88 percent of the Meharry pioneers are male compared with 87 percent of the Howard pioneers.

Analysis of Table 13 reveals that the dates of birth of the 50 Meharry pioneers range from 1851 (for Dr. James Jamison) to 1948 (for Dr. Herman Mabrie). Relative to their years of graduation from Meharry, the first male (Dr. Jamison) received his M.D. degree in 1877 while the first female (Dr. Georgia E. Patton-Washington) received her degree in 1893. The latest pioneering graduate in this table (Dr. Mabrie) earned his degree in 1973. These dates of birth and graduation are generally comparable with those for the pioneering graduates of HUCM.

In Table 13 below, note that names in boldface type are those individuals whose biographical sketches appear in chapter 4. The symbol (#) means date unknown.

Table 13—Black Pioneer Graduates of Meharry Medical College

NAME BIRTHPLACE LIFE SPAN	PIONEERING ACHIEVEMENTS AS AFRICAN AMERICANS	M.D. YEAR	UNDERGRAD. COLLEGE AND YEAR
Adom, Edwin N.A. Ghana 1939–	Blind black physician and psychiatrist in U.S (certified in psychiatry in 1978)	1968	University of Pennsylvania 1963
Avery, Clarence S. LA 1926–	President, California Medical Association, 1985?	1949	Xavier University 1945
Bent, Michael J. # Unknown	Dean, Meharry Medical College, 1941	1921	Unknown
Bernard, Louis J. LA 1925–	Board certified surgeon, University of Oklahoma College of Medicine, 1959 President, Oklahoma City Surgical Society, 1968	1950	Dillard University 1946
Boyd, Robert F. TN 1858–1912	Founder, Boyd Infirmary, 1893 Founder and president, National Medical Association, 1895–98	1882	Central Tenn. College and Fisk University #
Brown, Dorothy PA 1919–	Woman fellow, American College of Surgeons, 1959	1948	Bennett College 1941
Burton, John F. TN 1913–	Certified, forensic pathologist, American Board of Pathology, 1964	1941	Fisk and Tenn. State universities 1933
Butler, Henry R. NC 1862–1931	Chair, NMA Executive Board, 1895 President, Georgia Medical, Dental and Pharmaceutical Association #	1890	Lincoln University[1] 1887
Callender, Clive O. NY 1936–	NIH Postdoctoral Fellow in Transplant Immunology, 1971–73 Member, National Task Force on Organ Procurement and Transplantation, 1984	1963	Hunter College 1959
Chatman, Donald L. LA 1934–	President, American Association of Gynecologic Laparoscopists #	1960	Harvard University 1956
Clifford, Maurice C. DC 1920–	Vice president for medical affairs, 1978–80, and president, 1980–86, Medical College of Pennsylvania	1947	Hamilton College 1941
Cooper, Edward S. SC 1926–	President, American Heart Association, 1992	1949	Lincoln University[1] 1946

Table 13, *continued*

Name Birthplace Life Span	Pioneering Achievements as African Americans	M.D. Year	Undergrad. College and Year
Cowan, James R. DC 1916–	State Commissioner of Health, New Jersey, 1970–74 Assistant U.S. secretary of Defense, 1974	1944	Howard University 1939
Crump, Edward P. MS 1910–	One of three elected to Nashville Academy of Medicine, 1955 (with Hansen and Walker)	1941	Fisk University 1934
Davidson, Ezra C., Jr. MS 1933–	Chair, Obstetrics and Gynecology, Drew Medical School, 1971– Chair, College of Obstetrics and Gynecology, 1990–91	1958	Morehouse College 1954
Francis, G. Hamilton BWI 1885–1963	One of first two Interns, Hubbard Hospital, 1911 Founder, NMA House of Delegates, 1935	1911	Berkeley Institute of Bermuda 1907

Gladden, James R.
NC
1911–1969
	Certified, American Board of Orthopaedic
	    Surgery, 1949
	Fellow, American Academy of Orthopaedic
	    Surgeons, 1951
	First resident, HUCM's Orthopaedic Surgery Program #
		1938	Long Island
			University
			1934?

Hale, John H. TN 1879–1944	Major figure on Meharry Faculty, 1905–1944 Chief of surgery, Meharry, 1938–44 Cofounder, Millie E. Hale Hospital, 1916	1905	Walden University 1903
Hansen, Axel USVI 1919–	One of three elected to Nashville Academy of Medicine, 1955 (with Crump and Walker)	1944	Fisk University 1941
Jackson, Marvin A, GA 1927–	President, D.C. Society of Pathologists, 1964–65	1951	Morehouse College 1947

Jamison, James M.[2]
Unknown
1851–1921
	Graduate, Medical Department of Central
	    Tennessee College (became Meharry), 1877
	President, Tennessee Colored Medical
	    Association, 1880?
		1877	Unknown

Jones, Ernest J. LA 1943–	President, Georgia Academy of Family Physicians	1971	Texas Southern University #
Lambright, Middleton H., Jr., MO 1908–	Full staff appointment, Cleveland Hospitals, 1946 Assistant dean, Medical University of South Carolina, 1960–72	1938	Morehouse College and Lincoln U.[1] 1934

Table 13, *continued*

Name Birthplace Life Span	Pioneering Achievements as African Americans	M.D. Year	Undergrad. College and Year

Leavell, Walter F.
IL
1934–
	President, Minority Affairs Section, AAMC
	    Group on Student Affairs, 1969
	Cofounder, National Association of Minority
	    Medical Educators (NAMME), 1975
	Fulltime president, Drew University of
	    Medicine and Science, 1987–91
		1964	University of
			Cincinnati
			College of
			Pharmacy
			1957

Lynk, Miles V. TN 1871–1957	Publisher of medical journal, 1892 Suggested organization of National Medical Association (NMA), 1895	1891	Walden University 1900
Mabrie, Herman J., III TX, 1948	Otolaryngology resident, Baylor Affiliated Hospitals, 1975–78 Otolaryngologist in the United States, 1978?	1973	Howard University 1969
Majors, Monroe A. TX 1864–1960	Organized second Black Medical Association (Lone Star) in U.S., 1886 M.D. West of Denver, Colo., 1888	1886	Central Tenn. College 1882?

Manley, Audrey F.
MS
1934–
	Woman chief resident, Cook County Childrens'
	    Hospital, 1962
	Woman assistant surgeon general, U.S. Public
	    Health Service, 1988
	Woman deputy assistant secretary for health, U.S.
	    Department of Health and Human Services, 1989
		1959	Spelman
			College
			1955

McKinley, John F. Unknown #	Alumni faculty member at Meharry, 1883	1879	Unknown
Moore, Eddie S. VA 1935–	Chair of pediatrics, predominantly white school (University of Tennessee) #	1961	Johnson C. Smith University #
Patton-Washington, G.[2] TN 1864–1900	Woman graduate, Meharry Medical College (with Anna D. Gregg), 1893 Woman M.D. in Tennessee #	1893	None?
Perry, John E. TX 1870–1962	Founder, Perry Sanitarium, Kansas City, Mo., 1910 (became Wheatley-Provident Hospital, 1915)	1895	Bishop College 1891
Phillips, Jasper T. TN 1884–19??	Monitor, Tenn. State Medical Boards, 1913–14	1913	Fisk University 1907

Quinland, William S.
BWI
1885–1953
	Recipient, Rosenwald Fellowship for
	    Advanced Medical Study, 1920
	Member, American Association of Pathologists
	    and Bacteriologists, 1920?
		1919	Oskaloosa
			College
			1918

Entry continues

Table 13, *continued*

Name Birthplace Life Span	Pioneering Achievements as African Americans	M.D. Year	Undergrad. College and Year
Quinland, William S. *continued*	Certified, American Board of Pathologists, 1937 Fellow, American College of Pathologists, 1947		
Rann, Emery L., Jr. WV 1914–	Member, Mecklenburg County (N.C.) Medical Association, 1954 (vice president, 1958)	1948	Johnson C. Smith U. 1934
Reed, Theresa Greene MD 1923–	Woman epidemiologist, 1968 Founder, Mound City (St. Louis) Women Physicians Association, 1963	1949	Virginia State College 1945
Reid, Edith C., NJ 1934–	First woman and first black, New York State Board of Medicine #	1951	Hunter College 1947?
Robinson, Luther D. VA 1922–	Author of books on psychology of the deaf # Honorary D.Sc., Gallaudet College, 1971	1946	Virginia State College 1943
Robinson, Paul T., AR 1898–1966	Founder and editor, *Journal of New Orleans Medical, Dental and Pharmaceutical Association,* 1938 Founder, Robinson Infirmary and Clinic, 1950	1931	Bishop College 1917
Rolfe, Daniel T. FL 1902–1968	Founder of Alpha Omega Alpha, Meharry Medical College #	1927	Florida A&M University 1925
Roman, Charles V. PA 1864–1934	Editor, *JNMA,* 1908–18 Chair, ENT, Meharry, 1904–1931	1890	Hamilton Coll. Institute (Canada) #
Sampson, Calvin C. MD 1928–	Resident, Philadelphia's Episcopal Hospital, 1952–56 One of first certified, clinical pathology, 1957 Founder, HUCM Department of Allied Health Professions, 1971	1951	Hampton University 1947
Smith, Earl B. MO 1920–	Governor, American College of Surgeons (representing Surgery Section of NMA) #	1949	Lincoln U.[3] 1942 and Fisk U. 1944
Thomas, William McK. TX 1903–1958	Member, External Advisory Group, U.S. Public Health Service, 1954–59	1930	Wiley College 1926
Tyson, William G. GA 1900–	Member, American Academy of Allergy, 1946	1926	Howard University 1922

Table 13, *continued*

Name Birthplace Life Span	Pioneering Achievements as African Americans	M.D. Year	Undergrad. College and Year
Walker, Matthew LA 1906–1978	One of three elected, Nashville Academy of Medicine (with Crump and Hansen), 1955	1934	New Orleans University[4] 1929
Wells, Josie E. Unknown #	Woman Teacher at Meharry # Secretary, George W. Hubbard Hospital, 1910	1904	Unknown
West, Lightfoot A. Unknown 18??–1942	A founder of National Hospital Association	#	Rust College #
Whitten, Charles F. DE 1922–	Chief, Pediatrics Department, Detroit Receiving Hospital, 1956–62 Associate dean, Wayne State Medical School, 1976–	1945	University of Pennsylvania 1942
Wright, Charles H. AL 1918–	Founder, African Medical Education Fund # Founder, Afro-American Museum of Detroit, Mich. #	1943	Alabama State College 1939

[1] In Pennsylvania.

[2] Also in Table 7 because a first African-American graduate of a U.S. medical school.

[3] In Missouri.

[4] Now Dillard.

Whereas a substantial number of the HUCM pioneers were born in the Northeast (11 in the District of Columbia and 6 in New York state), most of the Meharry pioneers were born in the South (6 in Tennessee, 5 in Louisiana, and 4 in Texas).

Similarly, while the HUCM pioneers tended to complete their premedical studies in the North (27 at Howard University in Washington, D.C., and 4 at Lincoln University in Pennsylvania), the Meharry pioneers were more apt to have attended undergraduate college in the South (6 at Fisk University in Tennessee and 3 at Morehouse College in Georgia).

Further details about places of birth and undergraduate colleges are provided in Tables 17 and 18 that appear in chapter 10. That chapter also includes statistical comparisons (in Table 16) of the 75 graduates of Howard, the 50 graduates of Meharry, and the 164 graduates of other medical (and graduate) schools.

9

Black Pioneer Graduates of Other Colleges

Following the patterns used in chapters 7 and 8 for describing the graduates of the Howard University College of Medicine and Meharry Medical College, this chapter provides detailed information about the 164 black pioneer graduates of 70 other medical (and graduate) schools.

Analysis of Table 14 reveals that 39 (24 percent) of the 164 are female. This is approximately twice the proportion of female pioneers who were identified from Howard (13 percent) and Meharry (12 percent).

In Table 14 below, note that names in boldface type are those individuals whose biographical sketches appear in chapter 4. The symbol (#) means date unknown.

Table 14—Black Pioneer Graduates of Medical or Graduate Schools Other Than Howard and Meharry

NAME BIRTHPLACE LIFE SPAN	MEDICAL SCHOOL AND YEAR	PIONEERING ACHIEVEMENTS AS AFRICAN AMERICANS	UNDERGRAD. COLLEGE AND YEAR
Adams, Numa P.G. VA 1885–1940	Rush 1924	Dean, Howard University College of Medicine, 1929–40	Howard University 1911
Adebonojo, Festus O. Nigeria 1931–	Yale 1960	Chair of Pediatrics, East Tennessee State University College of Medicine, 1988	Yale University 1956
Alcena, Valeria Haiti 1934–	Einstein 1973	Author of *The Status of Blacks in the U.S. of A.: A Prescription for Improvement,* 1992	Queens College 1970
Alexander, Joseph L. AL 1929–	Louisville 1955	Surgical chair, King-Drew University of Medicine and Science, 1971	Fisk University 1951
Alexander, Walter G. VA 1880–1953	Boston College 1903	Co-founder, *JNMA,* 1909 Founder, N.J. Medical Society, 1909 Founder, N.J. State Medical Association, 1939?	Lincoln University[1] #

Table 14, *continued*

NAME BIRTHPLACE LIFE SPAN	MEDICAL SCHOOL AND YEAR	PIONEERING ACHIEVEMENTS AS AFRICAN AMERICANS	UNDERGRAD. COLLEGE AND YEAR
Amos, Harold NJ 1919–	Harvard 1952 (Ph.D.)	Department chair, Harvard Medical School, 1979	Springfield College 1941
Augusta, Alexander T. VA 1825–1890	Trinity of Toronto 1856	Commissioned in U.S. Army, 1863 Medical school faculty (one of original five), HUCM, 1868 Head, Freedmen's Hospital # Applied (with Purvis and Tucker) to D.C. Medical Society, 1869—all rejected	None?
Ayer, Vernon A. Unknown 1891–	Harvard #	Certified, American Board of Preventive Medicine and Public Health, 1950	Unknown
Barnes, William H. PA 1887–1945	University of Pennsylvania 1912	Certified specialist (ENT), 1927 Founder, Society for Promotion of Negro Specialists in Medicine, 1931	Central High School of Philadelphia #
Barnett, Herman A.[2] TX 1926–1973	Galveston 1953	Surgical house staff in deep south (Galveston), 1953 Member, Texas State Board of Medical Examiners #	Huston-Tillotson College 1949
Bateman, Mildred M. GA 1922–	Medical College of Pa., 1946	Director, West Virginia Mental Hygiene Department, 1962	Johnson C. Smith University 1941
Blevins, George, Jr. IL 1949–	Arkansas 1990 (Ph.D.)	Ph.D., University of Arkansas College of Medicine, 1990	University of Arkansas, Pine Bluff 1986
Boone, John D. NY 1922–	Long Island 1946	Certified, American Board of Anesthesiology, 1955	Unknown
Bousfield, Midian O. MO 1885–1948	Northwestern 1909	Commander, army hospital in World War II #	University of Kansas 1907
Bowen, Clotilde D.[2] IL 1923–	Ohio State 1947	Woman lt. colonel in U.S. Army, 1965 Woman colonel in U.S. Army, 1968	Ohio State University 1943
Bristow, Lonnie R. NY 1930–	New York University 1957	Member, American Medical Association Board of Trustees #	Morehouse College 1953

Table 14, *continued*

Name Birthplace Life Span	Medical School and Year	Pioneering Achievements as African Americans	Undergrad. College and Year
Brooks, Roosevelt AL 1902–1985	University of Illinois 1930	Member, medical school faculty, University of Illinois, 1937	Unknown
Brown, Lucy H. NC 1863–1911	Medical College of Pennsylvania 1894	Founder, hospital and nurse training school, Charleston, S.C. #	Unknown
Brunson, Milton E. AR 1947–	Arkansas 1980	Completed obstetrics and gynecology residency, University of Arkansas Medical School, 1985	Philander Smith College and University of Arkansas, Little Rock #
Callis, Henry A. NY 1887–1974	Rush 1922	Diplomate, American Board of Internal Medicine, 1940	Cornell University 1909
Cardozo, William W. DC 1905–1962	Ohio State 1933	A founder, Alpha Omega Alpha (AOA), HUCM, 1955 Investigator of sickle cell anemia	Ohio State University 1929
Carson, Benjamin S. MI 1951–	Michigan 1977	Neurosurgery resident, Johns Hopkins, 1978–83 Director, Department of Pediatric Neurosurgery, Johns Hopkins, 1985–	Yale University 1973
Carson, Simeon L. NC 1882–1954	Michigan 1903	Founder, private hospital in Washington, D.C., 1919	University of Michigan 1903
Carter, Edward A. VA 1882–1958	Iowa State University 1907	Ranked first of 55 on state medical board examination #	Iowa State University 1903
Carty, Claudia T. NY 1950–	Johns Hopkins 1975	Female orthopaedic surgeon, 1982 Female member, American Academy of Orthopaedic Surgeons # Female orthopaedic faculty member, Johns Hopkins University School of Medicine #	Vassar College 1971
Chinn, Chester W. Unknown 1899–1978	University of Michigan 1925	Certified, American Board of Ophthalmology, 1934	Ivy League College?
Chinn, May E. MA 1896–1980	Bellevue 1926	Woman graduate, Bellevue Hospital Medical College, 1926 Intern, Harlem Hospital, 1926	Teachers College Columbia 1921

Table 14, *continued*

Name Birthplace Life Span	Medical School and Year	Pioneering Achievements as African Americans	Undergrad. College and Year
Cole, Rebecca J.[2] PA 1846–1992	Medical College of Pennsylvania 1867	Second woman M.D.	Institute for Colored Youth, 1963
Cornely, Paul B. French West Indies 1906–	University of Michigan 1931	Doctor of Public Health, 1934 President, Physicians Forum, 1961 President, American Public Health Association, 1969–70	University of Michigan 1928

Crawford, Alvin H.[2]
TN
1939–
	Tennessee
	1964
		Pediatric orthopaedic fellow, Boston
		   Children's (Harvard) Medical
		   Center, 1971
		Professor, orthopaedic surgery,
		   University of Cincinnatti College
		   of Medicine, 1981
		Editor, *Journal of Pediatric
		   Orthopaedics,* 1987
			Tennessee
			A&I College
			1960

Crumpler, Rebecca L.[2] Unknown 18??–19??	N.E. Female Medical College 1864	Graduate, N.E. Female Medical College, 1864 Woman M.D. in U.S.	Unknown
Curtis, Austin M., Sr. NC 1868–1939	Northwestern 1891	Intern, Chicago's Provident Hospital, 1891 Surgeon, Cook County Hospital, 1896 Chair, surgery, HUCM, 1928	Lincoln University[1] 1888

Dailey, Ulysses G.
LA
1885–1961
	Northwestern
	1906
		One of 4 members, American College
		   of Surgeons, 1942
		Cofounder (with Giles) and fellow
		   (with Stubbs), International College
		   of Surgeons, 1945
		Founder (with Hunter and Kenney),
		   John A. Andrew Clinical
		   Society, Tuskegee, Ala., 1918
			Dillard
			University
			1902?

Daly, Marie M. NY 1921–	Columbia 1948 (Ph.D.)	Woman Ph.D. in chemistry, 1948	Queens College 1942

Davis, Harvey F.
VA
1896–
	Boston
	1923
		Certified, American Board
		   of Physical Medicine
		   and Rehabilitation, 1947
			Howard
			University
			1918

Debas, Haile T. Ethiopia 1937–	McGill 1963	Chair of Surgery, UCSF Medical School, 1987 Dean, UCSF Medical School, 1993	University of Addis Ababa 1958

Table 14, *continued*

Name Birthplace Life Span	Medical School and Year	Pioneering Achievements as African Americans	Undergrad. College and Year

DeGrasse, John V.S.
NY
1825–1868
	Bowdoin
	1849
		Graduate, Bowdoin Medical College
		  and second U.S. M.D. (with
		  White) 1849
		Member, medical association
		  (Mass. Medical Society), 1854
			Oneida
			Institute, 1854
			and Aubruk
			College, Paris #

Derham, James[3] PA 1757–18??	None	Physician in U.S., 1780s (learned from other M.D.s)	None

Dickens, Helen O.
OH
1909–
	University
	of Illinois
	1934
		Woman admitted to American College
		  of Surgeons, 1950
		Associate dean, University of Pa.
		  Medical School, 1969
			University of
			Illinois
			1932

Donnell, Clyde NC 1890–1971	Harvard 1915	Founder, Durham (N.C.) Academy of Medicine, 1918	Howard University 1911
Dorsette, Cornelius N. NC 1852–1897	Buffalo 1882	Early graduate, University of Buffalo Medical School, 1882 Licensed in Alabama # Founder, Hale Infirmary, 1890	Hampton University 1878
Dove, Dennis B. BWI 1947–	Cincinnatti 1972	AAMC administrative assistant for minority student affairs, 1969–70	Queens College 1967
Drew, Charles R. DC 1904–1950	McGill 1933	Organizer, blood bank, 1940 Director, first American Red Cross Blood Bank, 1941	Amherst College 1926
Elam, Lloyd C.[2] AR 1928–	University of Washington, Seattle 1957	Head, psychiatry department (Meharry Medical College), 1960–67	Roosevelt University 1950

Elders, M. Joycelyn
AR
1933–
	Arkansas,
	1960
		Director, Arkansas State Health
		  Department #
		Full professor, University of Arkansas
		  Medical School, 1976
		Surgeon General of the U.S., 1993
			Philander
			Smith College
			1952

Ellis, Effie O. GA 1931–	Illinois 1950	Ohio State director of Maternal and Child Health #	Spelman College 1933
Ferebee, Dorothy B. VA 1898? –1980	Tufts 1927	Medical director, Miss. Health Project, 1934–41	Simmons College 1923

Table 14, *continued*

NAME BIRTHPLACE LIFE SPAN	MEDICAL SCHOOL AND YEAR	PIONEERING ACHIEVEMENTS AS AFRICAN AMERICANS	UNDERGRAD. COLLEGE AND YEAR
Fitzbutler, William H.[2] CAN 1842–1901	University of Michigan 1872	Founder, Louisville National Medical College, 1888	None?
Forde, Kenneth A. NY 1933–	Columbia 1959	President, Society of American Gastrointestinal Endoscopic Surgeons, 1983	City College of New York 1954
Foster, Henry AR 1933–	Arkansas 1958	Director, Maternal and Infant Care Project, Tuskegee, Ala., 1971 President, Association of Professors of Obstetrics and Gynecology, 1993	Morehouse College 1954
Franklin, Eleanor GA 1929–	University of Wisconsin 1957 (Ph.D.)	Woman administrative officer, HUCM, 1970	Spelman College 1948
Frederick, Rivers[2] LA 1873–1954	Illinois 1897	Chief surgeon, Flint-Goodridge Hospital of New Orleans, 1904–1953	Dillard University 1893
Fuller, Solomon C. Liberia 1872–1953	Boston University 1897	Psychiatrist in U.S., 1899 Faculty member, Boston University Medical School, 1899	Livingstone College 1895
Gauntlett, Hughenna L.[2] Costa Rica 1915–	Loma Linda 1951	Woman certified, American Board of Surgery, 1968 Fellow, American Board of Surgery, 1970	Atlanta Union College? 1946
Gilbert, Artishia G. KY 1869–19??	Louisville Nat., 1893	Woman M.D. in Kentucky #	Louisville State University 1892?
Giles, Roscoe C.[2] NY 1890–1970	Cornell 1915	Diplomate, American Board of Surgery, 1938 Removed "Col" (with Payne and Roberts) from AMA Directory, 1940 One of first, American College of Surgeons, 1945 Founding fellow (with Dailey), International College of Surgeons, 1945	Cornell University 1911
Green, Frederick C. IN 1920–	Indiana 1944	Director, Children's Bureau, U.S. Dept. of Health and Human Services # Special assistant to dean, George Washington University Medical School, 1975–	University of Indiana 1942

Table 14, *continued*

Name Birthplace Life Span	Medical School and Year	Pioneering Achievements as African Americans	Undergrad. College and Year
Hall, George C. MI 1864–1930	Bennett (Chicago) 1888	Founder (with Williams and Wesley) Provident Hospital, 1891 Founder, Cook County Physicians Association, 1918? Organizer, first postgraduate course, Provident, 1918	Lincoln University[1] 1886
Hall, James L., Sr. Unknown #	Medical College of Maine, 1822?	Physician in U.S., 1822? (unverified)	Unknown
Harris, Bernard A. TX 1956–	Texas Tech 1982	Male M.D. astronaut, 1990	University of Houston, 1978
Harris, Bobby J. TX 1936–	Nebraska 1962	Certified, colorectal surgery, 1971	Union College and University of Nebraska 1958
Harris, Jean L.[2] VA 1931–	Medical College of Virginia 1955	Member, Medical College of Virginia house staff, 1955–58 Director, MCV Department of Community Medicine, 1973–78	Virginia Union University 1951
Harris, Stanley I. NY 1944–	Einstein 1974	Project medical director, Montefiore Comprehensive Health Care Center, 1979 Assistant vice president, ambulatory care, NYC Health and Hospital Corp., 1987 Acting chief medical officer, N.J. Blue Cross/Blue Shield, 1990	Marist College 1968
Henderson, Donald FL 1946–	Florida, 1972	Executive producer, "Health is Wealth" #	Howard University 1967
Hilliard, Robert L.M., TX 1931–	Galveston 1956	President, Texas State Board of Medical Examiners, #	Howard University 1952
Hinson, Eugene T. PA 1873–1960	Pennsylvania 1898	Cofounder, Mercy Hospital (Philadelphia), 1907	Institute for Colored Youth, 1892
Hinton, William A. IL 1883–1959	Harvard 1912	Professor, Harvard Medical School, 1949–53 Author, medical text on syphilis, 1936	Harvard University 1905

Table 14, *continued*

NAME BIRTHPLACE LIFE SPAN	MEDICAL SCHOOL AND YEAR	PIONEERING ACHIEVEMENTS AS AFRICAN AMERICANS	UNDERGRAD. COLLEGE AND YEAR
Holloman, John L. DC 1919–	Michigan 1943	President, NYC Health and Hospital Corporation, 1974–77	Virginia Union University 1940
Holmes, Hamilton E [2] GA 1941–	Emory 1967	Medical director, Grady Memorial Hospital #	University of Georgia 1963
Hoover, Eddie L. NC 1944–	Duke 1969	Second graduate, Duke University School of Medicine, 1969 Chair, surgery, SUNY-Buffalo, 1990	University of North Carolina, Chapel Hill 1965
Hope, Justin M. DC 1912–	Pennsylvania 1934	Certified, American Board of Psychiatry and Neurology, 1943	Unknown
Hunter, John E. VA 1866–19??	Western Reserve 1889	Chair, surgical section, NMA, 1906 Cofounder (with Dailey and Kenney), John A. Andrew Clinical Society, Tuskegee, Ala., 1918	Oberlin College 1885
Hyde-Rowan, Maxine MS 1949–	Case Western 1977	Woman neurosurgeon, 1985	Tougaloo College 1970
Irby, Edith Mae[2] AR 1927–	Arkansas 1952	Woman president, NMA, 1986	Knoxville College 1947
Jackson, Algernon B.[2] IN 1878–1942	Jefferson 1901	Fellow, American College of Physicians,1917	Indiana University #
Jemison, Mae C. AL 1956–	Cornell 1981	Woman M.D. astronaut, 1987	Stanford University 1977
Jenkins, Melvin E. MO 1923–	Kansas 1946	Pediatric endocrinologist, 1965 Tenured faculty member, University of Nebraska College of Medicine, 1969 Vice chair, pediatrics, University of Nebraska College of Medicine, 1971–73 Member, governing board, American Board of Pediatrics, 1983–89	University of Kansas 1944

Table 14, *continued*

Name Birthplace Life Span	Medical School and Year	Pioneering Achievements as African Americans	Undergrad. College and Year
Jenkins, Renee R. PA 1947–	Wayne State 1971	President, Society of Adolescent Medicine, 1989–90	Wayne State University 1967
Johnson, John B., Jr. AL 1908–1972	Western Reserve 1935	Staff, Georgetown University Hospital (with R. F. Jones), 1954	Oberlin College 1931
Johnson, Joseph L. PA 1895–19??	University of Chicago 1931	Tied for second M.D./Ph.D. (with Maloney); from University of Chicago, 1931	Penn State University 1919

Jones, Edith M.I.[2] *(See Irby, Edith Mae)*

Name Birthplace Life Span	Medical School and Year	Pioneering Achievements as African Americans	Undergrad. College and Year
Jones, Thomas A. Guyana 1873–19??	Boston College of Physicians and Surgeons, 1903	Founded obstetrical school for blacks, Gonzales, Texas, 1904	Howard University 1900
Jones, Verina M. OH 1865-19??	Medical College of Pennsylvania 1888	Woman M.D. in Mississippi #	Columbia S.C. State Normal School #
Julian, Percy L. AL 1899–1975	University of Vienna 1931 (Ph.D.)	Founder, Julian Laboratories, 1954 Founder, Julian Research Institute, 1964	DePauw University 1920
Just, Ernest E. SC 1883–1941	University of Chicago 1916 (Ph.D.)	Scholar, Woods Hole Marine Biological Laboratory # Recipient, first Spingarn Medal, 1914 Vice president, American Society of Zoologists, 1930	Dartmouth College 1907
Kenney, John A. Sr. VA 1874–1950	Shaw University 1901	Suggester of *JNMA*, 1908 Cofounder (with Hunter and Dailey), John A. Andrew Clinical Society, Tuskegee, Ala., 1918	Hampton Normal and Ag. Institute, 1897
Kittrell, Flemmie P. NC 1904–1980	Cornell 1938 (Ph.D.)	Woman Ph.D. in nutrition,1938	Hampton University 1928
Kountz, Samuel P. AR 1930–1981	Arkansas 1958	Chair, Department of Surgery, SUNY-Brooklyn Medical Center, 1972 President, Society of University Surgeons, 1974–75	University of Arkansas, Pine Bluff 1952

Table 14, *continued*

NAME BIRTHPLACE LIFE SPAN	MEDICAL SCHOOL AND YEAR	PIONEERING ACHIEVEMENTS AS AFRICAN AMERICANS	UNDERGRAD. COLLEGE AND YEAR
Lattimer, Agnes[2] TN 1928–	Chicago Medical 1954	Woman administrator, major hospital (Cook County), 1984–	Fisk University 1949
Laurey, J. Richard IL 1907–1964	Wayne 1933	Certified, American Board of Thoracic Surgery (and founder), 1949	Wayne State University. 1929
Lawlah, John W. AL 1904–19??	Rush 1932	Simultaneously dean, HUCM, and director, Freedmen's Hospital, 1941–46	Morehouse College 1925
Lawless, Theodore K. LA 1894–1971	Northwestern 1919	Certified, American Board of Dermatology and Syphilology, 1935	Talladega College 1914
Lawrence, Leonard E. IN 1937–	Indiana 1962	Assistant and associate dean, student affairs, University of Texas, San Antonio, 1983–	Indiana University 1958
Lee, Arthur B., Jr. NY 1936–	Boston 1961	Chair, surgery, Morehouse School of Medicine, 1984	Clark University 1957
Lee, Rebecca *(see Crumpler)*			
Leevy, Carroll M. SC 1920–	Michigan 1944	Chair, medicine, predominantly white medical school (Seton Hall), 1966–68	Fisk University 1941
Lewis, Julian H. IL 1891–	Rush 1917	Ph.D. in physiology, University of Chicago (first M.D./Ph.D.), 1915	University of Illinois 1911
Lloyd, Ruth S. DC 1917–	Western Reserve 1941 (Ph.D.)	Woman Ph.D. in anatomy, 1941	Mt.Holyoke College 1937
Logan, Myra A. AL 1908–1977	N.Y. Medical 1933	Woman fellow, American College of Surgeons #	Atlanta University 1927
Long, Irene D. Unknown 1950	St. Louis 1977?	Woman certified in aerospace medicine, 1991	Northwestern University 1973?
Malone, Thomas E. NC 1926–	Harvard 1952 (Ph.D.)	Associate director for extramural research, NIH, 1972–1977 Deputy director, NIH, 1977–1986 Acting director, NIH, 1981–1982	N.C. Central University 1948

Entry continues

Table 14, *continued*

Name Birthplace Life Span	Medical School and Year	Pioneering Achievements as African Americans	Undergrad. College and Year

Malone, Thomas E.
continued
		Associate vice chancellor for research,
		  University of Maryland Graduate
		  School, Baltimore, 1986–1988
		Vice president, biomedical research,
		  Association of American Medical
		  Colleges, 1988–1993	

Maloney, Arnold H.
BWI
1888–1955
	Indiana
	1929
		Tied for second M.D./Ph.D. (with Johnson)
		  (Ph.D., University of Wisconsin, 1931)
		Professor of pharmacology in the U.S.,
		  HUCM, 1931–53
			Naparima
			College
			1909

Maultsby, Maxie C., Jr., FL 1932–	Western Reserve 1957	Author, books on rational behavioral therapy #	Talladega College 1953
Maynard, Aubre D. Guyana 1901–19??	NYU 1926	Professor of surgery, predominantly white medical school (Columbia), 1961	City College of New York 1922
McBroom, Fletcher P.R. MS 1926–	Columbia 1953	Intern, UCLA Medical Center, 1953	University of Chicago, 1946 and Columbia University 1949
McCarroll, E. Mae AL 1898–	Medical College of Pa., 1925	Staff member, Newark City Hospital, 1946 Deputy health officer, Newark, N.J., 1953	Talladega College 1917
McKinney, Roscoe L. DC 1900–1978	University of Chicago 1930 (Ph.D.)	Ph.D. in anatomy, 1930	Bates College 1921
McKinney, Susan S. NY 1847–1918	NY Med College and Hospital for Women, 1870	Woman M.D., N.Y. state, 1870 Cofounder, Brooklyn Women's Hospital, 1881	None?
Minton, Henry McK. SC 1870–1946	Jefferson 1906	Second superintendant, Philadelphia's Mercy Hospital, 1920–1944	Philadelphia College of Pharmacy 1895
Moore, Ruth E. OH? 1903–	Ohio State 1933 (Ph.D.)	Woman Ph.D. in bacteriology, 1933	Ohio State University 1926

Table 14, *continued*

NAME BIRTHPLACE LIFE SPAN	MEDICAL SCHOOL AND YEAR	PIONEERING ACHIEVEMENTS AS AFRICAN AMERICANS	UNDERGRAD. COLLEGE AND YEAR
Mosell, Nathan F [2] CA 1856–1946	University of Pennsylvania 1882	Member, Philadelphia Co. Medical Society, 1888 Founder, Frederick Douglass Memorial Hospital, 1895	Lincoln University[1] 1879
Myers, Woodrow A., Jr. IN 1954–	Harvard 1977	Indiana State Commissioner of Health #	Stanford University 1973
Nickens, Herbert W. DC 1947–	University of Pennsylvania 1973	Director, HHS Office of Minority Health, 1986–1988 Vice president, AAMC Division of Minority Health, Education, and Prevention, 1988–	Harvard University 1969
Organ, Claude H., Jr. TX 1928–	Creighton 1952	Chair, surgery, predominantly white medical school (Creighton), 1971–82 President, SW Surgical Congress, 1984–85 Chair, American Board of Surgery, 1984–86 Editor, *Archives of Surgery,* 1989– Member, surgical resident review committee, 1986–1992	Xavier University 1948
Payne, Clarence H. KY 1892–1965	University of Chicago 1920	One of three removed "Col" (with Giles and Roberts) from AMA Directory, 1940	None?
Peck, David J.[2] PA 1800s	Rush 1847	Graduate, American medical school, 1847	Unknown
Peebles-Myers, Helen[2] NY 1915–	Wayne State 1943	Woman house staff, Detroit Receiving Hospital, 1943–47 Chief medical officer for salaried personnel, Ford Motor Co., 1977–85	Hunter College 1937
Peters, Jesse J. IN 1895–	Indiana 1920	Certified, American Board of Radiology, 1937	Tuskegee University #
Pierce, Chester M. NY 1927–	Harvard 1952	Member, American Board of Psychiatry and Neurology, 1970	Harvard College 1948
Pinn, Vivian W. VA 1941–	University of Virginia 1967	Early woman graduate, UVMS, 1967 Assistant dean, student affairs, Tufts Medical School, 1974–82 Woman chair, HUCM Pathology Department, 1982–90	Wellesley College 1963

Entry continues

Table 14, *continued*

Name Birthplace Life Span	Medical School and Year	Pioneering Achievements as African Americans	Undergrad. College and Year
Pinn, Vivian W. *continued*		Second woman president, National Medical Association (NMA),1989 Director, NIH Office of Research on Women's Health, 1991	
Poindexter, Hildrus A. TN 1901–1987	Harvard 1929	M.D./Ph.D./M.P.H., bacteriology and public health, 1937 Surgical and medical director, U.S. Public Health Service, 1947–65	Lincoln University[1] 1924
Pouissant, Alvin F. NY 1934–	Cornell 1960	Associate dean of students, Harvard Medical School, 1969–	Columbia College 1956
Priest, Marlon L. AL 1952–	Alabama 1977	Assistant vice president for health affairs, University of Alabama, Birmingham, 1988–	Florence State University 1974
Prothrow-Stith, Deborah B. TX 1954	Harvard, 1979	Woman Mass. Commissioner of Public Health, 1987–89	Spelman College 1975
Purvis, Charles B.[2] PA 1842–1929	Western Reserve 1865	Second faculty member (at HUCM) of any U.S. medical school, 1869 In charge of civilian hospital (Freedmen's), 1882 Member, D.C. Board of Medical Examiners, 1897–1904 (and see Augusta re D.C. Medical Society application)	Oberlin College 1862
Redmond, Sidney D. MS 1871–1948	Illinois Medical College, 1897	Ranked first of 250 on state of Mississippi medical examination #	Rust College 1984
Reid, Clarice D. W. AL 1931–	Cincinnatti 1959	National coordinator, NIH Sickle Cell Anemia Program, 1976	Talladega College 1952
Remond, Sarah P. MA 1826–1894	Santa Maria Nuova Hospital, 1868	One of first women trained in a medical school and teaching hospital (Italy), 1866–68	Bedford College for Ladies, London, 1861
Roberts, Carl G. IN 1886–1950	Medical Department of Valparaiso University 1911	One of first 4, American College of Surgeons, 1945 Graduate, Medical Department of Valparaiso University, 1911 Removed "Col" (with Giles and Payne) from AMA Directory, 1940	Fairmont Academy 1905

Table 14, *continued*

NAME BIRTHPLACE LIFE SPAN	MEDICAL SCHOOL AND YEAR	PIONEERING ACHIEVEMENTS AS AFRICAN AMERICANS	UNDERGRAD. COLLEGE AND YEAR
Rock, John S. NJ 1825–1866	American. Medical College 1852 or 53	One of first to earn M.D. degree in U.S.	None?
Santomee, Lucas Unknown 1600s	Unknown	M.D. in U.S. # (degree from Holland)	Unknown
Satcher, David AL 1941–	Case Western 1970	Chair, family medicine, Morehouse School of Medicine # Director, U.S. Centers for Disease Control, 1993	Morehouse College 1963
Shockley, Dolores C. MS 1930–	Purdue 1955 (Ph.D.)	Woman Ph.D. in pharmacology in U.S., 1955	Louisiana State University, 1951
Smith, Alonzo de G. NJ 1890–1970	Long Island 1919	Fulltime medical school faculty clinician, 1932 Certified, American Board of Pediatrics, 1936	Howard University 1913
Smith, James McC. NY 1811–1865	Glasgow University 1837	American to receive M.D. degree, 1837	Glasgow University 1835
Sterling, Rosalyn NY? 1950–	NYU 1974	Woman certified, American Board Thoracic Surgery, 1986 Director, Surgical Intensive Care Unit, King-Drew #	Rensselaer Polytechnic 1970?
Steward, Susan S.M.[2]	*(See McKinney, Susan S.)*		
Stewart, Ferdinand A. AL 1862–19??	Harvard 1888	Chair, surgery, Meharry, 1908	Fisk University 1885
Stubbs, Frederick D. DE 1906–1947	Harvard 1931	One of first 4, American College of Surgeons, 1946 Member, Harvard Chapter, AOA# Intern, white teaching hospital (Cleveland City), 1931 Thoracic surgeon, 1938 Member, American Board of Surgeons, 1943 Staff member, Philadelphia General Hospital #	Dartmouth College 1927
Sullivan, Louis W. GA 1933–	Boston University 1958	House staff, Cornell, 1958–60 Fellow, Thorndike Laboratory, 1961 President, Morehouse School of Medicine, 1981	Morehouse College 1954

Entry continues

Table 14, *continued*

NAME BIRTHPLACE LIFE SPAN	MEDICAL SCHOOL AND YEAR	PIONEERING ACHIEVEMENTS AS AFRICAN AMERICANS	UNDERGRAD. COLLEGE AND YEAR
Sullivan, Louis W. *continued*		Secretary, U.S. Department of Health and Human Services, 1989–93 President, Association of Minority Health Professional Schools #	
Thomas, James H. KY 1941–	Kentucky 1966	Professor, surgery, and chief, vascular surgery, KY # Program director, University of Kansas, 1979?	Morehead State University 1962
Thomas, Vivien T. LA 1910–1985	No M.D. Honorary LL.D., Hopkins 1976	Laboratory assistant to Alfred Blalock, M.D., Vanderbilt and Johns Hopkins College of Medicine, 1930–1972 Codeveloper, "blue baby" operation, 1944 Instructor in surgery, Johns Hopkins College of Medicine, 1977–79	None
Townsend, John L. OK 1932–	Oklahoma 1959?	Founder, Association for Academic Minority Physicians, 1976	Fisk University 1955
Tucker, Alpheus W. Unknown 18??–	Unknown	One of 3 presented to D.C. Medical Society, 1869 *(see Augusta and Purvis)*	Unknown
Tuckson, Reed DC 1951–	Georgetown 1978	Vice president, March of Dimes #	Howard University 1973
Turner, Deborah Ann IA 1950–	Iowa 1978	Woman certified gynecological oncologist in U.S., 1985	Iowa State University 1973
Turner, John P. NC 1885–1958	Shaw, 1906	Founder and president, Pa. State Medical, Dental, and Pharmacy Association, 1921 Police surgeon, Philadelphia, 1931–41	City College of New York 1903
Venable, Howard P. Canada 1913–	Wayne State 1939	Examiner, American Board of Ophthalmology, 1959	Wayne State University 1939
Vincent, Ubert C. NC 1892–1938	University of Pennsylvania 1918	Intern, major American hospital (Bellevue), 1918?	Shaw University 1914
Walker, Bailus, Jr. TN 1932–	Minnesota 1975	Commissioner of public health and chair, Mass. Public Health Council, 1983–87 Director, Mich. Department of Public Health, 1981–83	University of Kentucky 1971?

Table 14, *continued*

NAME BIRTHPLACE LIFE SPAN	MEDICAL SCHOOL AND YEAR	PIONEERING ACHIEVEMENTS AS AFRICAN AMERICANS	UNDERGRAD. COLLEGE AND YEAR
Ward, Joseph H. IN 1870–1956	Indiana Medical College #	Head, veterans hospital (Tuskegee), 1924–36	Unknown
Watkins, Levi, Jr.[2] KS 1945–	Vanderbilt 1970	Chief resident, surgery, Johns Hopkins, 1970–78 Assistant dean, Johns Hopkins, 1991	Tennessee State University 1966
Wesley, Allen A. IN 1856–19??	Northwestern 1887	Founder (with Hall and Williams) Provident Hospital, Chicago, 1891	Fisk University 1884
West, Harold D. NJ 1904–1974	University of Illinois 1937 (Ph.D.)	President, Meharry Medical College, 1952–66	University of Illinois 1925
Wheeler, Albert H. MO 1915–	University of Michigan 1944 (Ph.D.)	Fulltime professor, University of Michigan Medical School, 1952–59	Lincoln University[1] 1936
White, Augustus A.,[2] III TN 1936–	Stanford 1961	Surgical resident, Presbyterian Medical Center, 1962 Orthopaedic resident, Yale Medical School, 1963 Faculty member, Department of Surgery, Yale Medical School, 1969 President, Cervical Spine Research Society, 1978 Professor, Orthopaedic Surgery, Harvard Medical School, 1978	Brown University 1957
White, Thomas J. NY 1800s	Bowdoin 1849	Graduate, Bowdoin Medical College and second U.S. M.D. (with DeGrasse), 1849	None?
Wilkerson, Vernon A. MO 1901–1968	University of Iowa 1925	Ph.D. in biochemistry, University of Minnesota, 1932	University of Kansas 1921
Wilkinson, William H. MA 1944–	Einstein 1978	Chief (acting), Department of Ambulatory Care Services and director of Medical Clinics, Kings County Hospital Center, 1991 Chief, Section on Ambulatory Care, Department of Medicine, SUNY Health Science Center at Brooklyn, 1991	University of Massachusetts Amherst 1965

Table 14, *continued*

NAME BIRTHPLACE LIFE SPAN	MEDICAL SCHOOL AND YEAR	PIONEERING ACHIEVEMENTS AS AFRICAN AMERICANS	UNDERGRAD. COLLEGE AND YEAR
Williams, Alonzo D. AR 1951–	Arkansas 1979	Member, Arkansas State Medical 　　Board, 1985	Arkansas State University 1974
Williams, Daniel H. PA 1856–1931	Northwestern 1883	Founder (with Hall and Wesley), 　　Provident Hospital, 1891 Founder and vice president, NMA, 1895 Charter member (and fellow), American 　　College of Surgeons, 1913	Hare's Classical Academy 1877
Williams, John F. NY 1948–	George Washington 1979	Assistant dean, admissions, and chair, 　　admissions committee, George 　　Washington University, 1987	Boston University 1975
Wilson, Donald E. MA 1936–	Tufts 1962	Dean, predominantly white medical 　　school (University of Maryland), 　　1991	Harvard University 1958
Wright, Clarence W. GA 1912–1968	Ohio State 1965 (Ph.D.)	Ph.D. in anatomy, Ohio State, 1965	Wilberforce University 1932
Wright, Jane C. NY 1919–	NY Medical 1945	Associate dean, N.Y. Medical College, 　　1967 Member, Presidential Commission on 　　Heart Disease, Cancer, and 　　Stroke, 1964– Vice president, African Research 　　Foundation #	Smith College 1942
Wright, Louis T. GA 1891–1952	Harvard 1915	One of first graduates, Harvard 　　Medical School, 1915 Police surgeon, NYC, 1929 Second member, American College 　　of Surgeons, 1934 Founder, Harlem Surgical Society, 1937 Honorary fellow, International College 　　of Surgeons, 1950	Clark College 1911
Yancey, Asa G., Sr. GA 1916–	University of Michigan 1941	Member, So. Surgical Association, 1985 Associate dean, Emory Medical 　　School, 1972–89	Morehouse College 1937

---

[1] In Pennsylvania.

[2] Also in Table 7 because a first African-American graduate of a U.S. medical school.

[3] Also spelled Durham.

The earliest dates of birth for these pioneering graduates of medical schools other than Howard and Meharry are in the 1600s for Lucas Santomee and in 1754 for James Derham. The latest birth dates are 1956 for Bernard Harris and Mae Jemison. This span of birth dates is much wider than that for the pioneers from Howard, which ranged from 1865 to 1939, and from Meharry, which ranged from 1851 to 1948.

The earliest pioneers to graduate from medical schools other than Howard and Meharry were Lucas Santomee, who earned his M.D. on an unknown date from a medical school in Holland, and James Smith, who received his degree in 1857 from the University of Glasgow. The earliest documented pioneer graduates of medical schools in the United States were David Peck, who graduated from Rush in 1847, and Rebecca Lee Crumpler, who graduated in 1864 from the New England Female College, which later became the Boston University College of Medicine.

The most recent pioneer graduates of other medical schools are Mae Jemison, who earned her M.D. from Cornell University College of Medicine in 1981, and Bernard Harris, who completed Texas Tech Medical School in 1982. Both of them have the distinction of being the first African-American physicians to become astronauts, Jemison in 1987 and Harris in 1990.

As noted in previous chapters, the pioneer graduates of Howard tended to have been born in the north and those of Meharry to have been born in the south. In contrast, the 164 pioneer graduates of other schools were born in almost all of the U.S. states, districts, and territories and in eight foreign countries. Twenty were born in New York, 12 in Alabama, 10 each in North Carolina and Virginia, 9 in Pennsylvania, and 8 each in the District of Columbia, Georgia, and Indiana.

Similarly, while the Howard pioneers tended to have attended undergraduate college in the north and the Meharry pioneers to have done their premedical studies in the south, the pioneering graduates of the other medical and graduate schools attended undergraduate colleges throughout the United States and in six foreign countries. Eight of these graduates completed their premedical studies at Howard University, 6 each at Lincoln University in Pennsylvania and Morehouse College, 5 at Fisk University, 4 each at Harvard University and Talladega College, and 3 each at City College of New York, Oberlin College, Ohio State University, Queens College, Spelman College, the universities of Illinois and Kansas, and Wayne State University. Of these 14 major providers of undergraduate education, five (Fisk, Lincoln, Morehouse, Spelman, and Talladega) are historically black institutions.

Table 15 summarizes the 70 different medical and graduate schools attended by the 164 pioneers from institutions other than Howard and Meharry. The most frequently attended school was Harvard, with 12 graduates. Other schools providing a substantial number of African-American pioneers included the University of Michigan (9), University of Arkansas (7), Case Western Reserve University (7), Northwestern University (6), University of Pennsylvania (6), University of Illinois (5), Medical College of Pennsylvania (5), and Rush Medical College (5).

Table 15—Medical or Graduate Schools Attended by Black Medical Pioneers from Institutions Other Than Howard and Meharry

MEDICAL SCHOOL	YEAR ESTABLISHED	NUMBER OF GRADUATES
Existing U.S. Schools		
Alabama	1859	1
Albert Einstein	1955	3
Arkansas	1879	7
Boston University	1873	4
Case Western	1843	7
Chicago Medical	1912	1
Chicago-Pritzker	1924	4
Cincinnatti	1819	2
Columbia	1767	3
Cornell	1898	4
Creighton	1892	1
Duke	1925	1
Emory	1854	1
Florida	1956	1
Georgetown	1851	1
George Washington	1825	1
Harvard	1782	12
Illinois, University of	1881	5
Indiana	1903	4
Iowa	1869	3
Jefferson	1825	2
Johns Hopkins	1893	1
Kansas	1905	1
Loma Linda	1909	1
Louisville	1837	1
Michigan, University of	1850	9
Minnesota	1883	1
Nebraska	1881	1
New York Medical	1858	3
New York University	1841	3
Northwestern	1859	6
Ohio State	1907	4

Table 15, *continued*

Medical School	Year Established	Number of Graduates	
Oklahoma	1900	1	
Pennsylvania, Medical College of	1850	5	
Pennsylvania, University of	1765	6	
Rush	1837	5	
Saint Louis	1901	1	
Stanford	1908	1	
SUNY-Buffalo	1846	1	
Tennessee	1851	1	
Texas Tech	1969	1	
Texas, University of (Galveston)	1890	2	
Tufts	1893	2	
Vanderbilt	1874	1	
Virginia, Medical College of	1938	1	
Virginia, University of	1827	1	
Washington, University of (Seattle)	1945	1	
Wayne State	1885	4	
Wisconsin, University of	1907	1	
Yale	1812	1	
		Subtotal: 136	(85 percent of known schools)

Other Medical or Graduate Schools

American Medical College	1	
Bellevue	1	
Bennett	1	
Boston College	2	
Bowdoin	2	
Glasgow	1	
Illinois Medical College	1	
Indiana Medical College	1	
Long Island College Hospital	2	
Louisville National Medical College	1	
Maine	1	
McGill	2	
New England Female Medical College	1	
New York Medical College for Women	1	
Purdue	1	
Santa Maria Nuova Hospital	1	
Shaw University	2	
Trinity of Toronto	1	
Valparaiso University Medical Department	1	
Vienna	1	
Subtotal:	25	(15% of known schools)
Total known	161	(100% of known schools)
No medical school	2	
School unknown	1	
Total:	164	

10

Comparison of Pioneer Graduates of Howard, Meharry, and Other Schools

Although a few comparisons of the pioneering graduates of Howard, Meharry, and other medical schools have already been noted in chapters 8 and 9, this chapter provides complete comparisons of the major characteristics of the 75 pioneers from Howard, the 50 from Meharry, the 164 from other schools, totalling 289 African-American medical pioneers.

Table 16 displays comparative information concerning several key characteristics of these three subgroups and of the total group. For example, the data indicate that 81 percent of these 289 individuals were male, with the proportion of females varying from a low of 12 percent of the Meharry graduates through 13 percent of the Howard graduates to a high of 24 percent of the graduates of the other medical schools

Table 16—Comparative Information about Graduates of Howard, Meharry, and Other Medical or Graduate Schools

VARIABLE	HOWARD		MEHARRY		OTHER		TOTAL	
	No.	(%)	No.	(%)	No.	(%)	No.	(%)
A. Gender								
Male	65	(87)	44	(88)	125	(76)	234	(81)
Female	10	(13)	6	(12)	39	(24)	55	(19)
Total:	75	(100)	50	(100)	164[1]	(100)	289	(100)
B. Nature of pioneering achievements as African Americans								
Medical education (E) only	20	(27)	8	(16)	56	(34)	84	(29)
Organized medicine (O) only	17	(23)	17	(34)	28	(17)	62	(21)
Related activities (R) only	16	(24)	9	(18)	40	(24)	65	(22)
E and O	13	(17)	7	(14)	10	(6)	30	(10)
E and R	2	(3)	7	(14)	13	(8)	22	(8)
O and R	5	(7)	2	(4)	7	(4)	14	(5)
E, O, and R	2	(3)	0	(0)	10	(6)	12	(4)
Total:	75	(101)	50	(100)	164	(99)	289	(100)
C. Medical education "firsts" at alma mater	16	(21)	8	(16)	13	(8)	37	(13)

Table 16, *continued*

VARIABLE		HOWARD		MEHARRY		OTHER		TOTAL	
		No.	(%)	No.	(%)	No.	(%)	No.	(%)
D. Birthplace									
U.S. states and territories		26	(87)	21	(88)	27	(77)	34	(76)
Foreign countries		4	(13)	3	(13)	8	(23)	11	(24)
	Total:	30	(100)	24	(101)	35	(100)	45	(100)
E. Different undergraduate colleges									
United States		34	(100)	30	(94)	80	(89)	103	(90)
Foreign (or no college)		0	(0)	2	(6)	10	(11)	12	(10)
	Total:	34	(100)	32	(100)	90	(100)	115	(100)
F. Items in chronological tables[2]									
Medical education		20	(31)	8	(32)	49	(43)	77	(38)
Organized medicine		28	(43)	11	(44)	36	(32)	75	(37)
Related activities		17	(26)	6	(24)	27	(24)	50	(25)
	Total:	65	(100)	25	(100)	112	(99)	202	(100)

---

[1] These 164 individuals attended 70 different professional schools, 50 of them currently existing U.S. schools and 20 other medical (or graduate) schools.

[2] There are 78 items in the Medical Education table (Table 2) because its first entry is for a physician who attended no medical school. Conversely, there are only 49 different items in the Related Activities table (Table 4), but the 1964 entry is counted twice because it includes individuals from two different categories of medical school.

Twenty-nine percent of the 289 individuals did their pioneering in "medical education" only, 21 percent in "organized medicine" only, and 22 percent solely in activities closely related to medical education and organized medicine. The "other school" graduates had the highest percentage (34 percent) of pioneers in medical education only and the Meharry graduates had the highest percentage (34 percent) in organized medicine only. Twelve individuals were pioneers in all three categories, two of them (Drs. Cobb and Spurlock) having graduated from Howard and the remaining 10 (including Drs. Organ, Pinn, and Sullivan) from predominantly white medical schools. The Howard graduates had the largest proportion (43 percent) who experienced their medical education "firsts" at their alma mater.

The 289 pioneers in Table 16 were born in 45 different states, territories, and countries and attended 115 different undergraduate colleges, 103 of them in the United States.

Birthplaces by state and country are detailed in Table 17, and undergraduate colleges are listed in Table 18.

Of the 202 items selected to illustrate the chronological history of this pioneering, 38 percent are in the area of medical education, 37 percent in organized medicine, and the remaining 25 percent in related activities (Table 16). The historical items selected for the Howard and Meharry graduates tend to emphasize organized medicine while those for the "other" schools are more in the area of medical education. For specific historical milestones, see tables 2, 3, and 4 in chapter three.

Table 17—Birthplace of African-American Pioneer Graduates of Howard, Meharry, and Other Medical or Graduate Schools

BIRTHPLACE	ABBREV.	HOWARD	MEHARRY	OTHER	TOTAL
United States					
Alabama	AL	1	1	12	14
Arkansas	AR	2	1	7	10
California	CA			1	1
Connecticut	CT	1			1
Delaware	DE		1	1	2
District of Columbia	DC	11	2	8	21
Florida	FL	4	1	2	7
Georgia	GA	6	2	8	16
Illinois	IL	3	1	5	9
Indiana	IN	2		8	10
Iowa	IA			1	1
Kansas	KS			1	1
Kentucky	KY	1		2	3
Louisiana	LA	3	5	4	12
Maryland	MD	2	2		4
Massachusetts	MA	3		4	7
Michigan	MI			2	2
Mississippi	MS	1	3	4	8
Missouri	MO		2	4	6
New Jersey	NJ	1	1	4	6
New York	NY	6	1	20	27
North Carolina	NC	2	2	10	14
Ohio	OH	1		3	4
Oklahoma	OK			1	1
Pennsylvania	PA	2	2	9	13
Puerto Rico	PR	1			1
South Carolina	SC	3	1	3	7
Tennessee	TN	2	6	5	13
Texas	TX	2	4	6	12
Virginia	VA	3	2	10	15
Virgin Islands	VI		1		1
Washington	WA	1			1
West Virginia	WV	3	1		4
Wyoming	WY	1	0	0	1
Subtotal U.S		68	42	145	255

Table 17, *continued*

BIRTHPLACE	ABBREV.	HOWARD	MEHARRY	OTHER	TOTAL
Foreign					
British West Indies	BWI	5	2	2	9
Canada	CAN			2	2
Costa Rica	COS			1	1
Ethiopia	ETH			1	1
French West Indies	FWI			1	1
Ghana	GHA		1		1
Guyana	GUY			2	2
Haiti	HAI			1	1
Liberia	LIB			1	1
Nigeria	NIG	1		1	2
Panama	PAN	1	0	0	1
Subtotal foreign		7	3	12	22
Total known birthplaces		75	45	158	277
Birthplaces now unknown		0	5	7	12
Total:		75	50	163	289

Table 18—Undergraduate Colleges of African-American Pioneer Graduates of Howard, Meharry, and Other Medical or Graduate Schools

		NUMBER OF GRADUATES FROM SPECIFIED SCHOOLS			
UNDERGRADUATE COLLEGE[1]	STATE	HOWARD	MEHARRY	OTHER	TOTAL
United States Colleges					
Alabama State College	AL		1		1
Amherst College	MA	1		1	2
Arkansas State University	AR			1	1
Atlanta Union College	MA			1	1
Atlanta University	GA	1		1	2
Bates College	ME	1		1	2
Bennett College	NC		1		1
Bishop College	TX		2		2
Boston University	MA			1	1
Brown University	RI			1	1
Catholic University	DC	1			1
Central Tennessee College[2]	TN		2		2
City College of New York (CCNY)	NY	3		3	6
Clark College	GA	1		1	2
Clark University	MA			1	1
Columbia College	NY			1	1
Columbia University[2]	NY	2		1	3

Table 18, *continued*

Undergraduate College[1]	State	Howard	Meharry	Other	Total
Cornell University	NY			2	2
Dartmouth College	NH	1		2	3
DePauw University	IN			1	1
Dillard University	LA	2	1	2	5
Fisk University[2]	TN		6	5	11
Florence State University				1	1
Florida A&M University	FL	2	1		3
Hamilton College	NY		1		1
Hampton University	VA		2	3	5
Harvard University	MA	1	1	4	6
Howard University	DC	27	3	8	38
Hunter College	NY	1	2	1	4
Huston-Tillotson College	TX			1	1
Indiana University	IN	1		2	3
Iowa State University	IA			2	2
Johnson C. Smith University	NC	1	2	1	4
Knoxville College	TN	1		1	2
Lincoln University[2]	MO		1		1
Lincoln University[2]	PA	4	3	6	13
Livingston College	NC			1	1
Long Island University	NY		1		1
Louisiana State University	LA			1	1
Louisville State University	KY	1		1	2
Marist College	NY			1	1
Morehead State University	KY			1	1
Morehouse College[2]	GA	2	3	6	11
Morgan State University	MD	1			1
Mount Holyoke College	MA			1	1
New Orleans University	LA		1		1
New York University	NY	2			2
North Carolina Central University	NC			1	1
Northwestern University	IL	1		1	2
Oberlin College	OH	1		3	4
Ohio State University	OH			3	3
Oneida Institute[2]	NY			1	1
Oskaloosa College	??		1		1
Pennsylvania State University	PA	1		1	2
Philadelphia College of Pharmacy	PA			1	1
Philander Smith College[2]	AR	1		2	3
Queens College	NY	1		3	4

Table 18, *continued*

UNDERGRADUATE COLLEGE[1]	STATE	HOWARD	MEHARRY	OTHER	TOTAL
Rensselaer Polytechnic Institute	NY			1	1
Richmond Normal School	VA	1			1
Roosevelt University	IL	1		1	2
Rust College	MS		1	1	2
Shaw University	NC	1		1	2
Simmons College	MA			1	1
Smith College	MA			1	1
Spelman College	GA		1	3	4
Springfield College	MA			1	1
Stanford University	CA			2	2
State Normal School, Columbia	SC			1	1
Storer College	WV?	1			1
Talladega College	AL	1		4	5
Teachers C, Columbia	NY			1	1
Temple University	PA	1			1
Tennessee A & I College	TN			1	1
Tennessee State University[2]	TN		1	1	2
Texas Southern University	TX		1		1
Tougaloo College	MS			1	1
Tuskegee University	AL	1		1	2
Union College[2]	NY			1	1
University of Arizona	AZ	1			1
University of Arkansas at Pine Bluff	AR			2	2
University of Chicago[2]	IL	1		1	2
University of Cincinnatti College of Pharmacy	OH		1		1
University of Georgia	GA			1	1
University of Houston	TX			1	1
University of Illinois	IL			3	3
University of Indiana	IN			1	1
University of Kansas	KS			3	3
University of Kentucky	KY			1	
University of Massachusetts, Amherst	MA			1	1
University of Michigan	MI			2	2
University of Nebraska[2]	NE			1	1
University of North Carolina at Chapel Hill	NC			1	1
University of Pennsylvania	PA	2	2		4
Vassar College	NY			1	1
Virginia State College	VA	1	2		3
Virginia Union University	VA			2	2
Walden University	TN?		2		2
Wayne State University	MI			3	3
Wellesley College	MA			1	1
Wilberforce University	OH			1	1
Wiley College	TX		1		1

Table 18, *continued*

UNDERGRADUATE COLLEGE[1]	STATE	HOWARD	MEHARRY	OTHER	TOTAL
Xavier University of Louisiana	LA		1	1	2
Yale University	CT			1	1
Subtotal, U.S. colleges (total = 81 percent)		74	48	135	257

Foreign or No College

Aubruk College[2]	France			1	1
Bedford College for Ladies	London			1	1
Berkeley Inst. of Bermuda	Bermuda		1		1
Central H.S. of Philadelphia	PA			1	1
Fairmont Academy	IN?			1	1
Glasgow University	Scotland			1	1
Hamilton Collegiate Institute	Canada		1		1
Hare's Classical Academy	PA?			1	1
Institute for Colored Youth	PA			2	2
Ivy League College?	??			1	1
Naparima College	??			1	1
University of Addis Ababa	Ethiopia			1	1
No College	N/A	1	1	9	11
Subtotal, foreign or no college (total = 9 percent)		1	3	20	24
Total with known college information (total = 100 percent)		75	51	155	281
College information currently unknown		0	4	11	15
Total:		75	55	166	296

---

[1] A total of seven attended more than one college.

[2] Indicates that one or more of these graduates also attended other undergraduate colleges.

PART IV

CHALLENGES FOR
THE FUTURE

This final chapter consists of a brief summary of the major findings of the study and specific recommendations for meeting future challenges. These challenges include preparing more African Americans and individuals from other minority groups to apply to medical school, and encouraging them to consider careers in academic medicine and seek leadership roles in organized medicine.

11

Summary and Recommendations

Summary

Through extensive research in approximately 20 major sources, the study identified a total of 556 African-American pioneers in academic and organized medicine. Of these, 290 are the first African-American graduates of the 126 existing U.S. medical schools, and a total of 289 achieved other "firsts" in academic and organized medicine. Of the 289 pioneers, 75 are graduates of Howard University College of Medicine (HUCM), 50 of Meharry Medical College, and the remaining 164 of other medical or graduate schools.

A significant number (23) of the pioneering medical school graduates also became medical pioneers elsewhere. For example, Lloyd Elam, the first African-American graduate of the University of Washington (Seattle) School of Medicine, later became the first African-American chairperson of the department of psychiatry at Meharry Medical College. Similarly, Edith Irby Jones is not only the first African-American graduate of the University of Arkansas School of Medicine, but also the first female African-American president of the National Medical Association. Likewise, Levi Watkins, Jr., is both the first African-American graduate of Vanderbilt School of Medicine and the first African-American assistant dean at the Johns Hopkins University School of Medicine.

Although 96 percent of U.S. medical schools had at least one African-American graduate by the early 1990s, the median number of years from when these schools were organized to when they graduated their first African American was 27 years (19 years for the 145 males and 47 years for the 145 females).

The 290 first African-American graduates were born in 39 different states and attended 162 different undergraduate colleges. The states producing the largest number of these pioneers are New York (28), Texas (23), California (17), Ohio (16), Pennsylvania (16), Georgia (12), North Carolina (12), and Florida (11). Among the undergraduate colleges producing the largest number were Howard University (16), Morehouse College (6), Fisk University (4), Hunter College (4), Michigan State University (4), Ohio State University (4), Spelman College (4), Tennessee State University (4), and the University of Missouri at Kansas City (4).

Of the 289 pioneering graduates of Howard, Meharry, and other schools, a substantial proportion were pioneers in two or more categories. Fifty-one percent are pioneers in academic medicine, as faculty members and deans, for example; 40 percent are in organized medicine, such as presidents of medical societies; and 39 percent are in closely related activities, for example, as secretary of the U.S. Department of Health and Human Services. A total of 81 percent are male and 19 percent female.

The 289 medical pioneers came from 45 different states, territories, or countries. The largest number were born in New York (27), the District of Columbia (21), Georgia (16), Virginia (15), Alabama (14), and North Carolina (14). They attended 115 different undergraduate colleges, primarily Howard University (33), Lincoln University in Pennsylvania (13), Fisk University (11), and Morehouse College (11).

Regarding the medical colleges or graduate schools attended by the 164 pioneers from institutions other than Howard and Meharry, the major producers were Harvard University (12), the University of Arkansas (7), Northwestern University (6), the University of Pennsylvania (6), the University of Illinois (5), the Medical College of Pennsylvania (5), and Rush Medical College (5).

Research about the medical education of African Americans in the United States revealed that from 1868 to 1993 there existed a total of 15 predominantly black medical schools. When the Flexner Report was released in 1910, it recommended that a large number of all medical schools in the United States be closed. Of the eight racially black schools then in existence, only Howard and Meharry were encouraged to remain open. Subsequently, two other predominantly black medical schools, the Charles R. Drew University of Medicine and Science and the Morehouse School of Medicine, were opened in 1966 and 1978 respectively.

Of the 202 selected historical milestones highlighted in chapter 2, 38 percent of the selected milestones are in academic medicine, 37 percent in organized medicine, and 25 percent in related activities. These milestones span more than 300 years, extending from the 1780s, when James Derham was the first African American to practice medicine in the United States, to 1993, when Joycelyn Elders became the first African-American surgeon general of the United States.

All but three of the 33 biographical sketches in this book are based on lengthy interviews, while those for Claude Organ, and deceased pioneers W. Montague Cobb and Charles R. Drew, are derived from printed material. Twenty-one of the sketches are of males and 12 of females. An analysis of these sketches reveals that although most of the 33 individuals encountered significant racial and financial obstacles, they were able to overcome them by positive attitudes and hard work. Along the way, they also acknowledged having received substantial help from both blacks and whites.

Many of these 33 individuals contributed significantly to the advancement of racial harmony. They did this not only by personal example, but also by participating actively in integrated churches and similar organizations, serving on school desegregation committees, and encouraging their students to treat everyone with dignity and respect.

Data derived from the index of specialties shows that the 289 African-American pioneer graduates of Howard, Meharry, and other medical schools have been active in 39 different specialties ranging from aerospace medicine to zoology. The most popular of the medical specialties have been surgery (the specialty of 67, or 23 percent, of these 289 pioneers), internal medicine (32, or 11 percent), pediatrics (20, or 7 percent), public health (20, or 7 percent), obstetrics and gynecology (19, or 7 percent), and psychiatry (16, or 6 percent).

Recommendations

Challenging our society is the need to enable more youth from minority groups, especially African Americans, to be admitted to and graduated from medical school, to serve as role models in academic medicine, and to become leaders in organized medicine. If enough individuals heed the recommendations given here, it should increase the likelihood of meeting the Association of American Medical Colleges' challenge of admitting 3,000 minority medical students annually by the year 2000. Finally, the more minority group leaders we can attract to academic and organized medicine, the better the chances are that the United States can meet the national challenge of carrying out a movement toward health care reform that will meet the needs of all of our citizens, especially those from the largely underserved minority groups.

Several sources were consulted for the recommendations given here. First is the landmark article, "Predicting Minority Students' Success in Medical School" (Sedlacek and Prieto, 1990), that emphasized the importance of considering noncognitive variables in the admission of minority applicants. The eight noncognitive characteristics they emphasize are: 1) positive self-concept or confidence, 2) realistic self-appraisal, 3) understanding and dealing with racism, 4) preference for long-range over short-term or immediate goals, 5) availability of a strong support person, 6) successful leadership experience, 7) demonstrated community service, and 8) knowledge acquired in a given field.

The second source is an article entitled "Academic Medicine Shapes the Future" (Whiting, 1992), written by the African-American director of the faculty roster system of the Association of American Medical Colleges. Her article points out that salaries in academic medicine are now generally competitive with those in medical practice, that teaching and the academic environment are intrinsically rewarding, and that medical teachers can significantly influence the next generation of physicians.

Dr. Whiting also offers a number of practical suggestions to minority students considering careers in academic medicine. These include: 1) developing an area of interest in which you can become an expert, 2) obtaining research-related experience, 3) learning strong statistical and computer skills, 4) associating with a productive researcher and joining professional associations in your field of interest, 5) practicing good time management techniques, and 6) being open to criticism.

Our own research, particularly that based on the 33 biographical sketches, confirms the importance of the recommendations in these two articles. If a minority student wishes to become a physician, he or she will do well to develop as many as possible of the eight noncognitive attributes cited by Sedlacek and Prieto. Similarly, if a minority student is considering a career in academic medicine, he or she can profit from Whiting's six suggestions.

In addition to endorsing the above recommendations, we strongly encourage individual students and groups to consider the following:

1. African-American medical pioneers should consciously serve as role models and mentors to younger colleagues and to students.

2. Parents and teachers of African-American children should become aware, through this and similar publications, of the achievements of their African-American predecessors.

3. African-American premedical students and their advisors should become aware of those institutions (see Table 18) that have produced the largest number of African-American medical pioneers. They should also recognize, to their benefit, that the academic doors are open much wider today than during the times when most of the pioneers listed here obtained their education.

4. African-American medical students should become aware, through

reading the 33 biographical sketches in chapter 4 and their summary in chapter 5, of the many types of opportunities that have been and are still available in the fields of academic and organized medicine. Because of the understandable finding that almost all of the pioneers in this study were board certified, current students should also aim for eventual certification in a specialty, including those in the primary care area.

5. African-American physicians should be aware of the satisfactions to be derived from careers in academic medicine, and also the impact they can have on our society by becoming active in organized medicine. They should also provide maximum support and mentoring to young African Americans to help them overcome the overt and covert discrimination and the uneven quality of opportunities that still exist.

6. *Project 3000 by 2000* school coordinators, and other recruiters of minority medical students, should use the information given here to publicize the black pioneer graduates of their medical schools. They should also use the information about the hundreds of still-living pioneers to help identify pioneering alumni, faculty, or local practitioners who might assist them in their partnership-building and mentoring projects.

7. Medical school administrators should consider the possibility of celebrating past successes in minority student recruiting and retention, as was done by the University of Washington at St. Louis College of Medicine when they graduated their one hundredth African-American student. Similarly, administrators should consider honoring their outstanding individual African-American graduates or faculty members, as was done by the Universtiy of Pennsylvania College of Medicine when they featured Dr. Helen O. Dickens in a recent issue of *Penn Medicine* (Dinan, 1990).

8. Individuals interested in fostering racial harmony should be aware of the attitudes and techniques that are illustrated in many of the biographical sketches and highlighted in the racial harmony section of chapter 5. The authors' belief that racial harmony is an important societal goal is illustrated by the fact that two of the coauthors of this book are African-American and one is Caucasian. Our experience of

working together on this project reinforced our mutual friendship and respect.

9. Members of the media should feature some of the findings of this book when writing and producing radio and television programs. Additionally, the communications media should consider featuring some of the 33 individuals whose biographical sketches and photographs are available in chapter 4.

10. Scholars should continue to study the achievements of minority group members and to document them in publications such as this book. Only in this way can we be assured that the story of these individuals will be preserved.

APPENDIX A

Key Findings of the Study:
Black Pioneers in Medical Education[1]
Charles H. Epps, Jr., M.D.

Dr. Epps is dean of the Howard University College of Medicine, Washington, D.C. This letter to the editor appeared on page 546 of the July 1993 issue of Academic Medicine: Journal of the Association of American Medical Colleges.

African-American physicians have made significant—and often sadly overlooked—contributions to medicine and medical education. In an effort to acknowledge the achievements of pioneering African-American physicians, the *Journal of the National Medical Association (JNMA)* will publish a series of three articles on the subject this summer. "Black Medical Pioneers: African-American 'Firsts' in Academic and Organized Medicine," slated to appear in the August, September, and October 1993 issues of *JNMA,* was coauthored by Davis G. Johnson, a former AAMC staff member, Audrey L. Vaughan, an editor and writer at the Howard University College of Medicine, and myself.

In these three articles, we explore and celebrate the achievements of over 500 black medical pioneers, including (1) 290 of the first men and women graduates of the 126 currently existing U.S. medical schools, (2) 68 pioneering graduates of the Howard University College of Medicine, (3) 50 graduates of Meharry Medical College, and (4) 159 graduates of predominately white medical schools. The articles also feature biographical sketches of 33 black physicians that emphasize the obstacles they overcame and the help they received from both black and white people that enabled them to reach their professional goals.

Under the auspices of the AAMC's Section for Student Services, we gathered information from the AAMC's member schools about their first African-American graduates. Our findings revealed that (1) 96 percent of schools reported having had at least one African-American graduate; of all these black graduates, two-thirds received their M.D. degrees after 1960; (2) the median time lapse between the establishment of a medical school and the graduation of its first black M.D. was 19 years for men graduates and 45 years for women; and (3) the first 290 black graduates of currently existing medical schools received their undergraduate educations from over 160 different colleges; the largest number (16) attended Howard University as undergraduates.

As the AAMC and its member schools work to achieve the goals of *Project 3000 by 2000*—that is, to have at least 3,000 minority students per year admitted to U.S. medical schools by the year 2000—it seems especially important to recognize and applaud the accomplishments of pioneering African-American physicians. Their achievements, often attained in the face of grave obstacles and prejudice, blazed the trail that many now follow.

----

[1] The slight discrepancy between the number of pioneers cited in Dr. Epps' letter and the number of pioneers cited in the book is due to the addition of pioneers since this letter was published.

APPENDIX B

Scope and Value of the Study:
The Evolution and Significance of Black Medical Pioneers
Louis W. Sullivan, M.D.

Dr. Sullivan is president of the Morehouse School of Medicine and former secretary of the U.S. Department of Health and Human Services. This guest editorial appeared on page 901 of the December 1993 issue of the Journal of the National Medical Association.

Sir Isaac Newton put it this way: "If I have been able to see farther than others, it was because I stood on the shoulders of giants." Daniel Boorstin, the former librarian of Congress, has written that "Discoveries become episodes of biography, unpredictable as the new worlds the discoverers opened to us . . . this is a story without end." My own mentor, Dr. Benjamin Elijah Mays, the late president of Morehouse College, once said, "He who would be as great as his predecessor must be greater."

History is biography. We do learn, grow, and achieve through comparison with others. The past is prelude. And our historical achievements can generate the hope and accomplishment necessary for a more promising future. As the members of the National Medical Association work to overcome the shocking health disparities that plague our minority communities—disparities that are in part the result of racism, discrimination, indifference, and callousness—we must stand on the shoulders of those who have gone before. Hardship often ignites leadership, and our past has been blessed by men and women of timeless courage and vision who have provided a vital foundation for our practice of the healing arts. That is why I am proud to participate in the "Black Medical Pioneers" project published in the August, September, and October 1993 issues of this journal, and to recommend the following articles for your careful study.

As stated in the August issue, the "Black Medical Pioneers" project was conceived by Charles H. Epps, Jr, M.D., dean of the Howard University College of Medicine (HUCM), and himself a cutting-edge black pioneer in orthopaedic surgery. He enlisted two outstanding coauthors, Davis G. Johnson, Ph.D., a long-time consultant to HUCM and a former division director of the Association of American Medical

Colleges, and Audrey L. Vaughan, M.S., the public information officer and editor/writer at HUCM.

Entitled "Black Medical Pioneers: African-American 'Firsts' in Academic and Organized Medicine," the project report includes those who broke new ground as graduates from both predominantly black and white medical schools. In addition, the project was enlarged to identify the first African-American graduates of all 126 US medical schools and to include extended biographical sketches of 33 of the more than 500 pioneers who were identified.

Unfortunately, due to space limitations, the biographical sketches in the October issue had to be shortened. However, this is only a temporary delay. I've learned that the authors have tentative plans to produce an expanded hardcover edition of their publication that will include a detailed table of contents, a content analysis of the biographical sketches (particularly regarding obstacles encountered and overcome, help received from blacks and others, efforts to promote racial harmony, and advice to aspiring minority physicians), and a detailed index.

I am pleased that these articles appear on the thirtieth anniversary of Dr. W. Montague Cobb's 1963-64 presidency of the National Medical Association and honor his voluminous contributions as the acknowledged "principal historian of African Americans in medicine." Dr Cobb was a pioneer in every sense of the word, and his inspiration and enthusiasm for the profound power of remembrance has been transmitted by the authors.

I encourage everyone to make full use of these articles. They will be extremely helpful for developing materials to recruit more citizens from our minority communities into medicine and the sciences. These reports also can be used as the basis for audiovisual presentations about "Black Medical Pioneers." This information is also valuable as an historical reference for the 1995 centennial year of the founding of the National Medical Association. Finally, these articles provide a continuing foundation for the evolutionary contributions that are a daily hallmark of "Black Medical Pioneers."

I congratulate Dr. Epps, Dr. Johnson, Ms. Vaughan, and the *Journal of the National Medical Association* for a job well done. We owe them a tremendous debt of thanks.

Appendix C

Directory of United States Medical Schools[1]

Alabama

University of Alabama School of Medicine
  Birmingham, AL 35294
University of Southern Alabama School of Medicine
  Mobile, AL 36688

Arizona

University of Arizona College of Medicine
  Tucson, AZ 85724

Arkansas

University of Arkansas College of Medicine
  Little Rock, AR 72205

California

University of California, Davis, School of Medicine
  Davis, CA 95616
University of California, Irvine, College of Medicine
  Irvine, CA 92717
University of California, Los Angeles, UCLA School of Medicine
  Los Angeles, CA 90024
University of California, San Diego, School of Medicine
  La Jolla, CA 92093
University of California, San Francisco, School of Medicine
  San Francisco, CA 94143
Charles R. Drew University of Medicine and Science
  Los Angeles, CA 90059
Loma Linda University School of Medicine
  Loma Linda, CA 92350
University of Southern California School of Medicine
  Los Angeles, CA 90033
Stanford University School of Medicine
  Palo Alto, CA 94305

Colorado

University of Colorado School of Medicine
  Denver, CO 80262

Connecticut

University of Connecticut School of Medicine
  Farmington, CT 06030
Yale University School of Medicine
  New Haven CT 06510

District of Columbia

George Washington University School of Medicine and Health Sciences
Washington, DC 20037

Georgetown University School of Medicine
Washington, DC 20007

Howard University College of Medicine
Washington, DC 20059

Florida

University of Florida College of Medicine
Gainesville, FL 32610

University of Miami School of Medicine
Miami, FL 33101

University of South Florida College of Medicine
Tampa, FL 33612

Georgia

Emory University School of Medicine
Atlanta, GA 30322

Medical College of Georgia School of Medicine
Augusta, GA 30912

Mercer University School of Medicine
Macon, GA 31207

Morehouse School of Medicine
Atlanta, GA 30310

Hawaii

University of Hawaii John A. Burns School of Medicine
Honolulu, HI 96822

Illinois

University of Chicago Division of the Biological Sciences,
Pritzker School of Medicine
Chicago, IL 60637

University of Health Sciences/Chicago Medical School
North Chicago, IL 60064

University of Illinois College of Medicine
Chicago, IL 60680

Loyola University of Chicago Stritch School of Medicine
Maywood, IL 60153

Northwestern University Medical School
Chicago, IL 60611

Rush Medical College of Rush University
Chicago, IL 60612

Southern Illinois University School of Medicine
Springfield, IL 62794

Indiana

Indiana University School of Medicine
Indianapolis, IN 46202

Iowa

University of Iowa College of Medicine
Iowa City, IA 52242

Kansas

University of Kansas School of Medicine
Kansas City, KS 66103

Kentucky

University of Kentucky College of Medicine
Lexington, KY 40536
University of Louisville School of Medicine
Louisville, KY 40292

Louisiana

Louisiana State University School of Medicine in New Orleans
New Orleans, LA 70112
Louisiana State University School of Medicine in Shreveport
Shreveport, LA 71130
Tulane University School of Medicine
New Orleans, LA 70112

Maryland

Johns Hopkins University School of Medicine
Baltimore, MD 21205
University of Maryland School of Medicine
Baltimore, MD 21201
Uniformed Services University of the Health Sciences
Bethesda, MD 20814

Massachusetts

Boston University School of Medicine
Boston, MA 02118
Harvard Medical School
Boston, MA 02115
University of Massachusetts Medical School
Worcester, MA 01655
Tufts University School of Medicine
Boston, MA 02111

Michigan

Michigan State University College of Human Medicine
East Lansing, MI 48828

University of Michigan Medical School
Ann Arbor, MI 48109
Wayne State University School of Medicine
Detroit, MI 48201

Minnesota
Mayo Medical School
Rochester, MN 55905
University of Minnesota, Duluth School of Medicine[2]
Duluth, MN 55812
University of Minnesota Medical School, Minneapolis
Minneapolis, MN 55455

Mississippi
University of Mississippi School of Medicine
Jackson, MS 39216

Missouri
University of Missouri-Columbia School of Medicine
Columbia, MO 65203
University of Missouri-Kansas City School of Medicine
Kansas City, MO 64108
Saint Louis University School of Medicine
Saint Louis, MO 63104
Washington University School of Medicine
Saint Louis, MO 63110

Nebraska
Creighton University School of Medicine
Omaha, NE 68178
University of Nebraska College of Medicine
Omaha, NE 68198

Nevada
University of Nevada School of Medicine
Reno, NV 89557

New Hampshire
Dartmouth Medical School
Hanover, NH 03756

New Jersey
University of Medicine and Dentistry of New Jersey/New Jersey Medical School
Newark, NJ 07103
University of Medicine and Dentistry of New Jersey/
Robert Wood Johnson Medical School
Piscataway, NJ 08854

New Mexico

University of New Mexico School of Medicine
Albuquerque, NM 87131

New York

Albany Medical College
Albany, NY 12208
Albert Einstein College of Medicine of Yeshiva University
Bronx, NY 10461
Columbia University College of Physicians and Surgeons
New York, NY 10032
Cornell University Medical College
New York, NY 10021
Mount Sinai School of Medicine of the City University of New York
New York, NY 10029
New York Medical College
Valhalla, NY 10595
New York University School of Medicine
New York, NY 10016
University of Rochester School of Medicine and Dentistry
Rochester, NY 14642
State University of New York Health Science Center at Brooklyn
College of Medicine
Brooklyn, NY 11203
State University of New York at Buffalo School of Medicine and
Biomedical Sciences
Buffalo, NY 14214
State University of New York at Stony Brook Health Sciences Center
School of Medicine
Stony Brook, NY 11794
State University of New York Health Science Center at Syracuse
College of Medicine
Syracuse, NY 13210

North Carolina

Bowman Gray School of Medicine of Wake Forest University
Winston-Salem, NC 27157
Duke University School of Medicine
Durham, NC 27710
East Carolina University School of Medicine
Greenville, NC 27858
University of North Carolina at Chapel Hill School of Medicine
Chapel Hill, NC 27599

North Dakota

University of North Dakota School of Medicine
Grand Forks, ND 58203

Ohio

Case Western Reserve University School of Medicine
Cleveland, OH 44106

University of Cincinnati College of Medicine
Cincinnati, OH 45267

Medical College of Ohio
Toledo, OH 43699

Northeastern Ohio Universities College of Medicine
Rootstown, OH 44272

Ohio State University College of Medicine
Columbus, OH 43210

Wright State University School of Medicine
Dayton, OH 45401

Oklahoma

University of Oklahoma College of Medicine
Oklahoma City, OK 73190

Oregon

Oregon Health Sciences University School of Medicine
Portland, OR 97201

Pennsylvania

Hahnemann University School of Medicine
Philadelphia, PA 19102

Jefferson Medical College of Thomas Jefferson University
Philadelphia, PA 19107

Medical College of Pennsylvania
Philadelphia, PA 19129

Pennsylvania State University College of Medicine
Hershey, PA 17033

University of Pennsylvania School of Medicine
Philadelphia, PA 19104

University of Pittsburgh School of Medicine
Pittsburgh, PA 15261

Temple University School of Medicine
Philadelphia, PA 19140

Puerto Rico

Universidad Central del Caribe School of Medicine
Bayamon, PR 00621

Ponce School of Medicine
Ponce, PR 00732

University of Puerto Rico School of Medicine
San Juan, PR 00936

Rhode Island
  Brown University Program in Medicine
    Providence, RI 02912

South Carolina
  Medical University of South Carolina College of Medicine,
    Charleston, SC 29425
  University of South Carolina School of Medicine
    Columbia, SC 29208

South Dakota
  University of South Dakota School of Medicine
    Sioux Falls, SD 57117

Tennessee
  East Tennessee State University James H. Quillen College of Medicine
    Johnson City, TN 37614
  Meharry Medical College School of Medicine
    Nashville, TN 37208
  University of Tennessee, Memphis, College of Medicine
    Memphis, TN 38163
  Vanderbilt University School of Medicine
    Nashville, TN 37232

Texas
  Baylor College of Medicine
    Houston, TX 77030
  Texas A&M University Health Science Center College of Medicine
    College Station, TX 77843
  Texas Tech University Health Sciences Center School of Medicine
    Lubbock, TX 79430
  University of Texas Southwestern Medical Center at Dallas
    Southwestern Medical School
    Dallas, TX 75235
  University of Texas Medical School at Galveston
    Galveston, TX 77550
  University of Texas Medical School at Houston
    Houston, TX 77225
  University of Texas Medical School at San Antonio
    San Antonio, TX 78284

Utah
  University of Utah School of Medicine
    Salt Lake City, UT 84132

Vermont

University of Vermont College of Medicine
Burlington, VT 05405

Virginia

Eastern Virginia Medical School of the Medical College of Hampton Roads
Norfolk, VA 23501
Virginia Commonwealth University Medical College of Virginia School of Medicine
Richmond, VA 23298
University of Virginia School of Medicine
Charlottesville, VA 22908

Washington

University of Washington School of Medicine
Seattle, WA 98195

West Virginia

Marshall University School of Medicine
Huntington, WV 25755
West Virginia University School of Medicine
Morgantown, WV 26506

Wisconsin

Medical College of Wisconsin
Milwaukee, WI 53226
University of Wisconsin Medical School
Madison, WI 53706

---

[1] Information is taken from the *Directory of American Medical Education, 1991–92* (AAMC).

[2] The University of Minnesota, Duluth School of Medicine, is not included in Table 7; it is a two-year school and does not award the M.D. degree.

BIBLIOGRAPHY

Association of American Medical Colleges. *AAMC Directory of American Medical Education,* 1991–92. Washington, D.C., 1991.

Bennett, L., Jr. *Before the Mayflower: A History of Black America.* Chicago: Johnson Publishing Co., 1982.

Cass, J., and M. Birnbaum, *Comparative Guide to American Colleges,* 13th ed. New York: Harper and Row, 1987.

Cobb, W.M. "The Black American in Medicine." *Journal of the National Medical Association* 73 (1981) suppl.:1181–1244.

_____. *Medical Care and the Plight of the Negro.* New York: The National Association for the Advancement of Colored People, 1947.

Corner, G. W. *Two Centuries of Medicine: A History of the School of Medicine, University of Pennsylvania.* Philadelphia: J.B. Lippincott, 1965.

Curtis, J. L. *Blacks, Medical Schools, and Society.* Ann Arbor: University of Michigan Press, 1971 (especially chapter 1, "Historical Perspectives," pp.1–27).

Dinan, D. A. "Just Do It: Helen Dickens Speaks Her Mind." *Penn Medicine* 1990; 4(1):8–15.

Dyson, W. "Founding the School of Medicine of Howard University, 1868–1873." *Howard University Studies in History,* no. 10, Nov. 1929.

_____. *Howard University, The Capstone of Negro Education. A History: 1867–1940.* Washington, D.C.: The Graduate School of Howard University, 1941.

Eiler, M. A., T.J. Pasko, and M. Max. *Medical School Alumni, 1986 Edition.* Chicago: American Medical Association, 1986.

Epps, C. H., Jr., D. G. Johnson, and A.L. Vaughan. "Black Medical Pioneers: African-American 'Firsts' in Academic and Organized Medicine." *Journal of the National Medical Association,* 1993(85): 629–44, 703–20, and 777–96.

Flexner, A. *Medical Education in the United States and Canada: Report to the Carnegie Foundation for the Advancement of Teaching.* New York: Carnegie Foundation for the Advancement of Teaching, Bulletin No. 4, 1910.

Hawkins, W. L. *Afro-American Biographies: Profiles of 558 Current Men and Women.* North Carolina: McFarland and Co., 1992.

Howard University College of Medicine, Washington, D.C. Address of L.C. Loomis, M.D., Professor of Physiology and Microscopy, Delivered at the Opening of the First Course of Lectures, November 5, 1868. Washington, D.C.: Government Printing Office, 1869.

Johnson, D. G. *Physicians in the Making: Personal, Academic, and Socioeconomic Characteristics of Medical Students from 1950 to 2000.* San Francisco: Jossey-Bass, 1983.

LaBlanc, M. L., ed. *Contemporary Black Biography: Profiles from the International Black Community.* Detroit, Mich.: Gale Research Co., 1992.

Bibliography

Lamb, D. S., ed. *Howard University Medical Department, Washington, D.C.: A Historical, Biographical and Statistical Souvenir.* Washington, D.C.: R. Beresford, 1900.

Logan, R. W. *Howard University: The First Hundred Years, 1867–1967.* New York: New York University Press, 1969.

Logan, R. W. and M. R. Winston, eds. *Dictionary of American Negro Biography.* New York: Norton, 1983.

Macmillan Directory Division. *Marquis Who's Who: Directory of Medical Specialists, 25th Edition, 1991–1992.* Wilmette, Ill.: Macmillan Information Co., Inc., 1991.

Matney, W. C., ed. *Who's Who Among Black Americans.* 4th ed. Lake Forest, Ill.: Educational Communications, Inc., 1985.

Morais, H. M. *The History of the Afro-American in Medicine.* Rev. ed. Cornwells Heights, Pa.: Publishers Agency, under the auspices of the Association for the Study of Afro-American Life and History, 1978 (earliest edition published in 1967).

Organ, C. H., Jr., and M. M. Kosiba, eds. *A Century of Black Surgeons: The U.S.A. Experience* (2 vols.) Norman, Okla.: Transcript Press, 1987.

Petersdorf, R. G. "Not a Choice, An Obligation." *Academic Medicine* 1982; 67(2): 73-79.

Reed Publishing Co. *Marquis Who's Who in America, 1994.* 48th ed. New Providence, N.J.: Reed Publishing, Inc., 1993.

Sammons, V. O. *Blacks in Science and Medicine.* New York: Hemisphere Publishing Corp., 1990.

Savitt, T. L. "Abraham Flexner and the Black Medical School." In Barzansky, B., and N. Gevitz. *Beyond Flexner: Medical Education in the Twentieth Century.* New York: Greenwood Press, 1992.

Sedlacek, W. E., and D. O. Prieto. "Predicting Minority Students' Success in Medical School." *Academic Medicine*, 1990 (60): 161–66.

Shea, S., and M. T. Fullilove. "Entry of Black and Other Minority Students into U.S. Medical Schools." *New England Journal of Medicine* 1985 (313): 936.

Spradling, M. M., ed. *In Black and White: A Guide to Magazine Articles, Newspaper Articles, and Books Concerning More than 15,000 Black Individuals and Groups.* 3rd ed. (2 vols.) Detroit, Mich.: Gale Research Co., 1980.

Summerville, J. *Educating Black Doctors: A History of Meharry Medical College.* University, Ala.: University of Alabama Press, 1983.

The 1986 World Almanac and Book of Facts. New York: Newspaper Enterprise Association, Inc.; 1986.

Tomasson, R. E. "Goals for Racial Inclusion Elude the Latest Crop of Young Doctors." *The New York Times*, 1 April 1992, National Edition, p. B7.

Whiting, B. E. "Academic Medicine Shapes the Future." *Journal of the Student National Medical Association*, Summer 1992:26–30.

About the Authors

Charles H. Epps, Jr., M.D., is a 1951 graduate of Howard University and a 1955 graduate of the Howard University College of Medicine (HUCM). Dr. Epps, the first African-American president of both the Medical Society of the District of Columbia and of the American Orthopaedic Association, has also served as an assistant editor of the *Journal of the National Medical Association.* His publications include more than 100 journal articles, editorials, and book chapters, and he is the editor of *Complications in Orthopaedic Surgery,* the only text on this subject in the world's orthopaedic literature. He has been dean of HUCM since 1988. (A complete biographical sketch of Dr. Epps is included in chapter 4).

Davis G. Johnson, Ph.D., is a 1941 graduate of Amherst College and earned a Ph.D. in personnel psychology from Columbia University in 1951. He was dean of students at the SUNY-Syracuse Health Science Center from 1952 to 1963 and director of student studies and services at the Association of American Medical Colleges (AAMC) from 1963 to 1983. While at the AAMC, he was project director of their $1.5 million grant to bring more underrepresented minorities into the health professions. Dr. Johnson's publications include four books and over 100 journal articles. He has been a part-time consultant (with the rank of full professor) at HUCM since 1972.

Audrey L. Vaughan, M.S., is a 1965 graduate of Hampton University where she also earned a master of science degree in education in 1971. She taught English and history in the Virginia and New York public schools for more than ten years and at the State University of New York in Buffalo for five years. She was director of the minority affairs program at the SUNY-Buffalo School of Medicine from 1979 to 1981 and has worked at Howard University since 1981. Since 1989, Ms. Vaughan has been both the public information officer and the editor/writer at the Howard University College of Medicine.

INDEX OF SPECIALTIES

This index is limited to the 289 "black medical pioneers" listed in tables 12, 13, and 14. For some very early graduates, it is assumed they were general practitioners.

Aerospace Physicians
Harris, Bernard A.
Jemison, Mae C.
Long, Irene D.
Turner, Guthrie L., Jr.

Allergists
Tyson, William G.

Ambulatory Care Specialists
Wilkinson, William H.

Anatomists
Cobb, W. Montague
    (physical anthropologist)
Lloyd, Ruth S.
McKinney, Roscoe L.
Purvis, Charles B.
Wright, Clarence W.
Young, Moses W.

Anesthesiologists
Boone, John D.
Williams, John F.

Bacteriologists
Moore, Ruth E.
Poindexter, Hildrus A.
    (public health physician)
Wheeler, Albert H.
    (public health physician)

Biologists
Malone, Thomas E.

Cardiologists
Cooper, Edward S. *(internist)*
Curry, Charles L. *(internist)*
Johnson, John B., Jr. *(internist)*
McBroom, Fletcher P. R. *(internist)*
Reid, Edith C. *(internist)*

Chemists
Daly, Marie M.
Julian, Percy L. *(organic chemist)*
West, Harold D. *(biochemist)*
Wilkerson, Vernon A. *(biochemist)*

Dermatologists
Cave, Vernal G.
Gathings, Joseph G. *(syphilologist)*
Hinton, William A. *(syphilologist)*
Kenney, John A., Jr.
Lawless, Theodore K. *(syphilologist)*

Emergency Physicians
Priest, Marlon L.

Endocrinologists
Alexis, Carlton P. *(internist)*
Franklin, Eleanor I.
Jenkins, Melvin E. *(pediatrician)*
Titus-Dillon, Pauline *(internist)*
Townsend, John L. *(internist)*

Epidemiologists
Reed, Theresa Greene

Family/General Practitioners
Atkinson, Whittier C.
Brown, Lucy H.
Chinn, May E.
Cole, Rebecca J.
Crumpler, Rebecca Lee
Derham (Durham), James
Dorsette, Cornelius N.
Fitzbutler, William H.
Francis, G. Hamilton
Hall, James L., Sr.
Jamison, James Monroe
Jones, Ernest J.
Jones, Sarah G. B.
Kenney, John A., Sr.

Lynk, Miles V.
Matory, William E. *(surgeon)*
McKinley, John F.
McKinney (Steward), Susan Smith
Minton, Henry McK.
Mossell, Nathan Francis
Patton-Washington, Georgia E.
Peck, David Jones
Phillips, Jasper T.
Rann, Emery L., Jr.
Remond, Sarah P.
Rock, John S.
Santomee, Lucas
Satcher, David *(internist)*
Smith, James McC.
Steward, Susan McKinney Smith
Tucker, Alpheus W.
Weddington, Wilburn H.
Wells, Josie E.
West, Lightfoot A.
White, Thomas J.
Williston, Edward D.

Gastroenterologists
Blevins, George, Jr.
Forde, Kenneth A.
Henderson, Donald
Wilson, Donald E.

Internists
Adams, Numa P. G.
Alcena, Valeria
    (hematologist and oncologist)
Alexis, Carlton P. *(endocrinologist)*
Bristow, Lonnie R.
Cooper, Edward S. *(cardiologist)*
Greene, Charles R.
Harris, Jean Louise *(pediatrician)*
Henry, W. Lester, Jr.
Irby (Jones), Edith Mae
Jackson, Algernon B.
Johnson, John B., Jr. *(cardiologist)*
Leavell, Walter F.
Leevy, Carroll M.
McBroom, Fletcher P. R. *(cardiologist)*
Miller, Russell L., Jr.
    (clinical pharmacologist)
Payne, Howard M. *(pulmonologist)*

Peebles-Myers, Helen Marjorie
Prothrow-Stith, Deborah B.
    (public health physician)
Reid, Clarice D.W. *(hematologist)*
Reid, Edith C. *(cardiologist)*
Satcher, David *(family practitioner)*
Simmons, Arthur H.
Smoot, Roland T.
Sullivan, Louis W.
Thompson, Alvin J.
Thomson, Gerald E.
Titus-Dillon, Pauline *(endocrinologist)*
Townsend, John L. *(endocrinologist)*
Tuckson, Reed *(public health physician)*
Wilkinson, William H.
Williams, Alonzo D.

Microbiologists
Amos, Harold *(immunologist)*
Bent, Michael J.

Neurosurgeons
Barber, Jesse B., Jr.
Carson, Benjamin S.
    (pediatric neurosurgeon)
Greene, Clarence S.
Hyde-Rowan, Maxine
Odeku, E. Latunde

Nutritionists
Kittrell, Flemmie P.

Obstetricians and Gynecologists
Brunson, Milton E.
Chatman, Donald L.
    (gynecologicall laparoscopist)
Clifford, Maurice C.
Davidson, Ezra C., Jr.
Edwards, Lena F.
Ferebee, Dorothy Boulding
Foster, Henry W., Jr.
Gilbert, Artishia G.
Hall, George C.
Hinson, Eugene T. *(surgeon)*
Irby (Jones), Edith Mae
Jones, Thomas A.
Jones, Verina M.
Lowry, John E.

Murray, Peter M.
Ross, Julian W.
Steptoe, Robert C.
Turner, Deborah Ann
(*gynecological oncologist*)
Wright, Charles H.

Ophthalmologists
Bath, Patricia E.
Brooks, Roosevelt
Chinn, Chester W.
Cowan, Claude L., Sr.
Hansen, Axel
Venable, Howard P.

Orthopaedic Surgeons
Carty, Claudia Thomas
Crawford, Alvin H.
Epps, Charles H., Jr.
Gladden, James R.
Holmes, Hamilton Earl
White, Augustus A., III

Otolaryngologists
Barnes, William H.
Mabrie, Herman J., III
Morman, William D.
Roman, Charles V.

Pathologists
Burton, John F. (*forensic pathologist*)
Jackson, Marvin A.
Jason, Robert S.
Mann, Marion
Pinn, Vivian W.
Quinland, William S.
Robinson, Paul T.
Sampson, Calvin C. (*clinical pathologist*)

Pediatricians
Adebonojo, Festus O.
Bethel, Agnes Lattimer
Butler, Henry R. (*surgeon*)
Cardozo, William W.
Crump, Edward P.
Elders, M. Joycelyn
(*public health physician*)
Ellis, Effie O. (*public health physician*)

Epps, Roselyn P.
Ferguson, Angella D.
Green, Frederick C.
Harris, Jean Louise (*internist*)
Harris, Stanley I.
Hunter, Gertrude C. T.
Jenkins, Melvin E.
(*pediatric endocrinologist*)
Jenkins, Renee
(*adolescent medicine physician*)
Manley, Audrey F. (*neonatologist and
public health physician*)
Moore, Eddie S.
Scott, Roland B.
Smith, Alonzo de G.
Whitten, Charles F.

Pediatric Surgeons
Rosser, Samuel B.

Pharmacologists
Maloney, Arnold H.
Miller, Russell L., Jr. (*clinical
pharmacologist and internist*)
Shockley, Dolores C.

**Physiatrists (Physical Medicine and
Rehabilitation)**
Davis, Harvey F.

Physical Anthropologists
Cobb, W. Montague (*anatomist*)

Physiologists
Hawthorne, Edward W.
Johnson, Joseph L.
Lewis, Julian H.
Rolfe, Daniel T.

Plastic Surgeons
Garnes, Arthur L.
Porter, Vincent

Psychiatrists (and Neurologists)
Adom, Edwin N. A.
Bateman, Mildred M.
Bowen, Clotilde D.
Comer, James P. (*child psychiatrist*)

Elam, Lloyd C.
Fuller, Solomon C.
Hope, Justin M.
Lathen, John W.
Lawrence, Leonard E.
Maultsby, Maxie C., Jr.
Nickens, Herbert W.
Pierce, Chester M.
Pouissant, Alvin F.
Robinson, Luther D.
Spurlock, Jeanne *(child psychiatrist)*
Williams, Ernest Y.

Public Health Physicians
Ayer, Vernon A. *(public health and
    preventive medicine physician)*
Bousfield, Midian O.
Cornely, Paul B.
Cross, Edward B.
Elders, M. Joycelyn *(pediatrician)*
Ellis, Effie O. *(pediatrician)*
Higginbotham, Peyton R.
Holloman, John L.
Manley, Audrey F. *(pediatrician)*
McCarroll, E. Mae
Myers, Woodrow A., Jr.
Poindexter, Hildrus A. *(bacteriologist)*
Prothrow-Stith, Deborah B. *(internist)*
Rimple, Hubert M.
Standard, Raymond L.
Thomas, William McK. *(surgeon)*
Tuckson, Reed *(internist)*
Turner, Guthrie L., Jr.
Walker, Bailus, Jr.
Wheeler, Albert H. *(bacteriologist)*

Pulmonologists
Payne, Howard M. *(internist)*

Radiologists
Alexander, Leslie L.
Allen, William E., Jr.
Anderson, John A.
Donnell, Clyde
Lawlah, John W.
Peters, Jesse J.

Surgeons
Alexander, Joseph L.
Alexander, Walter G.
Augusta, Alexander T.
Avery, Clarence S.
Barnett, Herman A.
Bernard, Louis J.
Boyd, Robert F.
Brown, Dorothy
Butler, Henry R. *(pediatrician)*
Callender, Clive O. *(transplant surgeon)*
Carson, Simeon L.
Carter, Edward A.
Clement, Kenneth W.
Coleman, Arthur H.
Cowan, James R.
Curtis, Austin M., Sr.
Dailey, Ulysses G.
Debas, Haile T.
DeGrasse, John V. S.
Dibble, Eugene H.
Dickens, Helen O.
Dove, Dennis B.
Drew, Charles R.
Forde, Kenneth A.
    (gastrointestinal endoscopic surgeon)
Frederick, Rivers
Freeman, Harold P. *(oncologist)*
Gauntlett, Hughenna L.
Giles, Roscoe Conkling
Hale, John H.
Harris, Bobby J. *(colorectal surgeon)*
Hilliard, Robert L. M.
Hinson, Eugene T. *(gynecologist)*
Hoover, Eddie L.
Hunter, John E.
Ish, George W. S., Jr.
Kountz, Samuel P.
Lambright, Middleton H., Jr.
Lee, Arthur B.
Leffall, LaSalle D., Jr.
Logan, Myra A.
Majors, Monroe A.
Marchbanks, Vance H.
Matory, William E. *(family practitioner)*
Maynard, Aubre D.
Miller, Ross M., Jr.

Organ, Claude H., Jr.
Payne, Clarence H.
Perry, John E.
Redmond, Sidney D.
Roberts, Carl G.
Sinkler, William H.
Smith, Earl B.
Stewart, Ferdinand A.
Syphax, Burke
Thomas, James H.
Thomas, William McK.
　　(public health physician)
Thompson, Solomon H.
Turner, John P.
Walker, Matthew
Ward, Joseph H.
Warfield, William A.
Watkins, Levi, Jr. *(cardiac surgeon)*
Wesley, Allen A.
White, Jack E. *(oncologist)*
Williams, Daniel Hale
Wright, Jane Cooke
Wright, Louis T.
Yancey, Asa G., Sr.

Thoracic Surgeons
Laurey, J. Richard
Spellman, Mitchell W.
Sterling, Rosalyn
Stubbs, Frederick D.

Urologists
Becker, Leslie E., Jr.
Francis, Milton A.
Garvin, Charles H.
Jones, R. Frank
Vincent, Ubert C.

Zoologists
Epps, Anna Cherrie *(immunologist)*
Just, Ernest E.

No Specialty
Thomas, Vivien T.

Index of Names

Symbol (#) = first name unknown. Names in boldface type are pioneers.

A

Aaron, Ruth, 147
Abernathy, Ralph, 122
Adams, John, 59–60
Adams, Numa P.G., v, 14, 25, 28, 48, 135, 183, 235
Adebonojo, Festus O., 183, 236
Adom, Edwin N.A., 178, 236
Aitken, George T., 60
Albro, Helen Tupper, 66, 89
Alcena, Valeria, 183, 235
Alexander, John, 48
Alexander, Joseph L., 183, 237
Alexander, Leslie L., 169, 237
Alexander, Raymond, 53
Alexander, Sadie, 53
Alexander, Virginia, 52, 53
Alexander, Walter G., 183, 237
Alexis, Carlton P., 26, 63, 65, 169, 234, 235
Allen, Janice G., 147
Allen, Venita Carol Newby Thweatt, 152
Allen, William E., Jr., 29, 169, 237
Als, Ann V., 146
Ammerman, Harvey, 60
Amos, Harold, 184, 235
Anderson, John A., 31, 169, 237
Andrews, Augua, 147
Armstrong, Davill, 152
Arnett, Lawrence Calvert, 154
Atkinson, Whittier C., 33, 34, 35, 169, 234
Aubry, Alvin Joseph, Jr., 155
Augusta, Alexander T., 9, 10, 24, 29, 32, 33, 184, 237
Austen, W. Gerald, 82–3
Avery, Clarence S., 31, 178, 237
Ayer, Vernon A., 184, 237
Azlein, Arthur, 108

B

Babcock, Charlotte, 112
Barber, Jesse B., Jr., 34, 169, 235
Barnes, William H., 29, 184, 236
Barnett, Herman A., 155, 184, 237
Barnett, Margaret Edwina, 150
Bateman, Mildred M., 184, 236
Bath, Patricia E., 5, 169, 236
Battis, Sandra Dian, 147
Baucom, Karen, 151
Baucom, Sharon, 151
Beahrs, Oliver, 83
Beasley, Jean, 152

Beck, William, 107–08
Becker, Leslie E., Jr., 169, 238
Bee, Venette Jones, 150
Beinecke, Walter, 82
Benjamin, Sabrina Ann, 155
Bell, J.C., 136
Belton, Ruby Lavonzelle Sturgis, 153
Bennett, Arlene, 153
Bent, Michael J., 25, 28, 178, 235
Bernard, Louis J., 178, 237
Bernard, Viola, 112
Bertram, Elizabeth, 149
Bethel, Agnes Lattimer, 147, 192, 236
Bethune, Mary McCloud, 112
Birnie, James, 114
Blevins, George, Jr., 184, 235
Blizzard, Robert M., 76
Boaz, Franz, 49
Bogdonoff, Morton, 126
Bogerty, Sharon Ann, 154
Boise, Gladys, 104
Boland, Robert J., 156
Boone, John D., 184, 234
Boorstin, Daniel, 221
Bourne, Blanche, 65
Bousfield, Midian O., 184, 237
Bowell, Paul, 151
Bowen, Clotilde D., 34, 153, 184, 236
Bowen, James L.N., 149
Bowling, Marcia Clair, 150
Boyd, Robert F., 29, 178, 237
Braxton, Maceo, 155
Brayboy # *Reference* **Maultsby**, 94
Brazeal, B.R., 114
Brigety, Reuben Earl, 149
Bristow, Lonnie R., 184, 235
Brooks, George W., 149
Brooks, Roosevelt, 185, 236
Broome, Rochelle A., 153
Brown, Dorothy, 29, 178, 237
Brown, Lucy H., 185, 234
Brown, Roland K., 71
Brown, Rowine, 89
Brown, Tanya L., 151
Bruce, Samuel, 152
Brunson, Milton E., 185, 235
Bryant, Estella Louise, 155
Bulger, Roger, 126
Burger, Cliff, 123
Burnett, Carol E., 146
Burton, John F., 178, 236

Bush, Barbara, 115
Bush, George, 113, 115
Bush, Sydney Claye, 148
Butler, Henry R., 29, 178, 236, 237
Butzel, Fred, 50
Byers, James F., 153

C

Cain, Rogers, 151
Caldwell, Charles, 88
Callender, Carl, 41
Callender, Clive O., 34, 39–42, 132, 133, 178, 237
Callender, Fern, 42
Callis, Henry A., 30, 185
Campbell, Emmett, 148
Campbell, Lori Margaret, 149
Cannon, Linda Jean, 151
Capel, Denise L., 155
Cardozo, William W., 34, 185, 236
Carson, Benjamin S., 185, 235
Carson, Simeon L., 185, 237
Carter, Edward A., 149, 185, 237
Carter, George Clay, 146
Carter, Thomas, 156
Carter, William Beverly, 154
Carty, Claudia Thomas, 185, 236
Carven, Judith Berwick, 146
Cassell, William E., 115
Cates, Marjorie Ransome, 150
Cave, Herbert, 41
Cave, Vernal G., 41, 169, 234
Chapman, John, 121, 123
Charles, Roderick Edward, 150
Chatman, Donald L., 178, 235
Chavers, Blanche Marie, 156
Cheek, James E., 63
Cherot, Frances Justina, 154
Chinn, Chester W., 29, 185, 236
Chinn, May E., 185, 234
Christian, Cora LeEthel, 150
Clark, Jack Lewis, 153
Claybon, Patience Hodges, 146
Clement, Kenneth W., 170, 237
Clemmons, Joan E., 154
Clifford, Maurice C., 27, 28, 178, 235
Clowney, Doris L., 150
Cobb, Alexzine Montague, 42
Cobb, William Elmer, 42
Cobb, W. Montague, v, xiii, xiv, xv, 3, 14, 17, 20, 26, 34, 39, 42–5, 59, 62, 71, 82, 84, 86, 97, 107, 118, 131, 132, 133, 140, 167, 168, 170, 204, 214, 222, 234, 236
Cole, Maceola L., 154
Cole, Rebecca J., 24, 153, 186, 234
Coleman, Arthur H., 31, 34, 170, 237
Coleman, Marjorie S., 155

Coleman, William, Sr., 107
Collins, Natalear R., 148
Comer, James P., 26, 31, 45-7, 132, 133, 170, 236
Cooper, Edward S., 35, 178, 234, 235
Cornely, Paul B., 25, 30, 47-51, 62, 118, 132, 133, 186, 237
Cotman, Henry Earl, 149
Cowan, Claude L, Sr., 170, 236
Cowan, James R., 34, 179, 237
Cox, Betty Louise, 147
Crawford, Alvin H., 154, 186, 236
Crawford, Robert, 110
Crear, John Richard, Jr., 147
Creed, Cortland Van Rensselaer, 156
Cross, Edward B., 170, 237
Crump, Edward P., 30, 179, 236
Crumpler, Rebecca Lee, 24, 147, 157, 186, 192, 200, 234
Cureton, R.E., 114
Curry, Charles L., 170, 234
Curtis, Austin M., Sr., 24, 33, 186, 237

D

Dailey, Darlene, 155
Dailey, Ulysses G., 29, 30, 186, 237
Dales, Richard Charles, 146
Daly, Marie M., 25, 186, 234
Davidson, Ezra C., Jr., 179, 235
Davis, Harvey F., 186, 236
Deas, Bernard W., 154
Debas, Haile T., 27, 28, 186, 237
DeGrasse, John V.S., 24, 28, 29, 187, 237
De la Coates-Johnson, Roy, 147
Dent, Lemsuel Leon, 151
Densley, Theodore R., 153
Derham, James *Also* **Durham**, 24, 187, 200, 214, 234
Dibble, Eugene H., 33, 170, 237
Dickens, Daisy Jane, 51
Dickens, Helen O., 26, 30, 51-4, 132, 133, 187, 217, 237
Diggs, Edward Oscar, 152
Donnell, Clyde, 187, 237
Dorsette, Cornelius N., 187, 234
Dove, Dennis B., 34, 187, 237
Dowell, Arnold, 100
Drew, Charles R., xv, 33, 35, 39, 54–7, 71, 82, 116, 118, 127, 128–29, 131, 132, 133, 139, 140
    187, 214, 237
Duhaylongsod, Francis, 99
Dukes, Delilah, 148
Dunn, Van, 104
Durham, James *See* **Derham**
Dyson, Walter, 14

E

Ebert, Paul, 83
Ebert, William Frederick, 153
Easterling, Ruth Marguerite, 155

Edwards, Lena F., 34, 170, 235
Elam, Lloyd C., 26, 156, 187, 213, 237
Elders, M. Joycelyn, 27, 35, 187, 214, 236, 237
Ellis, Albert, 94
Ellis, Effie O., 187, 236, 237
Ellsworth, Rita Ann, 151
Epps, Anna Cherrie, 26, 67, 167, 170, 238
Epps, Charles H., Jr., v, viii, xii, xiii-iv, 6, 7, 31, 44, 57–60, 62, 132, 133, 134, 135, 167, 171, 219, 220, 221, 222, 233, 236
Epps, Roselyn P., 32, 59, 60–2, 132, 133, 134, 171, 236
Evans, Doris A., 147

F

Fabrega, Marco, 148
Falconer, Etta, 104
Favazza, Barbara Starks, 156
Fearing, Jeffrey J., xv
Feffer, Henry, 60
Ferebee, Dorothy Boulding, 62, 187, 235
Ferguson *(Plessy vs. Ferguson)*, 12
Ferguson, Angella D., 63–5, 110, 132, 133, 171, 236
Ferguson, Ira A., 129
Ferguson, Lloyd, 59
Fineburg, Harvey, 105
Fisher, Ada M., 156
Fisher, Kathryn A., xvi
Fitzbutler, Sarah Helen, 150
Fitzbutler, William H., 151, 188, 234
Flangin, Kathryn Haley, 155
Flax, Martin A., 102
Flexner, Abraham, 12–13, 16, 20
Flowers, Loma K. Brown, 147
Fluellen, William, 75
Forde, Kenneth A., 188, 235, 237
Foster, Henry W., Jr., 7, 188, 235
Foutz, Charles Douglas, 155
Fowler, J.C.G., 153
Fox, Janice Marie, 151
Fox, Paul J., 154
Fraad, Lewis, 79
Francis, G. Hamilton, 29, 179, 234
Francis, Milton A., 171, 238
Franklin, Eleanor I., 27, 65-8, 132, 133, 188, 234
Franklin, Luther, 65
Franklin, Rose, 65
Fraser, Sarah Lougen, 154
Frazier, Johnnie Paris, 155
Frederick, Rivers, 149, 188, 237
Freeman, Harold P., 34, 171, 237
Fuller, Solomon C., 25, 33, 188, 237
Furstenberg, A.C., 127, 129

G

Gamble, Robert Lee, 150
Gamble, Vanessa N., xiv, xv, 7, 14, 15

Gardner, Mary Louise, 149
Garnes, Arthur L., 171, 236
Garvin, Alan, 148
Garvin, Charles H., 33, 171, 238
Gathings, Joseph G., 171, 234
Gauntlett, Hughenna L., 150, 188, 237
Gelhorn, Alfred, 53
George-LaBrie, Johnett Peyton, 156
Gibbons, Wayne L., 153
Gibbs, Rose Delores, 154
Gilbert, Artishia G., 33, 171, 188, 235
Giles, Roscoe Conkling, 30, 33, 148, 188, 237
Gladden, James R., 30, 179, 236
Gladdis, Otis, Jr., 147
Goldberg, Arthur, 72
Goldberg, Dorothy, 72, 74
Gollman, Jacqueline Blutcher, 149
Gordon, William, 148
Graham, Marva, 153
Graham, Sandra, 104
Gray, Amelia Cobb, xv, 43
Gray, Carol L., 155
Green, Deborah, 148
Green, Frederick C., 188, 236
Greene, Charles R., 171, 235
Greene, Clarence S., 26, 30, 171, 235
Greengard, Joseph, 89
Gregg, Anna D., 151
Gregory, Kimberly, 148
Griffin (Levy), Agnes O., 148
Griffin, John, 114
Grimes, William Thomas, Jr., 147
Guillory, Charleta, 150

H

Haile, Alan D., xv
Hale, John H., 179, 237
Hall, Anita, 107
Hall, Everlyn Lilease, 154
Hall, George C., 25, 33, 189, 235
Hall, James L., Sr., 147, 189, 234
Hamilton, Grace Towns, 129
Hanlon, C. Rollins, 83
Hansen, Axel, 30, 179, 236
Harden, K. Albert, 49, 50, 67
Harper, John, 149
Harris, Bernard A., 35, 189, 200, 234
Harris, Bobby J., 30, 189, 237
Harris, Jean Louise, 156, 189, 235, 236
Harris, Patricia Pelhem, 151
Harris, Stanley I., 189, 236
Hart, Alrundus, 150
Hawthorne, Edward W., 67, 71, 97, 172, 236
Hayes, Freddie Lee, 151
Hayes-Jordan, Andrea, 99

Healy, Bernadine, 101
Henderson, Donald, 189, 235
Henderson, George Cortez, Jr., 150
Henderson, Purvis S., 52
Henry, Johnny Lee, 155
Henry, W. Lester, Jr., 26, 31, 32, 68–71, 97, 120, 132, 133, 168, 172, 235
Henson, Mattie, 71
Higginbotham, Peyton R., 172, 237
Hilfiker, James F., 64
Hill, Elizabeth Webb, 51, 53, 149
Hilliard, Robert L.M., 189, 237
Hinson, Eugene T., 189, 235, 237
Hinton, William A., 26, 189, 234
Holleb, Arthur, 83
Holloman, John L., 34, 190, 237
Holmes, Hamilton Earl, 148, 190, 236
Holthaus, Joseph, 100
Hood, Rodney Grant, 147
Hooks, Benjamin, 45
Hoover, Eddie L., 190, 237
Hope, Edward, 127
Hope, John, 127
Hope, Justin M., 29, 190, 237
Hornung, Philllip, 100
Houston, Earline, 154
Howard, Camilla, 66
Howard, Edwin Clarence J.T., 149
Howes, Edward, 71, 116, 118
Hubbard, Carol Jean, 156
Hucles, Howard, 59
Hughes, John Irison, 149
Hunter, Charles, 72
Hunter, George Washington, 107
Hunter, Gertrude C.T., 71–4, 132, 133, 172, 236
Hunter, John E., 29, 190, 237
Hunton, Benjamin L., 91
Hurley, Marja Marie, 148
Hyde-Rowan, Maxine, 190, 235
Hymes, Critty Lillette, 150

I

Imes, Thomas C., 149
Ingram, Judith Ann, 151
Irby (Jones), Edith Mae, 17, 31, 146, 190, 191, 213, 235
Ish, George W.S., Jr., 172, 237
Ison, Luther, 65
Ison, Rose, 65

J

Jackson, Algernon B., 150, 190, 235
Jackson, Howard, 122
Jackson, James Edwin, 149
Jackson, Marvin A., 107, 179, 236
Jackson, Morris, 146
Jackson, Redney Mark, 151

Jallah, Edwin Markham, 146
James, Tyshawn M., 150, 157
Jamison, James Monroe, 151, 177, 179, 234
Jason, Robert S., 25, 64, 82, 90, 107, 118, 167, 172, 236
Jemison, Mae C., 34, 190, 200, 234
Jefferson, Mildred F., 149
Jenkins, Barbara, 78
Jenkins, Melvin E., 26, 31, 65, 74–7, 79, 110, 132, 133, 190, 234, 236
Jenkins, Patricia Ann, 150
Jenkins, Renee R., 77–9, 132, 133, 191, 236
Jenifer, Franklyn G., 44
Jenson, Mary Jane, 112
Jerrell, Mary L., xvi
Johnson, Charles W., 81
Johnson, Davis G., v, xii, xiii, 91, 132, 219, 221, 222, 233,
Johnson, Green G., 147
Johnson, John B., Jr., 34, 71, 191, 234, 235
Johnson, Joseph L., 25, 118, 191, 236
Johnson, Martha, 81
Johnson, Mary C., xvi
Johnson, Mordecai, 14
Johnson, Travis, 148
Johnson, Wade A., 153
Jones, Alise M., 151
Jones, Edith M.I. *See* **Irby**
Jones, Ernest J., 179, 234
Jones, Janis Adelaide, 155
Jones, Joyce, 150
Jones, Marjorie Earline, 152
Jones, Philip Wayne, 155
Jones, R. Frank, 29, 30, 34, 107, 172, 238
Jones, Ronald Wayne, 155
Jones, Sarah G.B., 167, 172, 234
Jones, Stella Pinkney, 155
Jones, Thomas A., 33, 191, 235
Jones, Verina M., 191, 235
Jones, Wendell E., 151
Julian, Percy L., 118, 191, 234
Just, Ernest E., 33, 84, 86, 191, 238

K
Kennedy, John F., 104
Kenney, John A., Jr., 172, 234
Kenney, John A., Sr., 29, 33, 191, 234
Kerr, Lorin, 48, 51
Kershaw, Randi D., xvi
King, Coretta Scott, 123
King, Martin Luther, Jr., 28, 122, 128
Kittrell, Flemmie P., 25, 191, 235
Kluttz, Brenda Mills, 148
Knott, Albert Paul, 152
Kountz, Samuel P., 27, 31, 42, 191, 237
Kowalewski, Joseph, 81
Kreidle, Katherine V., 42
Kurtz, Louis, 42

Alibris Packing Slip

Ordered by:

Raili Maultsby
309 Yoakum Parkway #518
Alexandria, Va 22304
UNITED STATES

Ship to:

Raili Maultsby
309 Yoakum Parkway #518
Alexandria, Va 22304
UNITED STATES

PN #	Item ID	Alibris ID	Media Type	Title / Author	Order Date
15199780-3	METABASE007918B002949619		BOOK	African-American Medical Pioneers Epps, Charles H. Jr. Et. Al	Mar, 21 2006
				Near fine in near fine dust jacket	

Alibris Return Information

Alibris guarantees the condition of every item as it is described on our Web site. If you are dissatisfied for any reason, return your purchase within 30 days of receipt for a refund of the item price. We'll also refund shipping costs if the return was a result of our error. If you return an item more than 60 days after its shipment date, the item will be discarded and you will not be eligible to receive a refund.

For instructions on how to return your purchase, please visit http://www.alibris.com/returns

Problems? Questions? Suggestions? Send e-mail to Alibris Customer Service at info@alibris.com

L

Lamb, Daniel Smith, 14
Lambright, Middleton H., Jr., 26, 179, 237
Lancaster, Ronny, 7
Lark, Janice C., 154
Lathen, John W., 173, 237
Lattimer, Agnes *See* **Bethel**
Laurey, J. Richard, 30, 192, 238
Lawlah, John W., 25, 192, 237
Lawless, Theodore K., 29, 192, 234
Lawrence, Leonard E., 192, 237
Lawson, James, 121
Leavell, Ernest B., 79
Leavell, Grace, 79
Leavell, Pierce, 79
Leavell, Pierre, 79
Leavell, Vivian, 79
Leavell, Walter F., 31, 79–81, 132, 133, 180, 235
Lee, Arthur B., 192, 237
Lee, Daniel W., 153
Lee, Rebecca *See* **Crumpler**
Lee, Stanley, 126
Leevy, Carroll M., 26, 126, 192, 235
Leffall, LaSalle D., Jr., 27, 31, 32, 34, 42, 57, 81–4, 99, 100, 132, 133, 168, 173, 237
Levine, Rachmiel, 70, 71
Levy, Agnes O. Griffin, 148
Lewis, Hariette E., 152
Lewis, Joseph D., 153
Lewis, Julian H., 25, 192, 236
Lewis, Vivian Moon Sanford, 153,
Lloyd, Ruth S., 25, 67, 84–6, 132, 133, 192, 234
Lloyd, Sterling M., xii, xv, 84
Logan, Myra A., 192, 237
Logan, Rayford W., 14
Long, Irene D., 192, 234
Loomis, Lafayette C., 8
Louden, Henrynne Ann, 155
Love, Joseph Robert, 154
Lowry, John E., 173, 235
Lucas, Clarence A., Sr., 149
Luckey, E. Hugh, 114–15
Lynk, Miles V., 29, 180, 235

M

Mabrie, Herman J., III, 177, 180, 236
Maddox, A.R., 75
Madison, Constance G., 152
Majors, Monroe A., 180, 237
Mallette, Julius Q., 148
Malone, Thomas E., 192–93, 234
Maloney, Arnold H., 25, 71, 193, 236
Maloney, Pauline Weeden, 102
Manley, Albert E., 89
Manley, Audrey F., 87–9, 104, 132, 133, 180, 236, 237

Mann, Marion, xii, xv, 34, 67, 89–91, 107, 132, 133, 135, 168, 173, 236
Manning, Kenneth R., xiv, xv, 7, 8, 16, 20
Marchbanks, Vance H., 33, 35, 89, 173, 237
Markee, Rupert, 50
Martin, John D., Jr., 129
Martin, Marcus Lewis, 156
Mastroianni, Luigi, 53
Mathis, Charles Edward, III, 155
Matory, William E., 27, 173, 235, 237
Maultsby, Maxie, 92–5, 132, 133, 193, 237
Maynard, Aubre D., 193, 237
Mays, Benjamin Elijah, 114, 129, 221
McAnarney, Elizabeth, 79
McBay, Henry, 89
McBroom, Fletcher P.R., 193, 234, 235
McCarroll, E. Mae, 193, 237
McCleary, Beatrix Ann, 156
McCulley, Doris Jean Young, 154
McCullough, Deborah Lynne, 149
McDuffy, Clyde, 86
McIntosh, Janiece C., 153
McKinley, John F., 24, 180, 235
McKinney, Roscoe L., 25, 193, 234
McKinney (Steward), Susan Smith, 152, 193, 196, 235
Metcalfe, Ralph, 97–8
Meriwether, Wilhelm Delano, 148
Metoyer, Marie, 148
Migeon, Claude, 76
Miller, Marsha C., 150
Miller, Ross M., Jr., 173, 237
Miller, Russell L., Jr., 26, 27, 44, 95–7, 132, 133, 135, 167, 173, 235, 236
Minton, Henry McK., 193, 235
Mitchell, Lewis E., 153
Montgomery # *Reference* **Maultsby**, 94
Montier, Agnes Berry, 154
Moore, Eddie S., 180, 236
Moore, Ruth E., 25, 193, 234
Moorhead, James F., 152
Morgan, Mitchelene, 154
Morgan, Sherard York, 146
Morman, William D., 30, 173, 236
Morris-Grooms, Elaine W., 153
Morton # *Reference* **Syphax**
Mosby, Richard A., 155
Moses, Sharon Renee, 151
Mossell, Nathan Francis, 16, 29, 33, 153, 194, 235
Mudd, Emily, 53
Murphy, Mabel, 85
Murray, Johnson B., 154
Murray, Peter M., 29, 30, 32, 174, 236
Myers, Jack, 71
Myers, Woodrow A., Jr., 194, 237

N

Nabwangu, James, 150
Nailor, John Richard, 148
Nash, Edward B., 156
Ndiforchu, Cassandra J., 149
Newton, Sir Isaac, 221
Nickens, Herbert W., 34, 194, 237
Nejarian, John, 42
Njoku, George Chidi, 150
Noble, John, 105

O

Odeku, E. Latunde, 174, 235
Oliver, James, 151
Organ, Claude H., Jr., 27, 31, 39, 97–100, 132, 133, 136, 194, 204, 214, 238
Organ, Claude, Sr., 97
Organ, Elizabeth Mays, 100
Organ, Ottolena Pemberton, 97
Orr, Leo Earsel, Jr., 146
Oxley, Lucy, 148

P

Pannell, Corrine D., 107
Parker # *Reference* **Maultsby**, 94
Patterson, Gregory, 154
Patterson, Yvonne A., 153
Patton, Georgia Esther Lee, 151
Patton-Washington, Georgia E., 177, 180, 235
Payne, Clarence H., 33, 194, 238
Payne, Howard M., 34, 174, 235, 237
Peck, David Jones, 24, 154, 157, 194, 200, 235
Peebles-Meyers, Helen Marjorie, 156, 194, 235
Pemberton, Charles, 98
Pemberton, Dogan, 98
Pemberton, Diane Lorene, 147
Pennington, Abigail L., 152
Pepper, William, III, 16
Perkins, Beverly J., 149
Perkins, Frank, 118
Perry, Franklin D., 152
Perry, John E., 180, 238
Peters, Jesse J., 30, 194, 237
Petersdorf, Robert G., 71
Phillips, Jasper T., 180, 235
Pierce, Chester M., 194, 237
Pinkston, J. W., Jr., 129
Pinn, Vivian Winona, 32, 35, 100–02, 107, 132, 133, 194–95, 204, 236
Plessy *(Plessy vs. Ferguson)*, 12
Poindexter, Hildrus A., 25, 34, 195, 234, 237
Porter, Ernest Preston, 146
Porter, Vincent, 30, 174, 236
Pouissant, Alvin F., 26, 104, 195, 237
Prade, Margo Shamberger, 153
Price, Bebe Drew, xv
Priest, Marlon L., 195, 234

Prothrow-Stith, Deborah B., 103–05, 131, 132, 133, 195, 235, 237
Purvis, Charles B., 9, 10, 24, 29, 147, 195, 234

Q

Quinland, William S., 25, 30, 180–81, 236

R

Raines, Samuel L., 148
Randlett, Richard R., xvi
Rann, Emery L., Jr., 181, 235
Rappaport, Felix, 42
Reddick # *Reference* **Maultsby**, 94
Redmond, Sidney D., 195, 238
Reed, Theresa Greene, 181, 234
Reese, Errol, 126
Reid, Clarice D.W., 195, 235
Reid, Edith C., 181, 234, 235
Reid, James, 148
Remond, Sarah P., 195, 235
Revels, Harry, III, 154
Reynolds, Emma, 153
Reynolds, Walter, 153
Rice, Haynes, 18, 19
Richardson, Arthur P., 114, 129
Richmond, Julius, 73, 74
Rimple, Hubert M., 174, 237
Roberts, Carl G., 30, 33, 195, 238
Robertson, Gregory, xv
Robinson, Edwin Arzel, 153
Robinson, Luther D., 181, 237
Robinson, Mary Helen, 153
Robinson, Paul T., 181, 236
Robinson, William Anthony, 155
Rock, John S., 196, 235
Rolfe, Daniel T., 181, 236
Roman, Charles V., 33, 181, 236
Rosenberg, Mark, 105
Rosenthal, Ira, 89
Ross, Julian W., 25, 29, 30, 174, 236
Rosser, Samuel B., 31, 174, 236
Rowan, Carl T., 7
Rubenstein, Boris, 84, 86
Rumph, Frank, 149

S

St. John, Edward Thomas, 147
Sammons, Vivian O., xv
Sampson, Calvin C., xii, xiv, xv, 26, 34, 105–08, 132, 133, 181, 236
Sanders, George, 151
Sanders, Patricia Ann, 146
Santomee, Lucas, 196, 200, 235
Satcher, David, 196, 235
Schultz, Frederick W., 110
Scott, C. Waldo, 129
Scott, Floyd Earl, Jr., 154

Scott, Lawrence W., 147
Scott, Roland, B., 60–1, 62, 65, 108–10, 132, 133, 168, 174, 236
Scott, William H., 123
Scruggs, Karen LaFrance, 156
Scudder, John, 54
Scuka, Clayton L., 150
Seabron, Zyn, 148
Sealy, Joan R., 149
Senhouse, Miriam, 152
Shadd, Eunice P., 149
Shafiq, Florence Battle, 149
Shaw, James, 148
Shockley, Dolores C., 26, 196, 236
Shwartz, Samuel, 62
Simmons, Arthur H., 174, 235
Simmons, Jacqueline, 151
Simmons, Richard, 42
Sims, Angelica Valencia, 149
Sinai, Nathan, 50
Sinkler, William H., 174, 238
Smith, Alonzo de G., 29, 30, 109, 196, 236
Smith, Earl B., 181, 238
Smith, Bradley Donald, 84
Smith, Hilda B., 43
Smith, James McC., 24, 196, 200, 235
Smith, Jewel Irvin, 148
Smith, Kevin S., 150
Smith, Mary Elizabeth Morris, 84
Smith, Paul Jeffrey, 149
Smith-Blair, Gayle, 155
Smoot, Roland T., 174, 235
Smothers, Ruth Louise, 146
Snead, David Roland, 152
Spackman, Dora, 9
Spalding, Hughes, 129
Spaulding, Jean Gaillard, 148
Spellman, Mitchell W., 27, 175, 238
Spivak, Howard, 105
Spurlock, Jeanne, 26, 31, 34, 111–12, 132, 134, 167, 175, 204, 237
Standard, Raymond L., 175, 237
Stanfield, Eunice, 149
Starzl, Thomas, 42
Steptoe, Robert C., 175, 236
Sterling, Rosalyn, 31, 196, 238
Stephenson, W. H. C., 152
Steward, Susan Smith *See* **McKinney**
Stewart, Donald Wallace, 150
Stewart, Ferdinand A., 25, 196, 238
Stewart, Mae, 50
Stith, Charles, 104
Strauss, Maurice, 126
Stubbs, Frederick D., 25, 30, 196, 238
Stubbs, Judy M., 152
Stull, Virginia Elizabeth, 155
Sullivan, Louis W., viii, xiv, xv, 6, 27, 35, 113–15, 132, 134, 196–97, 204, 221, 235

Sullivan, Samuel William, Jr., 146
Sutler, Martin R., 129
Sweatt, James Leonard, III, 156
Syphax, Burke, 42, 56, 59, 82, 116–18, 132, 134, 175, 238

T

Tardy, Walter J., Jr., 156
Tarpley, John, 123
Tate, Harold F., 150
Tate, Jamesetta Ward, 150
Taylor, Paulus Clayton, 156
Tellis, Claude Jenkins, 150
Terry, E. Clayton, 71
Texeira, Antonio Dias, 71
Texeira, Carrie Jackson, 71
Thomas, James H., 197, 238
Thomas, Vivien T., 197, 238
Thomas, William McK., 181, 237, 238
Thompson, Alvin J., 175, 235
Thompson, Emma Ruthlyne, 154
Thompson, Levester, 149
Thompson, Solomon H., 175, 238
Thompson, Virgil, 153
Thomson, Gerald E., 175, 235
Titus, Hilma A., 119
Titus, Patrick A., 120
Titus-Dillon, Pauline, 27, 119–20, 132, 134, 175, 234, 235
Tollette, Truman B., 146
Townsend, John L., 31, 197, 234, 235
Travernier, Joseph, 148
Travis, Thomas Matthew, 156
Tucker, Alpheus W., 29, 197, 235
Tuckson, Reed, 7, 197, 235, 237
Turner, Guthrie L., Jr., 175, 234, 237
Turner, Deborah Ann, 31, 197, 236
Turner, John P., 29, 33, 197, 238
Tutu, Desmond, 123
Tyson, William G., 181, 234

V

Van Dunn # *Reference* **Prothrow-Stith**, 104
Vaughan, Audrey L., v, xii, xiii, xv, 132, 219, 221, 222, 233,
Vaughan, Tracie L., xvi
Venable, Howard P., 30, 197, 236
Vincent, Ubert C., 25, 197, 238
Virgil, Carl Demardrian, 152, 156

W

Wagner, John Henry, III, 146
Walker, Bailus, Jr., 197, 237
Walker, Maggie Laura, 129
Walker, Matthew, 30, 56, 127, 129, 181, 238
Walker, Jenee Barber, 156
Waller, Salvador B., xv

Wallis, Alan, 108
Walters, David Garth, 152
Ward, Joseph H., 33, 35, 198, 238
Warfield, William A., 176, 238
Warren, Sharon Jones, 152
Warren, W. Dean, 83, 129
Washington, Booker T., 11
Washington, LaRae H., 148
Waters, Ella, 41
Watkins, Levi, Jr., 27, 121–24, 132, 134, 155, 198, 213, 238
Watson, Carl Weber, 150
Watt, Robin Trudy, 152
Watts, Samuel, 73
Weathers, Donald Gregory, 151
Weaver, Michael, 151
Weaver, Yvonne Jackson, 147
Weddington, Wilburn H., 176, 235
Wells, Josie E., 182, 235
Wells, Peggy Jean Johnson, 151
Wesley, Allen A., 198, 238
West, Harold D., 26, 198, 234
West, Lightfoot A., 182, 235
West, William, 67
Wheeler, Albert H., 26, 198, 234, 237
White, Augustus A., III, 27, 154, 198, 236
White, Jack E., 27, 82, 176, 238
White, Thomas J., 24, 198, 235
Whiteman, Neville C., 152
Whitmire, Rogers O'Neil, 151
Whitten, Charles F., 27, 73, 182, 236
Whittico, James, 45
Wiley, Clarence L., 147
Wilkerson, Vernon A., 25, 198, 234
Wilkinson, Carolyn Cobb, 43
Wilkinson, William H., 198, 234, 235
Willard, Kim Maria, 152
Williams, Alonzo D., 199, 235
Williams, Arthur M., 152
Williams, Daniel Hale, 5, 29, 33, 153, 199, 238
Williams, Edward V., 150
Williams, Ernest Y., 176, 237
Williams, John F., 199, 234
Williams, Regina Lee, 151
Williams, Vivian L., 152
Willis, Adelaide, 148
Williston, Edward D., 167, 176, 235
Wills, Rebecca, 147
Wilson, Donald E., 27, 28, 31, 124–26, 132, 134, 199, 235
Wilson, Douglas S., 93
Wilson, Evelyn, 152
Wilson, Joanne Antoinette Peebles, 148
Wilson, Vernon, 74
Wittson, Cecil, 76
Wood, Edward T., 156

Woodard, Charles, 77
Woodard, Kristinza, 77
Woods, Elizabeth Hawkins, 149
Woods, Laura, 114
Wooley, Paul, 79
Wormley, James T., 9
Wragg, Robin Eleanor, 156
Wright, Charles H., 182, 236
Wright, Clarence W., 199, 234
Wright, Jane Cooke, 199, 238
Wright, Louis T., 25, 33, 199, 238

Y

Yarde, William L., 152
Yancey, Arthur H., 127
Yancey, Asa G., Sr., 27, 31, 127–30, 132, 134, 199, 238
Yancey, Bernise, 127
Yancey, Daisy Sherard, 127
Yeager, Curtis, 42
Yeargin-Allsopp, Marshalyn, 148
Yerby, Mark Smythe, 155
Young, Andrew, 123
Young, Lois Adelaide, 150
Young, Moses W., 25, 118, 176, 234

Z

Zeppa, Robert, 83
Zissi, Ifeanyi, A.O., 149

The W. Montague Cobb Scholarship Fund

The authors of **African-American Medical Pioneers**, Charles H. Epps, Jr., M.D., Davis G. Johnson, Ph.D., and Audrey L. Vaughan, M.S. Ed., have enthusiastically dedicated this volume to the memory of W. Montague Cobb, M.D., Ph.D. Each author had the pleasure of knowing Dr. Cobb personally. Dr. Epps knew Dr. Cobb over a period of several decades, first as his teacher, then as a fellow faculty member, and as a long-time friend and mentor.

Dr. Cobb, a 1929 graduate of the Howard University College of Medicine and a 1932 Ph.D. graduate of Western Reserve Hospital, was a well-known faculty member of the Howard University College of Medicine from 1932 to 1973 and chaired its department of anatomy from 1947 to 1969. He was a committed, dedicated instructor, always striving to make lectures in anatomy simple yet meaningful.

Dr. Cobb is recognized as the principal historian of the African American in medicine. For over 27 years, he served as editor of the *Journal of the National Medical Association (JNMA)*. More than 100 biographical sketches of African-American medical leaders were written by Dr. Cobb and published in *JNMA,* a collection which served as a major reference for this research on Black medical pioneers.

Approximately 85 percent of Howard's medical students receive financial assistance. This is consistent with the mission of the College of Medicine, which is to provide opportunity to all deserving students. To honor Dr. Cobb's long career of distinguished service to the students of the college, all royalties earned from the sales of **African-American Medical Pioneers** will be placed in an endowed fund that will provide scholarships for deserving students. The fund will be known as the W. Montague Cobb Scholarship Fund. It will be administered by the dean of the College of Medicine and awarded annually at its Honors and Awards Day ceremony.

Readers of **African-American Medical Pioneers**, with additional generosity, may support the Howard University College of Medicine's scholarship fund named in Dr. Cobb's honor. You have supported it with the purchase of this volume; an added incentive is to make it a memorable gift for someone special. With your additional book purchases, the publisher of this volume encourages you to request complimentary copies of the W. Montague Cobb Scholarship Fund bookplate, which is displayed on the next page. Please include with your book order both your name and the name of the recipient as you wish them to appear. Identify this information as:

BOOKPLATE—From:_____   To:_____.

Send to Betz Publishing Company, P.O. Box 1745, Rockville Maryland, 20850.

_____

gives this copy of

African-American Medical Pioneers

with great pleasure

to

_____

Royalties from the purchase of your copy of
African-American Medical Pioneers
have been used entirely to fund the
W. Montague Cobb Scholarship Fund
at the Howard University College of Medicine.